The Next Deal

The Next Deal

The Future of Public Life in the Information Age

Andrei Cherny

BASIC
BOOKS

A Member of the Perseus Books Group

Published by Basic Books,
A Member of the Perseus Books Group

ISBN: 0-465-00972-7
First Edition

A CIP catalog record for this book is available from the Library of Congress.

The paper used in this publication meets the requirements of the
American National Standard for Permanence of Paper for Printed Library
Materials Z39.48-1984.

10 9 8 7 6 5 4 3 2

Designed by Nighthawk Design

To my parents and brother, Daniel

There is one great basic fact which underlies all the questions that are discussed on the political platform at the present moment. That singular fact is that nothing is done in this country as it was done twenty years ago. We are in the presence of a new organization of society. Our life has broken away from the past. The life of America is not the life it was twenty years ago. We have changed our economic conditions absolutely, from top to bottom; and with our economic society, the organization of our life. The old political formulas do not fit the present problems; they read now like documents taken out of a forgotten age.

—WOODROW WILSON, 1912

Contents

PREFACE

*T*was the night before Christmas and all through the White House, not a creature was stirring—except for me. Actually, it was the afternoon before Christmas, but the White House really was practically deserted with the exception of this then 22-year-old speechwriter. Just about everyone who worked there had gone home to spend the day with their loved ones. Not having family in town or much else better to do, I had volunteered to write President Clinton's Saturday radio address for that week. It was a stirring and epic oration on expanded Medicare benefits for colorectal cancer screenings. You might remember it.

The plan had been to tape the speech in the early afternoon for delivery a few days later. I was supposed to be on hand in case Clinton had any questions. (As it would turn out, my only role was holding his dog, Buddy, so that he wouldn't bark during the taping.) But, as was his annual habit, Clinton had gone off to do last-minute Christmas shopping. So I sat alone in my office and waited and waited and waited. Finally, bored beyond belief, I left the building and wandered around downtown Washington. It was just about as empty. The Mall was barren—the malls were where the action was that day. I ended up in a local bookstore and there my eye caught a book that I had read several years earlier: the 1949 classic *The Vital Center.* Half a century ago, when Arthur Schlesinger wrote *The Vital Center,* it was an exposition on his age. Tempered by the despondence of the Great Depression, energized by the hope of the New Deal, and finally formed in the crucible of the Second World War, Schlesinger's generation came of age at a moment when the world was consumed by a global ideological struggle. In *The*

Vital Center, Schlesinger held out a revitalized liberal democracy as an alternative to totalitarian communism on one side and absolutist fascism on the other.

At that moment, Schlesinger's book seemed like much more than a reminder of a former era. In fact, President Clinton and those of us who worked in his administration were attempting to create a domestic version of this vital center—an alternative to the morally and intellectually exhausted options of New Deal liberalism and Reagan Revolution conservatism. Clinton himself had been saying this with various degrees of explicitness since before he began running for president. But what occurred to me as I saw *The Vital Center* sitting there on the shelf was that this was not going to work. The vision of a "Third Way" somewhere between—or beyond—traditional liberalism and conservatism would have to be more daring and farsighted if it were going to be a long-run solution and not just a short-term alternative. Events outside of Washington—particularly the rise of the Information Age with its different ways of working and living—would require a whole new set of ideas about what government does and why it does it. That moment in the Washington bookstore was when I first thought about trying to write a book that would explain clearly why today's America—and my generation in particular—is looking for a new role for government that is radically different from the one we had in the twentieth century.

In the months and years to come, I thought about but shelved that notion numerous times. But one thing kept on prodding me to return to thinking about this project: conversations I had with some of the brightest, most deservedly respected, visionary people in Washington. Nearly to a person, they all said the same thing: in this time of peace, prosperity, and the convergence of the two parties' policy positions, the great issues are gone in American politics, the debates are settled, the battles over.

If there is one central idea in this book, it is this: that there is, in fact, a big battle yet to be waged—remaking American government and community life so that they can reflect the values of the new Information Age. This is neither about broadband regulation nor computers in the classrooms nor putting government services on-line. It is about the bigger picture: completely rethinking government's mission, just as we have rethought the way business works over the past decade. New Economy companies find success to the extent that they can do something that was unthinkable for corporations a generation and a century ago—giving their customers a larger universe of choices, putting decision-making power into customers' hands, and personalizing services to fit the needs and desires of each individual. However, government still largely runs on the old business model—one-size-fits-all, cookie-cutter programs. We have an assembly line government in an Internet age. This disconnect is the big issue facing American politics—an issue that will only grow in importance as the Information Age takes root and those who were reared in it grow up. This book is about how to bridge that disconnect, about how to move America's public life from the twentieth century into the twenty-first.

The book starts with two introductory chapters that serve as the background to the book's main argument. In *What I Saw at the Devolution*, I discuss the politics of the 1990s—what President Clinton tried to accomplish, where he succeeded, and where he ultimately fell short. I believe history will give him a great deal of credit for realizing that Industrial Age ideas about government no longer fit the times. However, while Clinton ended the old debate about government, he failed to enunciate a compelling new vision for government's role. Left with no alternatives, Washington—a city whose swamps have been filled but whose morass grows ever deeper—now increasingly revolves around obsolete orthodoxies, purblind partisanship, and powerful interest groups with a vested dependence on the status quo. American politics today runs on the vapors of scandal and soundbites because its governing ideologies have run out of fuel.

In *The New Generation of Choice*, I describe the generation of Americans who will come to have the responsibility of leading the nation into the new century. They were born after the moral revolutions of the 1960s radically expanded their lifestyle choices and came of age at a time when technological revolutions give them a plethora of choices to make when they shop, work, learn, and play. Since the ability to make their own choices is a fundamental expectation, I call these young people the Choice Generation. As with previous generations, government will come to adapt to their outlook.

Having introduced the politics and the people that will shape the new century, I move to the main part of the book. Parts I, II, and III deal with the economy, government, and community respectively. The three parts tell parallel stories. In each area, they trace America's journey from the individualistic Agricultural Age of the nineteenth century to the hierarchical Industrial Age of the twentieth century to the decentralized Information Age of the twenty-first century. Part I: *The Fall and Rise of the Individual* analyzes the economy, following Americans' voyage from farms to factories to the technologically-based, empowering workplaces of today and tomorrow. During this long, strange trip the belief that individuals should be at the heart of the economy was lost—and now has been found again.

Part II: *The Choice Revolution* tells the story of how American leaders have responded to the times throughout the nation's history by adapting government to new conditions. The goal of those who have believed in progress has remained remarkably constant: working toward equality of opportunity. Yet, different moments have called for different ways to accomplish this. Thomas Jefferson promoted a bottom-up belief that would open the doors of democracy by expanding suffrage and protect the open frontier of the independent farmer from the encroaching power of the landed aristocracy and new manufacturers. In the Progressive Era, Woodrow Wilson sought to update this vision, breaking up the concentrated power of the new industrial corporations and giving more power to individuals. But in the battle of ideas, he was defeated by Theodore Roosevelt who advocated a different view—a top-down theory that built up centralized government programs to give workers security and to stand up to big businesses on behalf of the people. This was the view that dominated twentieth-century conceptions of government—in both Democratic and Republican administrations. I argue that the time has come for another big change: returning to the spirit of

Jefferson and Wilson and the bottom-up philosophy that animated their worldview. A Choice Revolution in government entails expanding democracy by taking decision-making power out of the hands of bureaucrats and powerful interests and giving it to ordinary Americans. I argue that all Americans should have the ability to make choices for themselves and their families now reserved for only the wealthiest: the privilege to choose schools for their kids, choose their own health care plans, choose how to save for their retirement.

Finally, Part III: *The New Responsibility* reminds us that more individual power doesn't mean more selfish individualism. With more choices, Americans—as the community involvement of the Choice Generation demonstrates—will be more likely to do more for their neighbors. Government should provide an extra push in this direction. The New Responsibility will ask Americans to adopt a greater burden in caring for their community and doing what Franklin Roosevelt said we'd all have to do so long ago: "shoulder our common load."

The philosopher George Santayana famously wrote that "those who cannot remember the past are condemned to repeat it." This book rests on the premise that the opposite holds true as well. Those who cannot remember the past might not be able to repeat it. The task for today's young people—the Choice Generation—is to replicate in our day the accomplishment of the Progressive Generation of Woodrow Wilson and Theodore Roosevelt. They rethought the rules of public life to fit the contours of a new America. Our job is to do the same.

This is a book about America's future, not a work of history. Although it does look at America's past through a particular prism, it does so in seeking to answer the desperate need for an understanding of where America now finds herself. Like ships lost in a fog, the more confused our leaders grow the louder they blare and bleat. Most are frantically searching for a roadmap in a world where too much of our politics is divorced from the past and from the story of American life.

Any attempt to retell history is, at its heart, an exercise in simplification. No canvass could ever be big enough to hold the thousand contradictory details and shadows of human life. Thus history is little more than myths backed up by evidence. But the myths a people tell, and the memories they hold true, can never be separated from "facts." Daniel Boorstin wrote that "Our American past always speaks to us with two voices: the voice of the past, and the voice of the present." By listening to yesterday—its history and its myths—perhaps we can gain a greater understanding of where we are today. And in listening to those dim, faint echoes of voices from a bygone world, perhaps we will hear their whisper in the wind, their directions on how to move forward.

The New Deal and the idea of government it embodied was a signal achievement of the twentieth century. Its basic parameters have long been accepted by both parties and it has become part of the fabric of American life. Personally, I am the product of the public school system (in fact, my junior high was built by the New Deal Works Progress Administration), I went to college with federal student loans and grants, my family relied on food stamps to get by when I was a child, my grand-mother awaits her Social Security check every month. But the New Deal was created as a response to the America of the last century. As the econ-omy and society changes, Americans want more: a new mission for government that responds to today's America. They are waiting for the next deal.

What I Saw at the Devolution

This work is not designed to set forth novel or startling political doctrines. It is intended rather as a report on the fundamental enterprise of reexamination and self-criticism which liberalism has undergone in the last decade. The leaders in this enterprise have been the wiser men of an older generation. But its chief beneficiaries have been my own contemporaries; and its main consequence, I believe, has been to create a new and distinct political generation.

—*Arthur Schlesinger, Opening words of* The Vital Center, *1949*

A SPECIAL DAY

"Only mad dogs and Englishmen go out in the midday sun." It should have been no surprise that, try as I might, I couldn't get this Noel Coward ditty out of my head. Washington, D.C.'s dog days of summer have been legendary since the swamp was first declared our nation's capital as the bastard child of a constitutional compromise—and the summer of 1997 was no exception. Search as I might, however, I found few canines and even fewer foreigners as the temperature rose to oppressive levels. Instead, looking around the South Lawn of the White House, I saw a very different—though no less peculiar—menagerie braving Washington's heat and humidity on this most August day.

If I had not known better, I would almost have thought it was a heat-induced mirage. Striding out of the White House through a flag-bordered path and headed toward a platform on the South Lawn, not arm in arm but close, were the then opposing leaders of American political power: Bill Clinton and Newt Gingrich. It reminded me of the comic books of my childhood, when DC Comics' Batman and Marvel Comics' Spiderman would team up, Superman would battle Muhammad Ali, or all the superheroes would gather together for a "special" issue that every kid just had to have. Along with Clinton and Gingrich on the platform in front of me, and certainly even hotter than I was because of the powerful camera lights trained in their direction, were Vice President Al Gore, House Majority Leader Dick Armey, Budget Chairman John Kasich, and dozens of members of Congress from both parties. They had come together to end nearly three decades of wanton fiscal insanity in Washington and sign the first balanced budget in a generation.

Since the moment I had started my job as Vice President Gore's senior speechwriter two months earlier, the push for a balanced budget had been at the center of my work. "Today is the reason I came to the White House," I wrote in my diary the day the budget deal was first announced. The provisions of the agreement would have a real impact on the millions of Americans who would benefit from the lower interest rates that would result from the balanced budget, from the plan's tax cut for middle-class families, from the health insurance it provided for low-income children, and from the college tuition assistance it offered. On top of all this, the achievement of a balanced budget after decades of debate and false starts was an important milestone for the country and for the New Democrat brand of thinking that Clinton had brought to the White House. I had come to Washington to make a difference. Now, the day after my 22nd birthday and less than two months since I had graduated from college, I was, Forrest Gump-like, standing in a sacred spot on a truly historic day.

But gnawing at my pride was a profound disquietude. At first I couldn't identify its source. The event was proceeding almost exactly as planned. Logistical preparations had begun days earlier in the West Wing basement office of Communications Director Ann Lewis. There, every last detail was haggled out—from the programs (parchment embossed with the presidential seal) to the invitees (over one thousand guests) to the music (answering a demand for "patriotic music," one meeting participant was forced to defend the choice of the Marine Band. "The Marine Band is 'the President's Own,'" she sputtered. "They're about as American as you can get—and they're pretty wonderful!"). A top White House official poked her head in on her way out on the town that Friday evening and made sure the staff understood the significance of what we were doing. "This is the president's day," she directed. "Let's make it special for him."

Although the show was proceeding as planned, my uneasiness grew steadily stronger. The day was bigger than even the president of the United States. The assembled potentates had come to lower the curtain on something larger than three decades of budget deficits. Along with its specific importance, the balanced budget had a symbolic significance as well. Though I didn't realize it just then, I was witnessing the end of the political history of twentieth-century America. As historian John Lukacs has pointed out, internationally, the twentieth century really lasted from Franz Ferdinand's assassination and the beginning of World War I in 1914 to the moment when East Europeans tore apart the Iron Curtain with their bare hands and ended the Cold War in 1989. In that "short century," the forces of democracy and freedom faced off against monarchy, fascism, and communism—and emerged triumphant. Similarly, American politics of the twentieth century lasted from August 1910, when former President Theodore Roosevelt unveiled his New Nationalism vision of big government, to August 1997, when President Bill Clinton acknowledged that expanding centralized, top-down, bureaucratic government was a thing of the past.

It is no accident that these events occurred when they did. Roosevelt and his cousin Franklin, who put the New Nationalism into practice, lived in a time when centralized, assembly line factories were the cutting edge. They defined Americans' thinking about how the world should be ordered and structured. Bill Clinton came to power at a moment when this world was rapidly retreating and being replaced by a New Economy that was—perhaps above all else—intrinsically skeptical of centralized power and institutions, including government as Americans have come to know it. Clinton's signing of the balanced budget was a recognition of the awesome power the global financial markets now have in shaping American prosperity; it sent a clear message to Americans that government would live within its means, abiding by the same rules as the middle class; but most of all it made clear that the old, traditional choices about government had stopped being viable. Democratic big government programs and huge Republican tax giveaways—both types of government by "hot check"—were no longer live options.

As the ceremony went on, I began to realize why I was so anxious. When I was very young, my parents ran a small theater company in Los Angeles. I had grown up backstage, memorizing all the actors' parts and knowing when the audience would laugh far before they had any inkling of an impending guffaw. This predictability gave me comfort. Now, as the budget signing dragged on, an idea gnawed at me: a page was turning—and no one had their lines for the next act. In the years since that hot summer of 1997, politics has stumbled and bumbled along, without moving forward. The new lines still have not been written. This is the unfinished business of American politics.

A CRISIS OF THE OLD ORDER

Noticing the rest of my White House colleagues, and trying desperately to fit in and to avoid passing out, I took the lead of the men and doffed my suit jacket, slinging it ever so casually over my shoulder. I strained—unsuccessfully—to keep my mind from drifting during the interminable speeches. Watching the behavior of the assembled crowd, an observer might not have realized that this was such a crucial new beginning for the president, his party, and the nation. Over there was Press Secretary Mike McCurry sharing a laugh with a couple other staffers under the shade of a gnarled old tree. There was one of my colleagues, in his late

20s and—like Thomas Hobbes' life in a state of nature—"nasty, brutish, and short," sidling up to a pretty summer intern. There was a cluster of staffers from the First Lady's Office—Hillaryland, they called it—folding their programs into makeshift fans. And every so often, people would interrupt whatever they were doing to glance over at the made-for-TV production taking place before them.

It was indeed a special day for President Clinton—one that no one could have foreseen when he began his campaign for the White House. Running for president in 1992, Clinton had found a country gripped by a crisis of the old order. Confronted by the demise of the Cold War and the final death throes of the comfortable post–World War II economic arrangements, Americans felt certain of little more than decline—in their own standard of living, in the nation's economic well-being and social fabric, in their hopes for their children's future.

It was clearly a moment for creative, innovative leadership. But as the 1990s began, both parties were AWOL. The Republican Party gloried in the creed of greed and viewed crime and welfare as wedge issues to be exploited rather than problems to be solved. It had raised taxes on the middle class and presided over an era of dwindling growth. Education was an afterthought and Republican economic strategy was largely limited to the notion of rewarding those privileged with wealth and praying that their leftover trickle would sustain the nation.

At the same time, Americans saw a Democratic Party that had rejected its historic role as the tribune of the middle class. Many Democrats downplayed traditional values of work, family, responsibility, faith—labeling them the province of the Republicans. Paying more attention to rights than to responsibilities, to criminals than to victims, to bureaucrats than to entrepreneurs, to America's international sins than to its capacity for global good, the Democratic Party had lost its way.

Both parties concentrated on playing their assigned roles in the formulaic debate between "left" and "right" that characterized politics for most of the century—a debate that had become devoid of meaning, dependent on memory, derisive of the many. If American politics of the 1980s and early 1990s was a school dance, the Republicans would be locked in a chaste, but fervent embrace of economic elitism; the Democrats would be doing the *lambada* with cultural elitism; and America's middle class would be standing unobtrusively alone by the punch bowl. Politics was playing to those who favored French mustard—and ignoring those who used "French's." It rejected their interests and sneered at their values.

As the 1992 campaign got under way, few in Washington seemed to recognize this problem. But, far away from the glare of the national media's spotlight, a Democratic contender who had developed a cohesive critique of not only the Republican record but his own party's as well was preparing to step forward.

Arkansas' youthful, yet veteran, governor, Bill Clinton, was, as he described himself, "a different kind of Democrat." In a political career built—like most—on lucky breaks, one of Clinton's luckiest came early on. In 1974, he lost his first race—a run for Congress. Beginning his career on the state level instead, he gained a greater perspective on the changes transforming America. Of course, he paid a price for this distance from D.C. His name wasn't bandied about with breezy familiarity at the chardonnay and brie parties on the Upper East Side where campaign cash is collected. He did not become a powerful, beef-ingesting, pork-dispensing, perk-exploiting Capitol Hill baron. Yet his breathing distance from Washington allowed him to realize very early on that the Capital's political debates were increasingly irrelevant to a changing nation. Announcing his presidential candidacy in October of 1991, he further distanced himself from the most powerful leaders of his own party. "The small towns and main streets of America aren't like the corridors and back rooms of Washington," he intoned from the steps of Arkansas' Old State House. "People out here don't care about the idle rhetoric of 'left' and 'right' and 'liberal' and 'conservative' and all the other words that have made our politics a substitute for action."

Clinton demonstrated a clear willingness to challenge both the Democratic Party's political arrangements and its ideological orthodoxies. For more than a year, as chairman of the Democratic Leadership Council—a band of party rebels committed to building a new governing majority—Clinton had traveled the country speaking out on the party's need to change in order to keep up with the times. Now, as his presidential campaign got under way, Clinton would break forthrightly with his party's past.

THE COMING OF THE NEW COVENANT

I believe that together we have fulfilled the responsibility of our generation to guarantee opportunity to the next generation, the responsibility of our generation to take America into a new century, where there is opportunity for all who are responsible enough to work for it, where we have a chance to come together across all of our differences as a great American community.

—*President Bill Clinton, at the balanced budget signing, August 5, 1997*

On October 23, 1991, twenty days after he announced his candidacy, Clinton traveled to Georgetown University, his alma mater, to deliver the first in a series of three speeches that formed the intellectual foundation of his candidacy. By the time he finished delivering the third in mid-December, he was languishing in fourth place in the polls in New Hampshire and had managed to raise only half as much in campaign funds as the leading fund-raiser in the pack. However, the press realized the effectiveness of his message. For instance, Howard Fineman of *Newsweek* wrote that through this series of three speeches, "Clinton has cornered attention." Largely on the basis of these speeches, they anointed him with a front-runner status that he was to take all the way to the nomination.

The speech Clinton delivered that October day was one of the most eloquent given by an American politician in the past quarter century. Devoid of rhetorical bells and whistles, its power came from its honesty, from Clinton's willingness to speak truths that many politicians knew but few then had the courage to say.

Clinton thundered at those—rich, poor, and in between—whose

demand for special favors had undermined the basic American creed of fairness. He said it was time that all Americans—from corporate CEOs to deadbeat dads, from Congressional chieftains to welfare moms—were held to an equal standard of responsibility for their actions. He offered a "New Covenant, a solemn agreement between the people and their government, to provide opportunity for everybody, inspire responsibility throughout our society, and restore a sense of community to this great nation."

Like President Reagan's central themes of smaller government, lower taxes, and stronger defense, this triad—opportunity, responsibility, community—served as the guiding principles of Clinton's presidency. These ideas were at the core of most every speech he delivered as president, and certainly every major one. In 1991, they were not just idle slogans, but fundamental departures from the Democratic dogma of the previous twenty-five years. They underscored his "different kind of Democrat" claim—an assertion that was central to his ability to win the White House. It is no accident that Walter Mondale did not even use the word "responsibility" once in his convention acceptance address while Bill Clinton used it six times.

In his first presidential campaign, Clinton used "opportunity, responsibility, and community" to differentiate himself from both traditional Republican and Democratic nostrums. "Opportunity" was neither the no-growth economic record and indifference of the Bush years nor the government guarantee of equal results proffered by many Democrats—it was an outlook of rewarding hard work, encouraging strong economic growth, and above all else promoting access to education. His vision of "responsibility" included not just a promise to "end welfare as we know it," but an uncompromising demand for better corporate citizenship. Finally, his call for "community" rejected the loose principles of both the Left and Right, vowing to go "beyond every man for himself on one hand and the right to something for nothing on the other."

Clinton's New Covenant was less the basis for a new politics than a powerful reminder to the public that Clinton shared their distaste for the "brain-dead" old politics. Yet, it clearly reflected the raw resentments and muffled hopes of the average men and women who had seen both parties walk away from their historic commitments and get sidetracked by side issues. Unfortunately, as was once said of President William Howard Taft, if Clinton "were Pope he would think it necessary to appoint a few Protestant Cardinals." Once ensconced in office, Clinton brought into power a cadre of advisors and staffers who never bought into his message of change. He and his party paid a disastrous price for this in the 1994 midterm rejection.

In the summer of 1997, some of the White House staff gathered together in the ornately tiled Indian Treaty Room for a good-bye party for Donald Baer. The hard-driving former journalist who became Clinton's chief speechwriter and then communications director had helped engineer the president's political resurrection after 1994 and was one of the few true believers within the White House. As part of the "entertainment," the guests were treated to a parody of "We are the World," entitled "We are Don's World," written and performed by many of the White House speechwriters and communications staff. But it wasn't only the voices that were off-key.

> When we were down and out
> And there seemed no Hope at all
> Don helped build that bridge
> And now we're standing tall.

> Well well well, we're a community now.
> An opportunity to take responsibility
> In our churches, mosques, and synagogues.

Rising to deliver some brief words of thanks to Baer, President Clinton couldn't help but deliver a mild rebuke to his staff members. His smile never leaving his face, but his eyes betraying a profound disappointment, Clinton said, "The thing about that 'opportunity, responsibility, and community' is that for Don, they were never punch lines. They were what he believed in." As is often true, Clinton was also describing himself. But if he was disappointed in his staff, he might have seen where he fell short in leading them.

THE SON ALSO RISES

In signing the balanced budget, Clinton tried to make clear, once and for all, that Democrats would no longer peddle the shopworn planks of a bygone era. Whether it was free trade, welfare reform, fiscal responsibility, battling teen pregnancy, strong anticrime measures, use of military force abroad, or the death penalty, Clinton broke with the philosophy his party had promoted in recent years.

Yet, there is little assurance that his personal impact on the Democratic Party is necessarily anything more than ephemeral. From the very beginning, Clinton concentrated first and foremost on bringing change to the nation and saw bringing change to his party—if it happened—as a positive side-effect. Mere days after his election, the barons of congressional power flew down to Little Rock to meet with Clinton—an outsider who had explicitly campaigned against both the Democratic Congress and Washington, D.C., in general. Before the glare of the camera lights, these Washington pooh-bahs appeared with the crusading young reformer from the hinterlands and, in effect, took him under their left wing. "Don't worry, sonny," they seemed to say. "We'll show you how it's done." And Clinton followed their lead. His calls for cuts in bloated Capitol Hill staff and for the line-item veto vanished, he soft-pedaled his desire for campaign finance reform, and he suddenly became vague on the middle-class tax cut—once a centerpiece of his economic agenda.

From there forward, until his decisive break with congressional wisdom over the need for a balanced budget in the summer of 1995, Clinton chose accommodation over confrontation most every time. As president, he was seldom willing to expend his political capital in reconstructing the Democratic Party in his image. Most of his words and many of his actions pointed Democrats in a new direction. But when the forces defending the old party's apparatus and guarding its arrangements got in the way, he smoothed down the differences. This worked wonders for making peace; it was an enormous missed opportunity for remaking the Democratic Party.

Yet, while Clinton might have sped up the process, politics continued to change even without his active assistance. The same societal forces that had shaped Clinton in Arkansas were having an even greater impact in shaping the next generation of political leaders around the nation. As the 1990s progressed, it became increasingly apparent that the old ways of American politics were fading away. The story of one family in particular makes it clear that it is truly not your father's politics.

One would expect a moment of personal conversion to come while watching the sun rise over Machu Picchu, while running one's hands over the stones of the Great Wall of China, while traveling down the road to Damascus. It seems far less likely—and much less glamorous—for this moment of awakening to occur while campaigning for a state senate seat in St. Louis Park, a suburb of Minneapolis. After all, Saint Paul is one thing, St. Paul is another. Nevertheless, for one Minnesota politician, his successful first campaign put him in touch with voters who had concerns and outlooks very different from those of a previous generation.

The story begins 125 hundred miles away in a different world. On Halloween night 1936, the children of Theodore Mondale did not go door to door searching for candy. Their father was a stern and reverent preacher who frowned on the holiday's frivolity. Moreover, the tight grip of the Great Depression's seventh year left little levity in their tiny town of Ceylon, Minnesota. But there was another reason why the Mondale family was at home on this Halloween. Theodore Mondale had gathered his family to listen to the radio as Franklin Roosevelt brought his reelection campaign to a close with a stirring address at Madison Square Garden.

In a fiery speech, FDR sought to energize the Democratic Party's base of working Americans with a violent denunciation of the big business interests that he had battled during much of his first term. "I should like to have it said of my first administration that in it the forces of selfishness and of lust for power met their match," said Roosevelt, struggling to make his voice heard above the crescendoing cheers of the crowd. "I should like to have it said of my second administration that in it these forces met their master." Listening at his father's side, 8-year-old Walter Mondale was exposed to a brand of politics he would practice all his life.

That October night, as he called "the roll of honor of those that stood with us," Roosevelt saw an industrial democracy with powerful interests arrayed on either side of a wide chasm. In his New Deal, he built up a big government to guarantee equal opportunity and protect Americans from the vicissitudes of adversity.

A decade later, Walter Mondale became swept up in a small insurgent faction led by Hubert Humphrey that was fighting to bring the values of the New Deal to Minnesota. They were the children of FDR, the "distinct political generation" that Schlesinger had described. Attacked as an "upstart," Mondale laid into an old giant of Minnesota politics for being "a voice out of the past. A last gasp of the old farmer-labor group." He stated that his goal was to speak for a new "generation that has grown up to plague the normal and traditional way of doing things." In a world that changes much faster than the minds of the people who live in it, the challenge of politics in every age is to assess the world as it is and respond to it with honesty instead of nostalgia. When he was young, Walter Mondale met that challenge directly.

But by the 1970s, as Mondale reached the heights of national leadership, America was changing both economically and socially. Americans were less likely to pledge their loyalty to parties in exchange for particular programs, to companies in exchange for a lifetime job, to interest groups in exchange for favors.

While he was vice president, Walter Mondale stated that the Democratic Party's job was to "take care of its friends." That meant extending the reach of government to help those who had long been left out of the American Dream—the poor, minorities, struggling workers. Unfortunately, it also meant the care and feeding of the constituency groups that made up the party's special interest infrastructure by offering them specific promises and programs. Mondale believed that in addressing organized labor, he spoke to working people; in speaking to civil rights leaders, he addressed minorities; in talking with feminists, he appealed to women. "My premise has always been that there are more Democrats than Republicans, and if we can keep our own family relatively intact, chances are we'll win," he wrote in a memo to President Carter as they began their general election fight in 1980. He urged Carter to appeal "directly to our constituencies—Jews, labor, minorities, farmers, ethnics, women, environmentalists, etc." Running that fall against Ronald Reagan, Carter and Mondale did just that—and lost in a landslide.

Mondale's basic premise was no longer true. After half a century of change, the old New Deal coalition was but a memory. That coalition was the product of an industrial world that, by 1980, was slipping into antiquity. Burgeoning globalization and computerization were beginning to change America's economy—and Americans' political outlooks would necessarily follow suit. Unfortunately, that was not the lesson Walter Mondale took from his 1980 defeat. In his 1984 campaign for president, he succeeded as no candidate had before in gaining the support of old-style constituent groups. The price was that he seemed to sacrifice his independence. In one famous exchange during a 1984 debate, he refused to name a single issue on which he differed from organized labor. It wasn't that he couldn't, but that he wouldn't. He simply refused to disagree with the views of one of the constituent parts of the Democratic political machine.

The political rules Mondale had grown up with no longer applied. Increasingly independent-minded Americans cared more about whether politicians were friendly to their individual concerns than whether they were friends with a particular interest group. In the Democratic primaries, Gary Hart—who, upon his election to the Senate in 1974, associated himself with a generation of politicians whom he famously said were "not a bunch of little Hubert Humphreys"—was able to say that his campaign against Mondale was "a choice between the future and the past." The insurgents of '48 had become the old guard of '84. In November, Mondale carried only one state: his home state of Minnesota—by fewer than four thousand votes.

In 1995, the front-page headline of the *Minneapolis Labor Review* blared, "Mondale Betrays Labor." The *Minneapolis Star Tribune* asked, "What next? Michael Jordan sells Reeboks?" Yet, this apostate Mondale was not Walter, but his eldest child Ted—a state senator who, unlike his father, had found a subject on which he disagreed with organized labor. In the opinion of the president of the state's AFL-CIO, Mondale had "decided to stab his *friends* in the back."

It was Ted Mondale's deciding vote on a reform of the state's outdated workers' compensation program that earned him the enmity of the Minnesota AFL-CIO. But he didn't seem to mind all that much. For, like his father before him, he had also had a political epiphany. Yet, his revelation came not from hearing a voice over the radio, but going door to door during his first campaign in St. Louis Park. At age 33, he came face to face with a new reality.

As he tells the story: "I entered the race with the somewhat parochial view that politics is about what political label you wear and what interest groups you have on your side. I ended the race understanding that this kind of politics isn't relevant to regular voters. The people in St. Louis Park . . . care about their jobs, their families, and the future of their children."

Although he bears a striking physical resemblance to his father, Ted Mondale grew up in a very different world—not the industrial 1930s and 1940s, but amidst the social, economic, and technological transformations of the 1970s and 1980s. He wasn't the son of a minister, but of a leading national politician. This meant he was reared not in the small town of Ceylon, Minnesota, but in the fishbowl of Washington, D.C. As a young man, his rebellious streak drove him to take up motocross racing and jobs shoveling chicken droppings out of boxcars. As is usually the case with the errant sons of privilege, Mondale eventually found his way. He married and had three children. He traded up from motocross racer to Little League coach. He traded down from chicken excrement shoveler to lawyer and politician. But, along the way, he never lost his taste for rebellion.

As a state senator he advanced policies that fit the times, such as promoting economic growth, streamlining government, and cutting corporate subsidies, even though they might have been opposed by the Democratic Party's "friends." In 1998, he ran for the Democratic nomination for governor of Minnesota. As part of his campaign, he published not just a platform but a 130-page-long detailed book outlining exactly what he would do if elected. It contained new ideas that broke with the old assumptions of both parties.

Mondale staked much of his candidacy on his ability to attract younger voters to the Democratic Party. Unlike most contemporary politicians, he realized that the best way to do that was not with the latest music or most eye-catching computer graphics, but with policies that actually speak to young people's concerns. Together with Stan Greenberg, Clinton's pollster during the 1992 election, Mondale undertook a study of the political attitudes of voters below the age of 30 for the Democratic Leadership Council. As he put it, "There is a beginning consensus of beliefs among young voters all across the spectrum, whether liberal or conservative, Democratic or Republican, men or women. The consensus centers on three core beliefs—self reliance and responsibility, less costly government and hostility to intrusive government." He and Greenberg found that more than any other age group, young people believed that government's role was to empower people to do things for themselves—especially by reforming education. For these voters, Mondale said there was "nothing where the Democratic or Republican party is saying, 'Hey, this is how you're going to make it in the world.'" Throughout his gubernatorial campaign, Mondale warned that the Democrats had to change their tune or risk losing the votes of young people with no affinity for the old incantations.

But all his efforts weren't enough for Ted Mondale in 1998. Running against his party's status quo he ran into its entrenched interests in the primary election and ended up winning only 7 percent of the vote. Mondale lost to someone who could truly be described as "a little Hubert Humphrey"—Skip Humphrey, who embraced his father's policies much more wholeheartedly. To take on this traditional Democrat, the Republicans nominated a fairly traditional candidate of their own. And the two parties began playing out their appointed parts in this predictable contest.

Except, this time, there was a tiny twist—a 6'4", 250-pound tiny twist with a feather boa named Jesse Ventura. Decrying the stale politics of both parties and offering a breath of fresh air, Ventura secured the Reform Party's nomination and went on to win the governorship. And he did so with nearly 50 percent of young voters. In contrast, the Republican nominee received only about a third of these votes. As for Skip Humphrey, he won among voters over 60, collecting 40 percent of their vote. When it came to voters under 30, he received a paltry 16 percent.

Ventura's election was a signal from Minnesota's voters—especially its young voters. The old-style politics offered by both parties no longer appealed to them. Walter Mondale's world had disappeared. Now Minnesotans were demanding that his brand of politics pass as well.

Soon after the votes were tallied, Governor-elect Ventura lumbered past a group of waiting reporters. Since his campaign had been based more on his own personality and general outlook than any particular policies, they asked him if he had any thoughts about the types of proposals he might make as governor. He paused for a moment, blinked a few times, and replied, "I thought Ted Mondale wrote a good book."

AN UPHEAVAL OF POLITICS

By reassuring the bond market, appeasing the Federal Reserve, and nurturing low interest rates and high consumer confidence, the signing of the balanced budget accelerated an economy that had already been cruising along. It helped nourish the longest economic expansion in American history—one that has brought more prosperity to more Americans of all stations than ever before in the nation's history.

Yet, the economic story of the 1990s was not one of growth, but of transformation. In May of 1998, I worked with Vice President Gore on a major economic policy address to the Detroit Economic Club, the traditional forum for presidential candidates to deliver their economic platforms. As it happened, the day before he was to give the address, Chrysler and Daimler-Benz announced their merger. Sitting in the vice president's sunny West Wing office that morning, even the most senior officials of the country, including Treasury Secretary Robert Rubin, his deputy and successor Larry Summers, and National Economic Council chief Gene Sperling, regarded the development with hesitation. Finally, a senior White House political staffer spoke up and asked the question that was on everyone's mind: "This is a good thing. . . right?" He never got a straight answer. The vice president went ahead with his speech the following day, but much of the tone of triumphalism over America's manufacturing resurgence seemed strangely hollow at a time when profits flow through Stuttgart as easily as they do through Detroit.

Everywhere one turns brave new rules are taking the place of the old. A cursory glance at the headlines shows that we live in one of those rare moments when the tempo of history seems to move a little bit faster. In America and around the world, a series of epochal changes are altering nearly every aspect of our lives. Today, people, products, and ideas move across the globe with greater ease than our grandparents traveled across town. Rapid technological advancements are transforming our world bit by bit and byte by byte. The economy is driven by skills, learning, ideas, knowledge, innovation, and creativity. The centralization and hierarchy of workplaces defined by the assembly line has given way to the flexible, team-oriented atmosphere of many of today's modern offices. Many have thought about the implication of these changes for the economy, the workforce, and society, but far fewer have thought about the implications for government. Yet such thinking is urgently needed.

From America's beginning, a major part of our national story has been the tale of Americans adapting government to a changing economy. Throughout most of the twentieth century, political leaders built up a powerful government to provide Americans with security and protection from the adversities of the industrial world. Today, what Franklin Roosevelt called "the Machine Age" has been replaced by an age of computers and communication—new technologies that give individuals personal power. In response, the public is searching for a new role for government—one that corresponds to a world where personalized services put decisions and choices into the hands of the individual.

AND THEY'RE *STILL* RIGHT

Our citizens feel they've lost control of even the most basic decisions made about the essential services of government, such as schools, welfare, roads, and even garbage collection. And they're right.

—*Ronald Reagan, State of the Union Address, 1982*

Out there, you can hear the quiet, troubled voice of the forgotten middle class, lamenting that government no longer looks out for their interests or honors their values—like individual responsibility, hard work, family, community. They think their government takes more from them than it gives back and looks the other way when special interests only take from this country and give nothing back. And they're right.

—*Bill Clinton, "New Covenant" address, 1991*

Using forty souvenir ceremonial pens to write his name with a series of tiny strokes, Clinton signed the balanced budget. His signature marked the culmination of more than just the federal budget deficit. Together with his signature of the welfare reform bill the preceding August and with Vice President Gore's "Reinventing Government" initiative, it made real the stunning statement he made before the Congress and the nation in his 1996 State of the Union Address: "The era of big government is over."

Public antipathy toward big government had never really been about the size of government itself, but about its character. Most citizens—in fact, most people who work in government—would be very hard pressed to state whether any particular program in the federal budget costs $1 billion, $10 billion, or $100 billion.

What so exercised Americans was a government that seemed out-of-touch, out-of-date, and out-of-control. By reforming a welfare system that was paying able-bodied adults to sit at home instead of helping them find work, Clinton ended the most egregious case of government being out of touch with Americans' basic values. By cutting more than three hundred thousand bureaucrats and promoting modern management practices in federal agencies, Vice President Gore's "Reinventing Government" project tried to bring government up to date in reflecting the ways America's successful businesses now run their operations. Now, by signing a budget that, for the first time in thirty years, would not spend more than it took in, Clinton was bringing government finances under control.

But in reality, his "era of big government is over" statement was more an acknowledgment than an announcement. The American people had made that decision over the course of the previous three decades. In 1964, 76 percent of the public trusted the federal government to "do what is right just about always or most of the time." Thirty years later, in 1994, that number had dropped to 21 percent. Barry Goldwater lost in a landslide that first year, Newt Gingrich strode to victory in the second.

In ending the era of big government, Bill Clinton was reflecting the public mood. The support for an expansion of government had disappeared. Americans have realized the Industrial Age has vanished and have little patience for the obsolete political debate that it produced.

Nevertheless, that debate still continues. Like a horror movie zombie, it is deceased, but does not know it; dead, but still stalking the earth. Today, the central fallacy of liberals is the idea that Americans want more of the same type of government they had in the twentieth century. The central fallacy of conservatives is the notion that Americans want a less active government. In fact, throughout the 1990s, public opinion surveys consistently showed that what Americans want is a decentralized, nonbureaucratic government—that is more active than ever. This finding is a perennial source of mirth for Washington political insiders who chortle at the misguided contradictions and silly assumptions of the American people. It turns out that the joke's on them.

Americans' new expectations from the public sector are completely in line with their new experiences in the private sector. In the Information Age, particularly with the Internet, they are able to do, read, hear, and see more than they ever have before. They have more buying and decision-making power than they ever thought possible. And all this new might flows not through a bureaucracy, but directly into their hands.

None of this, however, stopped Republicans in Congress from seeking to simply provide less government—attempting to eliminate the Department of Education and cut the school lunch program. Nor did it stop President Clinton, his wife, and Democrats in Congress from attempting one of the biggest expansions of government ever—the nationalization of the health care system. Believing fervently that antipathy toward government was due to the fact that the middle-class felt government was only helping the poor, the Clintonites were convinced that a large new middle-class entitlement program was not only smart public policy, but would put a new generation in the debt of the Democratic Party just as surely as the advent of Social Security and Medicare had done in years past. In a bitter defeat, their plan failed—and they never quite grasped why.

It was not that Americans didn't want universal health care coverage or had tired of activist initiatives. Polls showed they simply rejected an expansion of the outdated bureaucratic government delivery system. In the endless analysis on the demise of liberalism, this central idea is almost always lost. Americans in the 1970s, 1980s, and 1990s, did not turn their backs on liberals just because of McGovern, Vietnam, or the long hot summers and muddy hippies of 1960s radicalism. Centralized government's time passed because the industrial America that produced it disappeared. In seeking to succor Americans with universal health care, the Clintons were singing a great song—except they released it on an 8-track tape.

With the demise of health care reform, Democrats of all stripes lost their nerve. The New Deal dream had collapsed in public indifference and anger. Their compass had failed them, their map no longer fit the terrain. Figuring that the way to get the public's support was to travel more slowly down the same road, Democrats resolved to putter around the edges of big challenges.

With the drive for universal coverage collapsing in 1994, First Lady Hillary Rodham Clinton brought her "Give 'Em Health, Hillary" campaign to the American Nurses Association meeting in San Antonio. There, in a rousing speech that would have made the heroes of the Alamo proud, she called for an all-or-nothing battle to the death. "As Congress acts on health care legislation," she told the nurses, "you need to say as clearly as you can: 'This is not a time for incrementalism.'"

Five years later, while on a listening tour of upstate New York in anticipation of her Senate candidacy, Hillary Clinton revealed the extent to which politicians of both parties offered a constrained vision in response to a changing world. Addressing an audience in Cooperstown, she made it clear that from now on, government should refrain from major innovations. Recounting her experience with health care reform, she said, "Now clearly that approach did not work, and we're not going to go try that again, rest assured. . . . I come from the school of small steps now, the belief that making smaller changes, incremental changes that will help some people, is better than walking away." Even in Cooperstown, swinging for the fences is clearly a thing of the past.

Hillary had it right the first time—at least in part. The problem with her original health care plan was the size of its bureaucracy, not the scope of its ambition. Getting players on base is a good strategy to win the game, but only the long ball gets the crowd to its feet. "Inch-a-lotta" politics—hoping that if one steadfastly and successively crawls toward big changes instead of sprinting, the protectors of the status quo won't notice—may or may not be good legislative strategy, but is a poor way to energize an American public that is turning away from government in disgust and indifference.

Even more important, less of more of the same does not meet the main challenge facing both parties today: figuring out a successor principle to that of the New Deal. Over the course of the 1990s, both parties had their fundamental ideologies rejected by the public—health care reform for the Democrats, the Gingrich Revolution for the Republicans. In the wake of these political disasters, political leaders in both parties are lost, substituting tiny tinkers for real vision.

Of course, small, incremental, but worthy steps have their place. Throughout the 1996 campaign, Clinton advanced a series of ideas—school uniforms, teenage curfews, providing cellular phones to neighborhood watch groups—that were insignificant only to those who judge effectiveness by the size of the appropriation, and not the result. For working parents, these proposals had a bigger impact on their everyday lives than a great deal of what passes as important government actions.

In 1996, Clinton's symbolic issues were shorthand illustrations of the values behind his larger agenda of economic, education, and tax proposals—support for family values, belief in the power of government to empower individuals, rejection of the false choices of the past. But, in the few yet full years since the balanced budget, politicians of both parties have decoupled the small issues from the big ideas they represented. At a time when multiple transformations are reshaping the landscape of American life, political proposals from both parties are laughably small. A "Bill of Rights" for airline passengers, more money for child car seats, a fistful of dollars in tax cuts. Soon they stop being symbols and start being simple ways of conflating action and achievement. Especially at a time of epic change outside of Washington, puny proposals substituting for a real reform agenda transform the president of the United States into the mayor of the Munchkin City.

These piddling programs—in Emerson's words, "small, sour and fierce schemes"—have become just another excuse in a pattern of avoidance that has defined politics in Washington since the balanced budget deal was signed. Like third-rate newscasters with a broken teleprompter, politicians, rendered mute when it comes to statements of substance, have resorted to banter and stalling. Lost without a vision, both parties have sought to change the subject at every turn and hope they never have to answer what it is exactly that they now stand for.

In the meantime, the past few years have witnessed a domestic policy that has, much like America's international policy in the post–Cold War years, been adrift. In both instances, we have been left with a policy alternating between meddle and muddle—more activity and less thinking about the reasons for this activity. In neither case have national leaders stepped up to the task of developing successor doctrines to those that defined the twentieth-century debates. Today both political parties have failed to find a new governing vision, a new song of their own.

They don't even dare try. In the early 1990s, most of the "experts" were convinced that budget deficits were something Americans would have to simply learn to accept—much as they were convinced in the late 1980s that the Soviet Union would always exist, always be communist, and always guard over an Iron Curtain that ran like a scar through the heart of Europe. Those who said anything different would be politely humored for their naivete. The accepted wisdom, constrained visions, and small dreams of the political establishment served to sanctify the status quo as the boundary of public thinking.

It is this fundamental failure of imagination which, as much as timidity, explains why contemporary politicians—liberal, moderate, and conservative alike—turn to incremental solutions to tackle large-scale challenges. They simply cannot envision a form of government that is substantially different from the options the Democrats and Republicans have been presenting for the past seventy years. Even those officials who do have a flash of insight quickly bury it and hide it from view, confiding perhaps only to their spouses at night after the kids have gone to bed. Bold departures from the status quo are simply not acceptable cocktail party chatter among the Washington elite—in whose rarefied company a bemused and indulgent smirk is more deadly than the most passionate attack.

It's no accident that politics' idealism disappeared at the same time as its ideology. Both concepts rely on a fundamental optimism—a belief that, as Thomas Paine wrote, "we have it in our power to begin the world over again." There are some things that you might say in the company of your close friends that you wouldn't dare say before a crowd of thousands. In today's Washington, ideology and idealism are the exact opposites—

fine for rah-rah speeches, but not the province of serious adults. What
the times require, however, is a revival and renewal of both.

THE STUPIDEST TEA PARTY

I believe most of you have had the great pleasure of reading that
very delightful book of nonsense, *Alice Through the Looking Glass*,
the companion of *Alice in Wonderland*. Alice in the book, you
remember is seized by the hand by the Red Chess Queen, who races
her off at a breathless pace until both of them can run no further
for lack of breath; then they stop and Alice looks around and says:
"But we are just where we were when we started."

"O, yes," says the Red Queen, "you have to run twice as fast as
that to get anywhere else."

—*Woodrow Wilson, campaign address at Hartford, Connecticut,*
September 25, 1912

In June of 1995, congressional Democratic leaders went to the White
House to beg Bill Clinton not to submit a balanced budget plan. The
new Republican majority in Congress had done just that and now they
were on the run. House Democratic Leader Dick Gephardt compared
the situation to the epic battle scene in the movie *Braveheart*. Just as Mel
Gibson's William Wallace had counseled his troops to "Hold! Hold!
Hold!" until the British were right on top of them before they unleashed
their long spears, Clinton should continue to let the Republicans pay
the political price for proposing cuts in Medicare before unveiling the
Democrats' own cuts.

Clinton disagreed. He argued—against these Democratic leaders and
almost all of his staff—that the American people expected political
progress, not just partisan wrangling and that new economic circumstances meant that government would have to change its ways. Less than
a week later, he broke with the party's past and much of its present by
submitting to the nation his own plan to balance the budget. The following year, he was reelected by a wide margin, while congressional

Democrats failed to win back control of Capitol Hill. And when the balanced budget was signed in 1997, many Democratic congressional leaders were nowhere to be found. They had voted against the deal. They were still counseling Democrats to "hold."

In *The Vital Center*, Arthur Schlesinger decried a breed of Democrats he called "Doughface Progressives"—Henry Wallace-type liberals, addled with sentimentality and with nary a bad word to say about Soviet communism. Today, the shame of the Democratic Party are those who are more interested in scoring political points than in achieving real progress. Usually, they confine their efforts to fighting to maintain the status quo in the face of Republican assaults on their most sacred programs and constituencies. They have given up on changing the world.

Like Alice and the Red Queen, they run themselves ragged without getting anywhere—because the land they are trying to reach is a figment of the past. Call them the Treadmillers. Deep down, Treadmillers—whose ranks include many Democrats on Capitol Hill—know they're not going to move forward, but they'll fight to the death to stay where they are. They work up a sweat and they get themselves and those who believe in them into fighting form—but they never get ahead.

Shackled by nostalgia and the convictions of yesteryear, the Treadmillers simply can't run fast enough to outdistance the world as it is. So, instead, they put out a blizzard of policies and proposals, cry out in impassioned speeches, and pour their energies into well-meaning petition campaigns. And, even when a slender ray of light breaks through the bleakness of government gridlock and they are successful in their endeavor, the average American is only slightly better off than when the whole rigmarole began. The world is simply moving faster than their ideas. Not just content to build castles in the clouds, they've moved in. Yet, in the meantime, in the land below the people are starved for real changes.

Republicans in Washington are no better—in fact, they are usually a good deal worse. They practice their own brand of this politics of avoidance. Call them the Blockheads. Unsure how to handle questions of education, crime, welfare, and so on, they seek to use "block grants" to transfer tax money from the federal bureaucracy to state bureaucracies. However, this does nothing to increase the choices and power of individual Americans. These block grants don't devolve power from Washington, just responsibility. Blockheads use shifting the bucks as an excuse for passing the buck. They wash their hands of any notion of progress or mutual obligations with the idea that it is always someone else's problem, someone else's child, someone else's job, someone else's school.

For most of a century, Americans have been offered a choice between THE program—big, bureaucratic, centralized, hierarchical, expert-controlled—and no program. Where once these options were fresh, now they are frustrating—disconnected from the modern world. The role of government in this new century should be to offer programs that each American can shape to fit their individual needs, outlook, insight, personality, and lifestyle. This is the idea that can renew, reshape, and realign American politics.

There is a real hunger today for a politics that is relevant to the modern world. The tough veneer Americans wear when they wade into political discussions is not cynicism, but skepticism. The former implies the absence of hope, the latter suggests hope dampened by experience. For at least a generation, Americans have been disappointed by leaders who failed to keep their word and failed to act with honor. They have been offered a choice largely between two unsatisfying options: Treadmillers and Blockheads. But despite it all, Americans have an instinctive feeling that there was a time when this nation believed in the possibility of politics. They are looking for a government that will respond to their world to give them that chance again.

A SILLINESS AT WASHINGTON

Down by the roadside near Appomattox Court House, Sheridan and Ord and other officers sat and waited while a brown-bearded little man in mud spattered uniform rode up. They all saluted him, and there was a quiet interchange of greetings, and then General

Grant tilted his head toward the village and asked: "Is General Lee up there?"

Sheridan replied that he was, and Grant said: "Very well. Let's go up."

The little cavalcade went trotting along the road to the village, and all around them the two armies waited in silence. As the generals neared the end of their ride, a Yankee band in a field near the town struck up "Auld Lang Syne."

—*Bruce Catton, conclusion of* A Stillness at Appomattox

While a red-jacketed Marine boomed "God Bless America" from the balcony of the White House, I still contemplated my discomfort. My mind raced back to a book I had been paging through in the beautifully ornate library of the Old Executive Office Building—the huge old building contained within the White House gates that houses almost all of the White House staff. Playing hooky from an awaiting assignment and wandering through the library's wonderful collection looking for a flash of inspiration, I had run across Bruce Catton's history of the final months of the Civil War, *A Stillness at Appomattox,* a book with a title so evocative of the time it describes—the instant when, after years of the bloodiest fighting Americans have ever seen, the two armies met, put down their swords, and the War of the Brothers ended.

As the platform participants milled around following the budget signing, I thought of the dreadfully uncomfortable moment that Robert E. Lee and Ulysess S. Grant faced as the surrender had been completed. For here, before my own eyes, another long and bitter war was coming to an end.

For sixty years, since Franklin Roosevelt marshaled the forces of the then tiny federal government to fight the Great Depression, the battle between the Democrats and Republicans had centered on their vision of the size of government. The New Deal social contract essentially said that government would act as your parent—tell you what to do and what not to do, make sure you ate your vegetables and got your dessert, punish you if you were bad, and give you some extra money to help you out if times were tough.

The Republican policies of Ronald Reagan accepted many of the same underpinnings. In effect, he said, "Your parents have been over-bearing and overprotective. You have to learn to make it on your own. It's time to cut the apron—and purse—strings." The theory was that of tough love, the reality was that of a deadbeat dad. Despite the rhetoric, the old commitments all stayed in place. It was only the money that dried up.

In *The Vital Center*, Arthur Schlesinger, then a young man, declared that "During most of my political consciousness this has been a New Deal country. I expect that it will continue to be a New Deal country." For nearly fifty years, he was right. If, as the historian William E. Leuchtenberg has written, American presidents live "in the shadow of FDR," then our view of government sat in the shadow of the New Deal. "The press is trying to paint me as now trying to undo the New Deal. I remind them that I voted for FDR four times," protested Ronald Reagan to his diary in 1982. Both parties argued endlessly about government's size and its reach, but the basic underpinnings and understandings of the New Deal—that an active government meant a bureaucratic one and that government's role was to act as a powerful counterforce to other big enti-ties—were largely accepted by all.

But with a Democrat signing a balanced budget and presiding over a retrenchment and devolution of government power, the old war over the New Deal ceased. The proponents of a larger federal government never waved the white flag; they simply disappeared from positions of serious responsibility. In fact, just about the only two places one can find old-style doctrinaire liberals anywhere near political power these days are in the think tanks and Washington pressure groups that publish report after mind-numbing report in order to justify their own existence and on television public affairs shows—an electronic Jurassic Park where TV producers who simply don't know any better provide a forum for breath-less pundits peddling extinct viewpoints.

The old debate over the New Deal ended because most Americans have given up on it. As most sports fans understand, the way to know that the game is over is not to watch the clock or listen for the buzzer. It's to look at the crowd. When they pack up their cushions and their coolers, the game is fairly certain to be done. Today, when it comes to politics, Americans are headed for the parking lot.

Voting and political interest have plummeted not because Americans are suddenly too weak-willed to make it to the ballot booth, too weak-minded to understand the issues, or too weak-stomached to swallow some negative political attacks. Americans are turning away from politics because the old debates are irrelevant to the ways they now live their lives.

Of course, most political insiders refuse to accept this fact. Just as the players on the field and their most die-hard fans still think that a last-minute turnover or a ninth inning grand slam will turn the tide, many Democrats and Republicans wait eagerly for the day when the public regains their appetite for centralized government programs or huge tax breaks.

Realizing this was not going to happen, Bill Clinton took Roosevelt's original pro-government thesis and Ronald Reagan's anti-government antithesis and combined them into his own synthesis: a smaller, less bureaucratic government that would still undertake big tasks on behalf of the American people. In a speech before the Democratic Leadership Council in December of 1996, he picked up on a theme which he had first laid out on the night of his reelection: that of a new "vital center" of American politics. "We've helped to forge a new American vision, a new consensus that can govern our country and move us all forward. The ground has shifted beneath our feet, but we have clearly created a new center—not the lukewarm midpoint between overheated liberalism and chilly conservatism, but instead a place where throughout our history, people of goodwill have tried to forge new approaches to new challenges . . . that vital center that has brought so much progress to our nation in the last four years; the vital, dynamic center from which we now must finish the work of preparing America for the 21st century."

While the auld acquaintance of the New Deal has, thankfully, not been forgot, Clinton led liberalism on an "enterprise of reexamination" no less "fundamental" than that which Schlesinger described in Roosevelt's generation. His synthesis closed the door on the antiquated New

Deal debate. However, in the end, Clinton's failure to set forth an original new thesis to replace the New Deal theory limited his ability to "create a new and distinct political generation."

America has paid a high price for this failure—not only in the loss of years to stillness that could have been used for intellectual progress, but in the price of silliness when seriousness is required. In that classic of American cinema, *Blazing Saddles*, the citizens of Rock Ridge build an exact replica of their town in order to thwart Hedley Lamarr's "great crusade to stamp out runaway decency in the West." The townspeople and the invading hordes duke it out in a huge brawl in the false front city, while the real Rock Ridge is empty. So too today, politics is played out in angry debates amidst a Potemkin Village facade of emotion-laden, focus-grouped issues that enrich campaign consultants and impoverish our politics. And meanwhile, the real issues remain untouched.

Politicians in both parties, unsure of where the nation is headed and how to respond to this new world, have been petrified into a convenient gridlock. The nation has been served a small politics of poll-tested pabulum and scorched-earth campaigns—unsound, yet full of fury; a slog through scandal and a war over minutia; an irrelevant politics built on quips and quibbles, seven-second sound bites and thirty-second attack ads. All the while, Americans feel more and more disengaged from a politics that has less and less relation to how they now live their lives.

WHAT COMES NEXT?

While I didn't know it at the time, the day of the balanced budget signing marked not only the end of an era of runaway deficits, but the culmination of Bill Clinton's presidency. Just five months later, any hope for more real substantive accomplishments and reforms was overtaken by the miasma of Monica.

Looking back on the 1990s, Bill Clinton was a political Moses. He led American government out of a philosophical enslavement to the New Deal debates that had defined public life for most of the twentieth

century, but had grown shop-worn and counterproductive in the new
Information Age. He led his people to the mountaintop. But, like
Moses, he was fated to be unable to lead them into the promised land.
He never was able to finish the job of showing the nation where to go
next.

Despite perceptions to the contrary, the Clinton administration fulfilled almost all its promises. The record is more mixed when it comes
to fulfilling its *promise*. Significant—in fact, remarkable—progress has
come in addressing many of the problems Clinton inherited when he
took office. Yet, far less has been done in taking positive, proactive new
steps to address the changes wrought by the Information Age on our culture, economy, and society. New circumstances are demanding a politics that won't merely try to shore up Machine Age structures, but builds
anew—with new initiatives and new institutions for our own time.

Clinton and Gore were right to work to restore public trust and government competency through the process of "reinventing government."
Today's government is smaller and more efficient. Yet, too often, all this
has given us is what Henry David Thoreau called "improved means for
unimproved ends." The trains run on time, but no one has changed
where they are going. This administration has changed how government
does things. Now the time has come to change what government does.

It could have been that I was just looking too hard for it. It could have
been they were thinking about the event's logistics. But as they prepared
to leave the platform at the balanced budget signing, their eyes met. Bill
Clinton and Newt Gingrich. Standing on the White House South Lawn.
One the leader of the party of Franklin Roosevelt, Lyndon Johnson, and
Hubert Humphrey. The other the leader of the party of Dwight Eisenhower, Barry Goldwater, and Ronald Reagan. And there I could swear I
saw it. A raised eyebrow. A curled lip. A tiny shrug. A look that said,
"Where now?"

The New Generation of Choice

Those who are born today are born into a world in which the foundations of the old order survive only as habits or by default. Scientific invention and blind social currents have made the old authority impossible. . . . Our time believes in change.

—*Walter Lippmann, 1914*

CHOOSE OR LOSE

The adventures you take are a result of your choice. *You* are responsible because *you* choose.

—*Edward Packard, Page 1 of* The Cave of Time

Edward Packard wasn't trying to rock the boat, he was simply looking for an easy way out. A successful 38-year-old New York lawyer, he did what successful 38-year-old New York lawyers do. Every morning he left his home in Greenwich, Connecticut, boarded the train headed to Manhattan, worked a long day on entertainment and anti-trust cases in his firm's offices high above the canyons of New York City, and then packed himself into the train heading back to Greenwich at night. And if he returned home early enough, his two daughters—9-year-old Caroline and 5-year-old Andrea—would greet him with a demand for a bedtime story starring an imaginary character named "Pete."

One night in 1969, bone-tired and with his head swimming, Packard found it so difficult to concentrate on the story that he asked Caroline and Andrea what they thought Pete should do next. Each had a different answer. Riding the train the next day, Packard wondered what would happen if somebody wrote a story with both paths as options. He tried his hand at doing just that with the manuscript for a book entitled "The Adventure of You on Sugar Cane Island." It was rejected by nearly a dozen New York publishers as being unsellable, and Packard put it away in a desk drawer for the better part of a decade.

In 1975, Packard read an article in *Vermont Life* magazine about a small publisher in the state that was looking for innovative ideas. Remembering his now dusty document, he submitted it to them and heard shortly afterward that it had been accepted. The book sold eight thousand copies—phenomenal sales for an alternative publisher. In 1979, the idea and the times finally met. A major national publishing house contracted to release a whole series of books based on Packard's concept. They decided to call the series Choose Your Own Adventure. The first book published was entitled *The Cave of Time*. Since then, 184 Choose Your Own Adventure titles have been published with hundreds of millions of copies in print—not to mention the dozens of popular series of children's books that have copied the format.

One of the best-selling children's book series in history, Choose Your Own Adventure books put the reader in the driver's seat. Reaching numerous forks in the road of the plot, the reader decides which path to take—whether to enter door #1 or door #2—and accepts the consequences. Their significance to the generation of young people who grew up with them shouldn't be overstated, but in their popularity one can glimpse an aspect of the era. Just as Horatio Alger's stories were a commentary on the new pathways to success of the Gilded Age and Nancy Drew and the Hardy Boys evoked the comfort of middle-class life after World War II, the Choose Your Own Adventure series was a perfect fit for a generation of Americans that has always been blessed with a short attention span, a fundamental belief in self-reliance, and an unbending desire to control their own lives.

TORCH SONGS

> There is a mysterious cycle in human events. To some generations much is given. Of other generations much is expected. This generation of Americans has a rendezvous with destiny.
> —*Franklin Roosevelt, speech before the 1936 Democratic National Convention*

Each generation is unique—in the world it sees and in the world it seeks to create. Demographers might tell us that a generation is a cohort born within a twenty-five-year span, yet what truly defines members of a generation politically is not their birthdates but a shared set of experiences and events that shape their outlook for the rest of their lives. Looking at America through the lens of generations is more than just a shorthand, it shows the long view: since nothing is more inexorable than aging, the attitudes developed in a generation's youth are ever more relevant for years to come. In the twentieth century, the Lost Generation of the 1920s had their "rendezvous with destiny" during the New Deal. Although Tom Brokaw opened his phenomenally successful book, *The Greatest Generation*, with the words of FDR in the above epigraph, he wrote about a subsequent generation—the generation of Americans who hoarded whatever food they could gather as children during the Great Depression and then went on to defeat the hordes of fascism as young adults a few years later. In describing the generation of Arthur Schlesinger, Ronald Reagan, and Frank Sinatra, Brokaw remembers his wartime childhood as a time when "the grown-ups all seemed to have a sense of purpose." Americans of all ages seem to remember this intrinsically. There was more to the catch in the audience's hearts in *Saving Private Ryan*'s final generational tableau at the cemetery of Omaha Beach than Steven Spielberg's cinematic mastery.

When the GIs came home, they went to college in droves, moved to the suburbs, raised their millions of children, and built the largest middle class the world has ever known. And all the while, they felt that their shared experiences gave them a bond. In 1946, when 29-year-old Lieutenant

John F. Kennedy ran for Congress, his slogan was "The New Generation Offers a Leader." Fourteen years later, their commanding general,
Dwight David Eisenhower, passed the torch of leadership to this new
generation. While their shared experiences did not breed ideological
conformity (Richard Nixon and George McGovern both grew up poor
and fought in World War II), they did bring shared perspectives on the
way the world worked.

A different "sense of purpose"—but that same sense of mission—was
evident in the lives of their children: those who came of age in the tumultuous 1960s. In 1962, a student at the University of Wisconsin named
Tom Hayden issued the Port Huron Statement on behalf of a generation "bred in at least modern comfort, housed now in universities, looking uncomfortably to the world we inherit." They responded by challenging authority in most every fashion and seeking to remake their
inherited world. Whether a member of the small number that joined in
the culture of protest or the vast mass that was affected by it and its rever-
berations, the Baby Boomers' identity was largely forged in those
crowded years. Though their political views may have changed over
time, their fundamental outlook hardly budged.

When it comes to the young people of today, most commentators say
that their "sense of purpose" is, at least, hard to discern. When it comes
to wondering how future Brokaws and Spielbergs will depict this generation, the question is met by, at best, a shrug. Yet, today's young people also grew up in a world of unique circumstances and, as with the
most important generations of the past, they, too, will come to remake
the world—and government—in their own image.

A GENERATION FOUND IN CYBERSPACE

If one listens to most young pundits, the self-appointed spokespeople of
America's youth, one would not be faulted for believing that young
Americans basically see the world as their parents did—only without the
love beads and disco. In print and on television, this fresh-faced, chirp-

ing, chattering geek chorus tries desperately to fit the modern world into
the prescribed norms of generational struggle left over from the culture
of the 1960s, attacking the supposed errors and shortsightedness of the
previous generation and whining about inequities of distribution. They
nostalgically wave the tie-dye shirt, but most young people ignore their
call.

In fact, today's young people, reared at the meeting point of two great
streams of change—technological and social—are responding with a
central unifying ethic all their own: that of *choice*. Born at a time when
they had more choices to make with fewer restrictions than ever before
in history and bred with an overwhelming desire to make these decisions
for themselves in every part of their lives, the 90 million Americans
between the ages of 5 and 30 might well be dubbed the "Choice Generation." For them, having and making choices is not just a question of
process, not just a luxury when ordering from a restaurant menu, not
just bubbling in the right Scantron space on a multiple-choice test. It
reflects their sense of self-confidence, their expectation that the world
can be conformed to their individual personalities, and their belief in
taking responsibility for themselves and their community. Exercising
choice defines their outlook in no uncertain terms. Choice is an end, not
just a means.

Who is the Choice Generation? The Choicers are defined not by their
common ages, but a common age—a moment in time when dramatic
changes are not just accepted, but expected. Compared to any other
cohort in history, they have grown up in a world that has radically
expanded the number of choices they get to—and have to—make. The
sociologist Alan Wolfe has written that "the general feeling in America
is that you are middle class if you say so." Similarly, you are a member
of the Choice Generation if you say so—if the world of largely unfettered choices in lifestyle and due to technology is familiar; if the demand
for personalized decision-making power when working and shopping is
second-nature.

To lay some benchmarks, however, one could say that most of the
Choice Generation was born between 1970 and 1995. The oldest of

them gained consciousness of the world around them as the American Industrial Age was rusting: factory gates were being padlocked, Japanese cars were buffeting Detroit, big business and big labor were in decline. The youngest began school with the millennium and only know the Information Age. They will laugh, in just a couple of years, when they are told there was a world before "dot-coms."

The years between 1970 and 1995 were years of transformation, America's cocoon years, when the economy strained to catch up and keep up with new technologies and globalization, when community life struggled to make sense of the changes the 1960s and its aftermath had bequeathed to American society, and when government tried to figure out its role and mission in a very different world. The Choice Generation grew up in a new world even as their parents worked to make the transition from the old.

The Choice Generation is clearly an evolving group—its values are continually reinforced as technology continues to provide more choices, more personalization, and more individualized power. The big three TV networks have been challenged in turn by cable, by more networks, by a thousand channels of satellite and digital cable programming. The movie theater competed first with the VCR, which lets viewers control what they watch and when they watch from the comfort of their couches. It now has to deal with DVDs that let viewers skip to their favorite scenes and soundtracks. With increasing frequency, young people have begun to eschew prepackaged music albums in favor of custom-created CDs made up of the songs *they* choose. Pagers appeared and were followed by cellular phones. Personal computers transformed America and were followed by Palm Pilots. Young people traded in record players for personal Walkmans and then for even more control with Discmans. Everywhere one looks the technologies that shape the lives of the Choice Generation are constantly and consistently trending toward giving the individual more personal power. More than half of the nation's minors have a television and CD player in their bedroom. No one watches them over their shoulders; they have a previously unimagined amount of power to shape the environment they live in.

Most fundamentally, the Internet has put them in control. They read whatever they want to read, buy whatever they want to buy, download photos of the hottest star of the moment. Moreover, they don't have to look at CNN's web page, they can look at their MyCNN page, which shows them only the topics they are interested in. They don't have to sift through the Web with the AltaVista search engine, they can search with MyAltaVista, which conforms itself to their "surfing" habits. At mybytes.com (with the slogan, "It's my web"), they can customize "my research tools," "my calendar," "my interests," "my life," and so on. At myway.com, where "you'll get all the information you need, the way you want it," they are welcomed "to the Internet's distinct, new personality. Yours." At Barbie.com, they can design their own doll to fit the specifications they choose. At Nike.com, they can design their own sneakers and even have their own name put on the shoes. The notion of "one-size-fits-all" is ever more obsolete in a world they are increasingly customizing to fit themselves.

And it isn't just their scores of gadgets, it's that they're the scions of Gidget. They were the first generation to grow up after the morality revolutions of the 1960s—post-Woodstock, post-"I Have A Dream," post-*Roe v. Wade*, post-Women's Rights, and post-Pill. They know no world other than that created by the lifting of taboos, the legalization of abortion, the growing acceptance of homosexuality, the end of the belief that women belong only in the kitchen, the widespread availability of contraceptives, the death-knell of legally enforced racial discrimination, the moment when Americans found out *Everything You Always Wanted to Know About Sex But Were Afraid to Ask*. Many Americans criticize these changes and that which they have wrought, but by and large, the culture—both pop and parental—that the Choice Generation grew up with celebrated the ability of individuals to make more free choices about how they will live their lives than ever before. The notion that they will be told how to live their lives from on high is not just repugnant—as it has been to previous generations—but foreign. The idea that strict, settled norms of behavior cover courtship, friendship, or appearance is quaint at best. The attempt to hold them to bygone standards is met with a viscerally negative reaction.

The Choice Generation's formative years were and are ones with more questions than answers. The Information Age has challenged old assumptions about the economy; the 1960s challenged basic assumptions about society. If new answers are to be found, it seems likely that the idea of individual choice will be at their heart. Choice defines this generation, seeking it gives them direction, and practicing it is something they're perfecting.

THE KIDS ARE ALRIGHT

While the Choice Generation is loath to criticize the choices of others, it generally shows a strong streak of personal responsibility in exercising those choices themselves. Tolerance is one of their preeminent values, but by many measurements, they do not tolerate the "anything goes" attitude of some of their parents and older siblings when it comes to their own lives.

The statistics tell a story. In 1975, 22 percent of high school seniors had tried stimulant drugs. In 1996, that number had dropped to 15 percent. Between 1985 and 1996, the percentage of high school seniors who had tried cocaine fell by nearly 60 percent. The percentage of teenagers attending church at least once a week is up by nearly 20 percent over the past two decades. Since 1989, the number of 15- to 24-year-olds who report involvement in the community is up by 16 percent, involvement in their religious and spiritual beliefs is up by 11 percent, and a self-declared "focus on family" is up by 8 percent. The percentage of young people who said they had "cheated" on a test or exam dropped from 66 percent in 1981 to 46 percent in 1992. Arrests of juveniles for violent crimes fell by 19 percent between 1994 and 1998—3 times the decline for adults. Suicide among teens, after rising since the 1950s, has been declining since 1994. Teen deaths from drunk driving are down 59 percent since 1982. In 1980, 72 percent of high school seniors said they had consumed alcohol recently. Sixteen years later, it was 51 percent—a bare majority of high school kids sneaking beers behind the bleachers.

After rising from the 1960s through the early 1990s, by 1998 pregnancy among high school age teenagers was at a forty-year low—down by 18 percent from 1991. In 1980, 48 percent of females used contraceptives during their first intercourse; by 1995 that number had increased by nearly two-thirds to 78 percent. Between 1991 and 1998, the percentage of teenagers who say they have never had sex rose by 11 percent. Hormones presumably rage no less than previously, but self-control seems to be on a definite upswing.

All of these numbers can be explained away if one really wants to. The rise of dangerous sexually transmitted diseases—especially AIDS—hangs like a cloud over young people, laws more strictly enforcing the drinking age have been put on the books, organizations such as Mothers Against Drunk Driving and the campaign against teen pregnancy have changed the public climate, numerous antidrug ads on television have shown young people what happens to "your brain on drugs." But the collective weight of the evidence demonstrates a streak of personal responsibility in the Choice Generation that is undeniable and indelible. They are matching their individual freedom to make decisions for themselves with a New Responsibility in making them.

As more and more Choicers enter adulthood, they are beginning to bring a restabilization of the American family after decades of unbalance. Between 1970 and 1990, the percentage of Americans who lived in traditional families of married couples with children under 18 plummeted from 40 percent to 26 percent. However, between 1990 and 1997, the number dropped just one percent more. Between 1985 and 1990, the divorce rate fell by 6 percent. Over the next five years, it fell by 13 percent. Although Choicers tend to marry later, they seem to do so because they are more careful and deliberate about whom they choose for their mate. In this area, as in many, they are not just making choices, they are making *informed* choices. This should not come as too much of a surprise. Half of their families were torn apart by divorce. Each year, the Gallup poll finds that between 72 percent and 79 percent of teenagers believe that "divorce laws are too lax," compared to 55 percent in 1984.

The Choice Generation's views on family were forged by the uncertainty of their own childhoods. During the 1970s the number of latchkey kids doubled and it has stayed high. Choicers wandered home alone and learned their values and life lessons from the glow of a television set. They were told not to talk to strangers and not to tell anyone who called whether their parents were home. They were surrounded by a wave of crime and fear in the 1980s and early 1990s that scared and scarred them to such an extent that, even though crime has dropped around the country to 1950s levels, it is still routinely a top concern for young people.

Their parents, feeling guilty about leaving their kids to go to work, were convinced that stern discipline was a thing of the past and often-times swung the pendulum in the opposite direction, abdicating many of their parental responsibilities. By the late 1980s a survey of teens revealed that 48 percent classified their parents as "cool"—compared to just 7 percent who called them "strict" and one percent who called them "nosy." Many of the parents of the Choice Generation adopted a "sink or swim" philosophy of parenting, entrusting young people with making their own choices about lifestyle and behavior at a very early age. Some thrived, others suffered—and became examples from whom their peers first learned about consequences.

When they were young and changing the world, the Baby Boomers' slogan was "Don't trust anyone over 30." Today, the Choice Generation doesn't trust anyone at all. In 1999, only 32 percent of young people said most people can be trusted. Fully 65 percent said most people should be approached with caution. Given the generally lonely world they grew up in, their response should be expected. Another 1999 survey found that teens spent 9 percent of their waking hours outside school with their peers, but 20 percent of those hours alone. It is no accident that their paradigmatic television show is called *Friends*.

Buffeted by change, surrounded by uncertainty, and fearful of abandonment, the Choice Generation exhibits a hunger for traditional values of stability and security—but it defines them in very different ways and seeks to get them through very different means. According to a 1999 survey, they place their highest priorities on "having a close-knit family," "gaining knowledge, education, and skills," and "becoming successful in a career." They aren't looking for guarantees from government or any big business—and they aren't looking to be handed anything on a silver platter. They are practical—not flaky. They are self-reliant—and they like it that way.

BALLOT-BOXED OUT

Nowhere is the Choicers' internal tension between skepticism about others and faith in themselves more evident—and more important— than in their views on citizenship and participation in the affairs of the larger world. Every generation looks upon its progeny and, like Harry MacAfee of Sweet Apple, Ohio, in *Bye Bye Birdie,* wonders, "Why can't they be like we were? / Perfect in every way / What's the matter with kids today?" But, in the early part of the 1990s, many Baby Boomers, convinced of the goodness of their youthful idealism, were especially vicious in their flagellation of their offspring. Despite their fears, today's young people have become neither the hyperacquisitive Alex P. Keaton of *Family Ties* nor the apathetic slackers of *Wayne's World.* They are a generation with a steel-strong sense of social conscience—one that defines its view of itself. In 1984, one would turn on the radio and hear Cyndi Lauper sing that "Girls Just Want to Have Fun" and Madonna proclaim that "We are living in a material world and I am a Material Girl." Fifteen years later, a radio listener would instead hear Jewel tell a receptive audience that "In the end, only kindness matters."

But all is not well. At collegiate conferences and foundation functions, academics and politicians alike join together in sanctimonious hand-wringing about young people's disengagement from public life. First, foremost—and often finally—they point to the fact that voter turnout among young people has plummeted. Over the course of the past twenty-five years, the turnout among all adults in presidential elections fell from 63 percent in 1972 to 54 percent in 1996. During those same years since 18-year-olds first gained the right to vote, turnout among 18- to 24-year-olds plunged from 50 percent to only 32 percent. In the 1998 midterm elections, less than one in five 18- to 24-year-olds bothered to go to the polls. Eight percent of 18- to 29-year-olds turned out to vote in the initial contested presidential primaries of the 2000 election.

The Choice Generation's political alienation extends beyond the voting booth. In 1966, when UCLA's annual nationwide survey of hundreds of thousands of incoming college freshmen was first administered, 58 percent of students believed that "keeping up to date with political affairs" was important. By 1997, that number had been cut by more than half—to just 27 percent.

Faced with this massive rejection of modern politics, most experts—rightly—castigate young people for failing to recognize how precious their right to vote is. Then they offer up excuses by saying that voting is too difficult for young people and that nobody asks them to be involved. In fact, voting turnout among young people continued to drop precipitously throughout the 1990s despite the much ballyhooed "Motor Voter" law easing registration and a multimillion-dollar media campaign from groups such as Rock the Vote that even included Madonna, clad in an American flag and little else, calling on young people to exercise their franchise. Finally, pointing to the much larger turnout among elderly voters, the learned scholars conclude with the hope that young people will turn back toward public life once they settle down and gain a few gray hairs.

On its face, this last point seems reasonable enough. Overall, 56 percent of senior citizens say they feel connected to government, while 44 percent feel disconnected. In contrast, 31 percent of young people feel connected, while fully 69 percent feel disconnected. One in three young adults feels "very disconnected" from government compared to only one in ten seniors.

However, on close inspection, the numbers reveal a deeper problem than mere youthful indifference to the political process. In a 2000 survey of college students, 63 percent disagreed with the statement, "I am waiting until I am older before I become politically engaged." Young people have logged off from politics not because they are young, but for a specific reason: government bears little relation to their world. When given a choice in 1999, 57 percent of Americans over 65 years of age referred to "*our* government," while 38 percent called it "*the* government." On the other hand, among 18- to 24-year-olds, less than a third referred to "*our* government," while 65 percent spoke of "*the* government."

This significant difference is about more than semantics—it is rooted in fact. For seniors, the stooped but unbowed survivors of Brokaw's "greatest generation" and Schlesinger's "distinct political generation," it is *their* government—one whose outlook and attitude was largely forged in the New Deal of their youth, one committed to upholding the values that defined American public life more than half a century ago.

Young people are turning away from government in droves, because, while its programs and policies still influence their lives for better and for worse, its principles are remnants of the world of dime novels and Dusenbergs. The Choice Generation grew up in a world where government itself has increasingly seemed a Machine Age anachronism—wasteful, corrupt, distant, and laden with bureaucracy. They order blue jeans tailored to their measurements by computer, but stand in endless lines to pick up forms at the Department of Motor Vehicles. They correspond instantaneously over the Internet with friends who are thousands of miles away and buy the best available airplane tickets to see them with a click of the mouse, but wait endlessly for "the next available operator" to take them off "hold" when it comes time to get a passport. Everywhere they turn, choices and decision-making power are thrust into their hands—except when it comes to government. In major areas such as public schools, health insurance, job training, or Social Security, government does not believe that they can make their own decisions. Choicers are disengaged from government because they see no reason to become engaged. They are disinterested because their interests are routinely ignored by a government run on outdated ideas. They are disconnected from government because government is disconnected from them.

This does not mean that the Choice Generation ignores the world around them—in fact, the exact opposite is true. In an editorial decrying the absence of young people from the ballot box and political involvement, the *San Francisco Examiner* headlined them "A Passive Generation." Yet, the Choice Generation shuns politics not because of selfish apathy, but in favor of selfless activity. The same benchmark UCLA survey that documented such an alarming drop in youth voter turnout showed that the percentage of college freshmen who reported performing volunteer activities in their senior year of high school rose from 62 percent in 1989 to 73 percent only eight years later.

At first glance, this might seem a paradox. It is, in fact, a reasonable and rational response. A generation that impatiently raps its fingers on the table when it takes more than a few seconds to download a web page from China, which expects packages sent from the other end of the continent to arrive by 10:00 A.M. the next morning, which finds it difficult to watch TV without a remote control in hand, which demands a piping hot pizza delivered to their front door in half an hour, has elected to bypass government through the immediacy of individual action. Reared with an expectation of instant gratification that grows ever stronger, the Choice Generation—both committed and practical—cares first and foremost about results. Unfortunately, they've learned not to expect them from government. Anything but "passive," they are an active generation unwilling to waste their time with a government that seems to have become a quicksand for energy and a black hole for idealism.

Instead, the Choice Generation has poured its efforts into community service—hard work with faster results. In 1999, an amazing 94 percent of 15- to 24-year-olds agreed with the statement that the "most important thing I can do as a citizen is to help others." Most are doing just that. In 1989, 55 percent of that age group said they had helped an elderly neighbor in the past year. Ten short years later, 87 percent reported that same activity—an increase of significantly more than half.

This cornucopia of conscience extends far beyond occasionally helping an old lady cross the street. Nearly three out of four college students perform volunteer service. On most college campuses, service captures the attention and leadership of the best and brightest students in the way that the protest movement did thirty years ago. Of Americans between the ages of 15 and 29 polled in 1998, 44 percent reported doing work for a community-based or grassroots effort within the past year. The discrepancy between community and political activity is jarring. In a 1999 survey, young people between 15 and 24 were queried about how they spent their time. Fifty-nine percent had volunteered in a religious organization and 53 percent had volunteered in the community. At the same time, 16 percent had participated in a political march or demonstration, 16 percent had volunteered in a political campaign, and 14 percent had joined a political or government organization.

The Choice Generation is not a generation of "slackers," but neither is it interested in pursuing the lost and symbolic causes of their parents' youth. Although nostalgic Baby Boomers and a few of their offspring may hunger for sit-ins and demonstrations, most Choicers are less interested in taking to the streets to protest for change than in actually producing those changes themselves. Nor do Choicers understand the faith that their grandparents, the New Deal generation, had in government. When John F. Kennedy reminded his generation to "ask what you can do for your country," he was referring to public service and its nobility—celebrating those who take part in the work of government. When the Choice Generation hears those same words, they instinctively think of a reading tutor.

In a 2000 survey from Harvard's Institute of Politics, 60 percent of the nation's college students felt that "community volunteerism" was a better way than "political engagement" of solving important issues facing the country. Only 36 percent chose the reverse. When it came to issues facing their communities, the disparity was even larger. It's not that the Choice Generation doesn't believe government can work in a positive way (60 percent think "government should help families achieve the American dream"), it's that they're almost positive that today's government is not working. It's not that they don't care about others, but that they care too much to pour their efforts into politics.

Bringing change in a democracy is always a slow and deliberate process. But government's changing to fit the times is not impossible. It is, in fact, inexorable. Yet this can be sped or slowed by the actions of involved individuals. It is wonderful that so many Choicers volunteer to help others, but it is not enough. Government still matters in the twenty-first century—perhaps more than ever. It needs to change so that the Choice Generation has a reason to be involved; the Choice Generation needs to get involved in order to lead government to change.

YOU SAY YOU WANT A REVOLUTION

Buried in the pages of the February 1999 issue of *National Geographic* magazine was an advertisement for a financial services company featuring a young woman kayaking down a river. The text read, "I have a MOTHER. I have a FATHER. I even have a BIG BROTHER. I DON'T need someone else looking out for me. I NEED someone who can help me look out for myself." While politicians of both parties peddle the warmed-over leftovers of New Deal paternalism, the Choice Generation will not turn back to political life until its own values of self-reliance and individual decision making find a home in the public arena. For politics to become relevant to them, Choicers will have to be able to refer to government as "*our* government."

In a study conducted in the bicentennial year of 1976, 41 percent of high school seniors said they enjoyed "the fast pace and changes of today's world." By 1988, as the first members of the Choice Generation graduated from high school, that number had risen to 56 percent. During the same period, the percentage who felt that "there is too much competition in society" fell from 37 percent to 20 percent. A 2000 survey asked teens and their parents to choose between "fitting in with friends" and "becoming outstanding." Parents chose "becoming outstanding" over "fitting in with friends" by only 50 percent to 43 percent. Their Choice Generation teen children, supposedly at the age most susceptible to peer pressure and most fearful of social ostracization, chose "becoming outstanding" by 69 percent to 26 percent. Unlike generations of the past, the Choicers welcome the rigors and risks of competition and are very comfortable with the tropes of individualism. Instead of recoiling from change, they are rushing into it—and they have little patience for institutions that fall behind.

It is true that not all generations are heard from equally in America's song. There are those quiet cohorts who march softly through the pages of our history—sturdy and sound, but leaving this nation much as they found it. Yet, in every moment of change and challenge, a generation has risen to lead America and bring its own values and experiences to the fore. The Choice Generation is likely to be one of the most important generations in American history. This is because it was born at the fulcrum—as the Industrial Age gave way to the Information Age. It exhibits characteristics that will be found in all Information Age generations to come and its actions will come to define the century ahead.

This is not the first time such a generation has appeared in America. A century ago, another generation was born at the fulcrum—as the Agricultural Age was replaced by the Industrial Age. The Progressive Generation grew up in an unsettling time of massive social and technological changes. Much as the Choice Generation was raised after the 1960s' culture wars over civil rights and Vietnam, the Progressives came of age after the 1860s' divisive and exhausting moral debates over the Civil War and Reconstruction. At a time of relative prosperity, with leaders like Teddy Roosevelt and Woodrow Wilson, they realized that the changes wrought by industrialization meant that the purpose and process of government would have to be radically transformed to fit the new world.

In turn, the Choice Generation will have to be the source of a Choice Revolution in government. This Choice Revolution would replace one-size-fits-all programs built on the notion of protecting citizens from adversity with new initiatives that put decision-making power in the hands of individuals and give them the tools for upward mobility. According to a report cited in the *Washington Post*, "When . . . young people were asked if they would consider public service or government work, the words most often used in reply were 'big,' 'intransigent,' and 'stifling'—the same words applied generations ago to business." Though business has caught up to the times, government lags behind. By the very nature of elections, politics will never respond to the decisions and desires of each individual. But this does not mean that government can't. As the Progressives built up a big, regimented, bureaucratic government to fit the age of assembly lines, it falls to the Choicers to create a government as decentralized and empowering as the businesses that are increasingly defining the future.

Everywhere one looks, the effects of the tremors of the Choice Revolution can be seen. The landscape of American life—what we expect from ourselves and from each other—is changing so fast that we hardly notice the new contours of our terrain. The upheavals of the Choice Revolution have changed the world of business. If history is any guide at all, government will be next.

In his book, *The New Democracy*, the Progressive journalist Walter Weyl wrote that a revolution "is simply a quicker turn of the wheel *in the direction in which the wheel is already turning.*" Men and women, famous and forgotten, often change the course of human events. But certain trends take on a life of their own. The wheel of the Choice Revolution is turning. It waits only for an extra push, from a new generation committed to progress, to make its force felt.

Thus it is only a matter of time. With ever growing pressure from a rising Choice Generation, government will come to embrace the Choice Revolution. As Humphrey Bogart might say: maybe not today, maybe not tomorrow, but soon, and for the rest of our lives.

PART I

The Fall and Rise
of the Individual

As I confess my belief in the common man, I know what I am
saying. The man who is swimming against the stream knows the
strength of it.

—*Woodrow Wilson, 1912*

*I*f we looked at government only through the lens of what we read in
the newspapers or see discussed on TV—through the prism of the
hurly-burly of heated battles in legislative chambers and on the hustings—it would appear to be a massive chaos. Interests battle interests,
candidates shift tactics based on whispered advice, politicians pander to
powerful constituencies. And on any given day, all this is true. But if we
take a step back, if we take the long view, daily fluctuations are subsumed
by larger trends.

Looking back over the course of American history, it is clear that
political ideas succeed or fail based on their ability to apply timeless values, such as justice, fairness, and opportunity, to a particular time. When
the nation's policies and programs become disconnected from everyday
experiences, when politics turns away from people, people turn away
from politics. This is what is occurring today as Americans grow ever
more disgusted with a political system that offers old answers to new
questions. Political ideas should be made to fit the times, not the other
way around.

At the beginning of the twentieth century, Robert LaFollette said, "It is incumbent upon the reformer who seeks to establish a new order to come equipped with a complete mastery of all the information upon which the established order is based." The search for this new order must be grounded in an understanding of the circumstances that call for new political ideas as well as those that gave rise to the old ones. LaFollette and the other Progressives lived and led at a time when the tide of history rose toward regimented enterprise and mass production of identical products. The Choice Generation lives at a time when history trends toward an economy driven by individuals' abilities and geared toward individual aspirations. The high-tech outputs of today's New Economy are often the stuff of futuristic science fiction, but some of its outlooks are the stuff of America's storied past—as the tale of one American city helps illustrate.

THE FORGE OF AMERICA

> I am monarch of all the forges,
> I have solved the riddle of fire,
> The Amen of Nature to need of Man
> Echoes at my desire;
> I search with the subtle soul of flame,
> The heart of Rocky earth,
> And out of my anvils prophecies
> Of the miracle years blaze forth.
> —*Richard Realf (1834–1878), "Hymn of Pittsburgh"*

Once America was an undiscovered country, an untrammeled wilderness where every step forward was an exploration, where a young man could set out in a New World with the confidence that no one was coming up behind him and no one stood in his way. It was out into this empty expanse that, in 1753, the colonial governor of Virginia sent a 21-year-old militia major named George Washington to survey the western lands. Embarking on his journey, Washington found himself at the spot where the Allegheny and Monongahela flow together to form the Ohio, and decided this would be an excellent place for a fort.

On the outskirts of the edge of Western civilization, Fort Pitt (later Pittsburgh) was a small and rarely noticed settlement. The village's taverns and workshops were not as much surrounded by farmland as they were an island in a sea of open land and small farms that seemed to go on and on forever and ever. But as the young Republic began to bustle, the excitement reached Pittsburgh as well. Or, at least, it passed through. Because of its strategic position, Pittsburgh was called the "Gateway to the West"—and for the thousands upon thousands of families who filtered through on their way to begin the American adventure of struggle and discovery, it was both a portal to new beginnings and a last chance to say good-bye to the world they had known.

One day in 1811, as the pioneers boarded their barges for the long and hazardous trip down the Ohio, they spied a machine whose premise would change the city and the world. On that day, Nicholas Roosevelt, a marine engineer from New York, launched the *New Orleans*, the first steam-powered boat on America's inland waterways. He set out down the river with his pregnant wife, Lydia; a daughter named Rosetta; and an enormous Newfoundland dog named Tiger.

Steam's power would bring to an end the comfortable certainties that had defined Americans' lives and the lives of their ancestors. It would usher in the Industrial Age.

But this transformation did not transpire overnight. On November 2, 1849, the *Pittsburgh Gazetteer* carried a small item which read, "A messenger boy by the name of Andrew Carnegie, employed by the O'Reilly Telegraph Company, yesterday found a draft for the amount of five hundred dollars. Like an honest little fellow, he promptly made known the fact, and deposited the paper in good hands where it waits identification." Over the next half century, through means honest and less so, this "little fellow" and others like him would forge an empire of steel that made Pittsburgh into a leading city of the world.

In the decades following the Civil War, *Fortune* magazine would recall in February of 1947, "when Pittsburgh was supplying the iron and steel for building the North and opening up the West, the growth of this area was one of the raw wonders of the nineteenth century world. Great mills proliferated up and down the narrow river banks, the building city staggered helter-skelter up precipitous hills and valleys, and some of the greatest U.S. fortunes were laid." These were the miracle years. By 1900, more wealth had likely "been beaten and torn from the 750 square miles of Allegheny County, whose capital is Pittsburgh, than from any other plot on earth."

In the year 1902, Pittsburgh was the fiery center of the industrial world. That year Allegheny County produced 34 percent of America's Bessemer steel, 44 percent of open hearth steel, 53 percent of crucible steel, and 59 percent of structural shapes—numbers that were once bandied about with awe and hubris. Exactly 86,636,680 tons were carried by railway and river—greater than the combined tonnage of London, New York, Antwerp, Hamburg, and Liverpool, which were the next five largest industrial cities in the world.

Discussing Pittsburgh in those days, economist John R. Commons of the University of Wisconsin would write, "Here our modern world achieves its greatest triumph and faces its gravest problem." Some of those problems were plain to see. The waste and refuse of industrial dynamism gave the city one of the highest death rates from cholera, dysentery, and typhoid fever of any large city in the world.

Other problems were less visible; less fatal, but perhaps more fateful. The process of industrialization replaced the open land of hardscrabble self-reliance, easy egalitarianism, and individual enterprise with a crowded, crammed, clamorous world of totem polls, orders, and order; a noisy, regulated realm of regimentation and haste. An English journalist visiting the Carnegie plant in nearby Homestead, Pennsylvania, in 1902, commented that "From the moment the ore is pitched into the furnace until the rail [is] finished, everything is done by machinery, and no man has a direct hand in the work." It was, atypical of the British, an exaggeration. Yet, where men were involved in the process, they were little more than biological extensions of the metal machines.

But Americans flocked to the factories. The old farms were disappearing and Pittsburgh was the land of the future—a gateway to the best hopes for prosperity. So hundreds of thousands of men worked away in the fiery furnaces of the forges, hour after eternal hour, watched over by stern taskmasters, lulled into the living sleep of repetition. Viewing Pittsburgh, Lincoln Steffens remarked, was seeing a land like "hell with the lid lifted."

Which is why the workers must have looked forward to the Fourth of July in 1902, a day of independence from the drudgery and dehumanizing toil of the factory. Some went out to Exposition Park to see the Pittsburgh Pirates play a doubleheader. Unfortunately, a late afternoon downpour caused such swelling of the Allegheny that the river began to flow into the outfield. This led to a new rule which stated that any ball hitting the water inside the park would be an automatic single. The following year, the Pirates would host Boston in the first World Series. Boston won, but, of course, this was a very, very long time ago.

Those who did not go "out to the ball game" (in the words of the song that became a hit six years later) on Independence Day 1902 might have gone to Schenley Park to hear the grandson of Nicholas Roosevelt's brother address the crowd. Boisterous and ebullient, Theodore Roosevelt—America's youngest president ever—was 43 years old and had been president for less than ten months. "When the morning gun salutes the sun tomorrow the greatest industrial center in the world will be ready to receive the chief executive of the most powerful and progressive nation on the earth," boasted the previous day's *Pittsburgh Press*. "That his words will be really momentous in their import is generally believed. He is expected to map out the policy of the administration and make clear his determination in regard to the burning questions of the day."

Having lived through the massive changes in America's economy and society that had picked up speed over the past decade, the people of Pittsburgh should have been as little surprised by what the barrel-chested, squeaky-voiced president mapped out as they were by the day's patriotic bunting and bands. Pittsburgh had seen its first automobile accident two years earlier; within the year the first movie theater in the world would open there. In 1900, when the Carnegie Institute for Technology had opened, there were ten thousand engineering students in the United States. A decade earlier there had been only one thousand.

The Pittsburghers who gathered together that day—be they old western Pennsylvania Scotch-Irish stock or new Slavic immigrants—understood that the world of small industries and individual initiative that they once knew was fast disappearing. That day, their president told them it was never to return. Although menacing storm clouds gathered in the distance, the sun shined brightly as Roosevelt proclaimed that the growth of what he called the nation's "great industrial tendencies" and the processes of impersonal mechanization were like the flow of the Mississippi River—inevitable, but something that could be "regulated and controlled by levees." A few years later, Woodrow Wilson would admit that "We shall never return to the old order of individual competition." A few years earlier, William Dean Howells agreed when he wrote in *The Rise of Silas Lapham* that "The day of small things was past, and I don't suppose it will ever come again in this country." They were wrong.

The flow of history is not like that of the Mississippi River which Theodore Roosevelt described—inexorably racing in a single direction, rushing toward a predetermined final destination. Swept up as we all are by the currents of our times we find it difficult to believe, but nevertheless it is true: there are moments, few but profound, in history as in nature, when the earth stops, stands still for the shortest instant, and begins to move in another direction. On the morning of December 16, 1811, as the Great Comet of 1811 hung overhead, the most powerful earthquake in America's recorded history struck the tiny town of New Madrid, Missouri. Damage was reported as far as Washington, D.C. Onboard the maiden voyage of the *New Orleans*, Nicholas Roosevelt "heard a rushing sound and a violent splash and saw large portions of the shore tearing away from the land and falling into the river." In Boston, a thousand miles away, ringing church bells tolled of the earthquake's strength. That day the Mississippi River changed direction and flowed backwards.

Today, enormous political, social, and economic tremors have reversed the flow of history and brought back "the day of small things." Everywhere one looks, the large-scale forces that defined life in the twentieth century—big government, big business, big labor—are in retreat. They are simply at a marked disadvantage in a world that moves at the speed of bytes; where technological momentum leaps toward putting power in the hands of individuals and relying on their native intelligence and skills. Labor unions continue to lose ground as a percentage of the workforce, even as an aggressive organizing campaign results in a net increase of members. Virtually all of the more than 20 million new jobs created in the economic boom of the 1990s were in small businesses. Even the big companies that define American business life today for so many are built on the premise of giving individuals personal choices and economic power. And today, the federal workforce, as a percentage of the American workforce, is the smallest it has been since before the New Deal that put Theodore Roosevelt's ideas into practice.

Nearly a hundred years after Teddy Roosevelt visited the old Pittsburgh, U.S. Steel's Irvin plant outside Pittsburgh has put the individual back at the center of its operations. There, new technologies and new theories of management have ended the rigid barriers that made workers mere sections of the machine. Workers are gaining sophisticated training and a greater degree of control over the way they do their jobs, and this is producing results. "When it works we see a lot more pride and better quality," says Walt Lonce, president of United Steelworkers Local 2227. Just as Americans in Teddy Roosevelt's day longed for a centralized, regimented government to protect them from the "great industrial tendencies," present-day Americans are increasingly looking to government to give them more personalized choices and more decision-making power. Today, everywhere one turns, the individual is back in charge.

A NEW WORLD

His brow is wet with honest sweat,
He earns whate'er he can,
And looks the whole world in the face
For he owes not any man.

—*Henry Wadsworth Longfellow,*
The Village Blacksmith, *1842*

America was born big. That bigness was not a source of fright, but of comfort. For with less than 4 million people—the population of the present-day state of South Carolina—spread over thirteen states, there was room enough for all. Room enough not just to prosper, but to find independence in everyday life just as the Republic itself had found independence in the world of nations. By and large, America was a land of farms and farmers—small farms and small farmers—who relied on their own efforts and would brook no notion that others would deign to be their masters. There were bonds of community, fellowship, and family; there were cities such as Boston, Philadelphia, and Charleston that served as centers of culture, commerce, and creativity; but Americans saw themselves, first and foremost, as individuals. Not islands separated from the rest of humanity, but free citizens who answered to no one and cherished a native chance of success through hard work. The exceptions to this outlook—slavery being the most notable—were all the more glaring because of their contrast to the nation's essential egalitarianism. Charles Dickens, visiting in the 1840s was aghast at the sight of American trains: unlike the elegant railcars of Europe, these had no first-, second-, or third-class carriages. Ebeneezer Scrooge and Bob Cratchit sat side by side—and it didn't occur to either one of them that things should ever be any other way.

Adam Smith wrote in *The Wealth of Nations* that "Plenty of good land and liberty to manage their own affairs their own way, seem to be the two great causes of prosperity" in distant America. Together, free land and freedom made America rich in both dollars and disposition. It was a time, as Herbert Croly wrote in *The Promise of American Life*, when "opportunity knocked at the door of every man, and the poor man of today was the prosperous householder of tomorrow." Thomas Jefferson assured those waiting by the door for a knock that no elite, no privileged group had been born, "booted and spurred, ready to ride" humankind. But for the average farmer—75 percent of the workforce when Jefferson was elected in 1800—this was more than an idle promise. For they held a trump card: the West.

The West was always a place that existed more in the mind than on a map. But Americans had always held tight to the promise of land where one could, through undeniable and often unbearable hardship and exertion, be as big as one dared to be. It offered an endless supply of opportunity and hopes. From at least the moment in 1716 when Virginia's heroic Governor Spotswood and his Knights of the Golden Horseshoe reached the crest of the Blue Ridge Mountains and peered into the lush Shenandoah Valley, the West had receded from Americans' advancing footsteps. It was, in Tennyson's words, an "untravll'd world, whose margin fades for ever and ever." Nineteenth-century Americans saw the West as a place where "you can look farther and see less than any other place in the world" and gave nary a thought to who—or what—they might have been overlooking. So, like the rising sun, Americans moved from east to west, subduing the untamed wilderness in their wake.

The West was more than an insurance against rising aristocracy, it was a formative experience; a national adventure starring the individual who battled the odds and the elements. As a frontier youth Abraham Lincoln was famed for his ability to split rails, yet the rise of the railroads—and the tide of industrialization their puffs of smoke steadily brought with them—split Americans off from their central saga. The centerpiece of the American story thus far, what Alexis de Tocqueville described as the tale of a people who "march across these wilds, draining swamps, turning the course of rivers, peopling solitudes and subduing nature," would come to an end. With the solitudes all peopled, the people would find that the individual-centered world they once knew and that formed their outlook—the society of farmers and shop owners; smiths, bakers, and small entrepreneurs—was coming to an end as well.

Swept into the presidency by the votes and voices of the common man, Andrew Jackson came to the White House in 1829. Submitting his first Message to Congress, the laconic general dispensed quickly with what did not even merit discussion: "The agricultural interest of our country is so essentially connected with every other, and so superior in importance to them all, that it is scarcely necessary to invite to it your particular attention." For most of the nineteenth century, agriculture and its individual, self-reliant lifestyle was American life itself. As the century closed that heritage was vanishing. "What greater affront to this tradition than the creation in 1889 of a cabinet post for agriculture, as if government needed a Department of American Citizens," noted Robert Wiebe in his influential work, *The Search for Order*.

As the nineteenth century began, Thomas Jefferson assumed the presidency in an Inaugural Address that assured his countrymen and women that theirs was a nation "with room enough for descendants to the thousandth and thousandth generation." Three generations later, room had run out. Richard Hofstadter, the famous historian, wrote that "Throughout most of the nineteenth century, ours was overwhelmingly a nation of farmers and small-town entrepreneurs—ambitious, mobile, optimistic, speculative, anti-authoritarian, egalitarian, and competitive." Americans liked it that way. It was the way things had always been. What's more, they never expected it to be any different. Yet, by the 1880s, a strange new word was being spoken by Americans for the first time; a foreign word for a foreign concept. The word was "nostalgia."

THE TURNING OF THE WHEEL

> For West is where we all plan to go some day. It is where you go when the land gives out and the old-field pines encroach. It is where you go when you get the letter saying: *Flee, all is discovered.*
> —*Robert Penn Warren*, All the King's Men

The historian George Dangerfield wrote that the United States received no respect from "the conservative and reactionary rulers of Europe" who gathered in 1815 at Vienna to waltz on the grave of the French Revolution. For them "the United States was no more than a grimy republican thumbprint upon the far margin of [the] page of history." But by the end of the nineteenth century, both Europe and America had changed— the latter more so. So on the occasion of the hundredth anniversary of the ratification of the Constitution and the four hundredth anniversary of Columbus's voyage across the ocean blue, the World's Fair came to America. After endless entreaties from Chicago's leading citizens, the city was awarded both the nickname "the Windy City" and the right to host the 1893 World's Columbian Exposition.

The Columbian Exposition was intended to celebrate American progress. In the years following the Civil War, with ever increasing speed and power, America had built, belched, and bought its way into becoming an industrial powerhouse. "We have been passing, as a people since 1876, through a period of prosperity unparalleled in the history of nations. It has been the golden age of American enterprise, American industry and American development. Wonders have been achieved in every branch of thought and in every line of trade," the Official Guide needlessly reminded visitors in language that would form the familiar chantings of boosters and spin doctors a century later.

In sixty short years, Chicago had grown from a village of less than four hundred people to the second largest city in the Western Hemisphere. Now, the past and the future would converge there as they rarely do. The overturning of the only lifestyle that Americans had ever known happened so fast that people saw the changes but had little understanding of the effects. The World's Fair pulled open the curtain on a new America. In a letter to his father, Karl Marx, right for once, wrote that "There are moments in life which mark the close of a period like boundary posts and at the same time definitely point in a new direction." In Chicago, 1893 was such a moment.

The fairgrounds were designed by Frederick Law Olmsted, Stanford White, and Louis Sullivan. Their elegance and order would launch the "City Beautiful" movement and bring urban planning to the fore. No longer would people be able to build where they wanted to build and what they wanted to build. Permits and zoning, regulations and commissions would now make such decisions. The twentieth century was kicking in its womb. At night the luminance of Edison's incandescent lights would shine so bright as to give the fairgrounds the name: the "great white city."

Americans were drawn toward the light. "The future is like heaven," James Baldwin once wrote, "Everyone exalts it, but no one wants to go there now." But they came to this future. Twenty-seven million people walked through the gates of the Columbian Exposition in the course of six months—one out of every four Americans. With the fourth transcontinental railroad just completed, they came from all over. For many—perhaps most—it was the farthest they had ever been and the farthest they would ever go.

It was well worth the trip. Tesla displayed his electric coil and Westinghouse his electric transformer and motor. Harry Houdini gave one of his first performances and Eadweard Muybridge thrilled fairgoers with one of the first examples of motion pictures. A promoter named Florenz Ziegfeld staged musical revues so popular that he eventually would move his "Follies" to New York. As John Philip Sousa conducted in the bandstand, listeners might have snacked on Cracker Jacks or chewed on Juicy Fruit gum—both introduced for the first time. They could have had their first taste of Aunt Jemima's syrup at breakfast and, for lunch, might have taken their first bite of a hamburger. And they might have started the strange custom of washing it down with their first gulp of a diet soda.

Taking time out from visiting the various exhibition halls, they could have sent their regards to the folks back home with the new innovation called a postcard. The kids could visit Davy Crockett Camp, described by the Official Guide as "a cabin erected by Mr. Theodore Roosevelt which is filled with relics and curiosities of interest to hunters and sportsmen." While scampering about, the children might have tried to remember the patriotic sentence that had been composed for the Exposition by a socialist named Francis Bellamy and which was sent to schools all across the country. It was entitled "the Pledge of Allegiance."

Dominating the fairgrounds was the first "wheel" built by George Washington Gale Ferris of Pittsburgh. Visitors to the fair—and especially Chicago children taking the day off from school—would squeal in delight and terror as the 264-foot-high Ferris wheel would hurtle them from the ground and carry 2,160 of them at a time high into the sky. And perhaps from that high vantage point, they could have seen the small building in the distance where a shy young academic was hammering shut the coffin of nineteenth-century America.

University of Wisconsin history professor Frederick Jackson Turner didn't have much time to tour the fairgrounds. He even missed a special performance of Buffalo Bill's Wild West Show because he was putting the finishing touches on the paper he was to deliver at a lecture series coinciding with the Exposition. It was a shame. For Buffalo Bill's show and Teddy Roosevelt's Davy Crockett Camp were to become even more of historical artifacts because of what he would say.

Following the presentation of a number of other academic papers—including Dr. Ruben Gold Thwaites' less than scintillating lecture on "Early Lead Mining in Illinois and Wisconsin"—on the sweltering night of July 12, Frederick Jackson Turner began his address by informing the assemblage of yawning scholars of the little-noticed revelation contained in the Census of 1890. "In a recent bulletin of the Superintendent of the Census for 1890," Turner said in opening, "appear these significant words: 'Up to and including 1880 the country had a frontier of settlement, but at present the unsettled area has been so broken into isolated bodies of settlement that there can hardly be said to be a frontier line. In the discussion of its extent, western movement, etc., it can not, therefore, any longer have a place in the census reports.' This brief official statement marks the closing of a great historic movement." It marked the closing of the frontier.

Continuing on, Turner discussed in depth America's western expansion—and how that expansion had formed the character of the nation and her people. "The frontier," he said "is productive of individualism." But, for consistency's sake, he should have said "was." For the frontier and the farms and the individualism they bred were fast becoming relics of another era. The railroad, the steam engine, the implements of industrialization had transformed the America of old. "And now," Turner said in concluding his remarks, "four centuries from the discovery of America, at the end of a hundred years of life under the Constitution, the frontier is gone, and with its going has closed the first period of American history." The Industrial Age had overtaken agrarian America.

Evidently, no one who was there that evening gave a second thought to Turner's remarks. Stepping out into the night air, they might have stumbled over to the Ferris Wheel and shelled out 50 cents for a spin on the metal monster—never realizing that they had just been informed of a mechanized revolution far greater than the one on which they were about to embark.

But the wheel of history never stops. Although it was not recognized at the time, the 1890 Census not only "closed the first period of American history," it opened the second period. For the first time, the United States Census Bureau grouped proprietors, managers, and clerks in one category and skilled craftsmen and unskilled operatives in another. Where once almost every American was an independent entrepreneur, now the classifications of Industrial Age stratification—white-collar and blue-collar workers—had been born.

Americans believe, somewhat uniquely, that what we count is a window on what counts. What the 1890 Census, Frederick Turner's thesis, and the Columbian Exposition showed was that what counted for Americans was changing. The individualist ways of the farm and the frontier were giving way to the ordered regiment of the industrial factory.

Henry Adams, confronted by the dynamism of the newfangled industrial world presented at the Columbian Exposition, felt he "had no choice but to sit down on the steps and brood." Bewildered, he wrote, "Chicago asked in 1893 for the first time whether the American people knew where they were driving." A few fast years later Adams, who longed for the glory of his family's lustrous heritage, remarked, "My country in 1900 is something totally different from my own country in 1860. I am wholly a stranger in it. Neither I, nor anyone else, understands it." For every statistical attempt to measure it, America had changed immeasurably in a matter of decades—and the pace of permutation would only increase. But for all of Adams' bewilderment, there were those who did understand the new ways of the coming century—and who would remake American life and Americans' lives in response.

THE INDIVIDUAL SUBMERGED

We have come upon a very different age from any that preceded us. We have come upon an age when we do not do business in the way in which we used to do business,—when we do not carry on any of the operations of manufacture, sale, transportation, or communication as men used to carry them on. There is a sense in which in our day the individual has been submerged.

—*Woodrow Wilson*, The New Freedom, *1912*

In the preface to his collected essays, Frederick Jackson Turner wrote of the "new age which is replacing the era of free lands and of measurable isolation by consolidated and complex industrial development." The frontier had not just disappeared from American life, it had been supplanted by industrialism as the driving force in the nation's consciousness. The spirit of discovery was transferred from Pike's Peak to Edison's laboratory, from the wagon train to the railroad. As Max Lerner wrote in his *America as a Civilization*, "Davy Crockett became Andrew Carnegie."

The two were not interchangeable. As representative symbols of their respective times, each brought fundamentally different values and divergent outlooks. In the world of "the King of the Wild Frontier," success for the average person was defined in terms of self-sufficiency and confidence. "I leave this rule for others when I'm dead," said Crockett. "Be always sure you're right—then go ahead." In Andrew Carnegie's factories, this sentiment would be as out of place as a coonskin cap.

There is an old joke in which a befuddled tourist in the Big Apple stops a New Yorker on the street and asks, "How do you get to Carnegie Hall?" The native answers, "Practice." But to be successful in the Carnegie steel mills, and in the America they came to represent, what was demanded was not practice, but persistence; not creativity, but obedience. Insight and inventiveness only got in the way of the machines, the experts, and the process. Frederic Harrison, a visiting Englishman in 1900, noted that "Life in the States is one perpetual whirl of telephones, telegrams, phonographs, electric bells, motors, lifts, and automatic instruments." But, for the everyday lives of ordinary Americans, what mattered was not just the Industrial Revolution's implements, but its implementations. Each set of technologies brings with it a certain fundamental logic about how the

world and the workplace should be organized. The tools of farming—
the plow and furrow and scythe—were designed for the use of individuals. The same is true of modern personal computers and hand-held
devices. Big factory machines had a pervasive logic all their own.

Perhaps the first to realize this was Frederick Winslow Taylor, the
ascetic and abstentious son of wealthy Pennsylvania Quakers. After a first-
rate career at Exeter Academy, and on the verge of accepting an offer of
admission to Harvard, Taylor did the unexpected. In 1874, he dropped
out of school and took a position as an apprentice machinist at the Enterprise Hydraulic Works, a pump manufacturing firm in Philadelphia. And
as he toiled away in this new industrial world, Taylor began to realize that
the new industrial workplaces would require new rules.

In the summer of 1893, Americans had flocked to Chicago to frolic
in the warmth of the future industrial era. Frederick Turner's small gray
cloud was lost in the bright spirit of possibility. But summer always ends
and every year has its winter. In December of 1893, Frederick Taylor
presented his first paper to the American Society of Mechanical Engineers. It was Taylor's opening shot in a campaign to rewrite the rules of
the American workplace. If Fred Turner believed the West had been
won, Fred Taylor was starting a new battle on the factory floor.

Taylor recognized that the values of the individualized workplaces of
the nineteenth century—of the small shops and stores where workers
took pride in craftsmanship and creativity—were incompatible with the
clang and clatter of Machine Age manufacturing. In 1816, there had
been 30 engineers in America. In 1850, when the Census first listed the
position, there were 2,000. By 1900, there would be 45,000. Taylor, the
chief engineer of the Midvale Steel Works, recognized that the order and
conformity of science and calculation would have to be brought to the
administration of workplaces involved in large-scale enterprises. In the
short span between 1889 and 1900 alone, for instance, the production
of rails shot up by nearly 40 percent and the production of raw steel
nearly doubled. The old individualized life of the farms would need to
give way to something new. The percentage of Americans involved in
industrial work increased by nearly two-thirds in the years between the

first blast at Fort Sumter and the last champagne-popping of the nineteenth century. Taylor demanded that these new workers "recognize as
essential the substitution of exact scientific investigation and knowledge
for the old individual judgment or opinion." Over the course of the next
century, workers were forced to meet Taylor's demand.

Taylor's preeminent goal was efficiency. Using a stopwatch and careful notation, he hung over workers like a hawk, recording every move
they made as they performed their jobs and tabulating how long it took
them. In his famous study at Bethlehem Steel, he scrutinized workers'
actions in order to "collect into one series the quickest and best move-
ments." Workers would then be paid and evaluated based on how fast
they could turn out "pieces" of product. Taylor called this central idea
of his theory the "Piece-Rate System."

Taylor wanted to turn men into machines—unadorned, methodical,
and static. Men entered the factory so that their muscles could be
exploited. They were asked to check their minds in at the front gate. "We
do not ask the initiative of our men. We do not want any initiative. All
we want of them is to obey the orders we give them, do what we say, and
do it quick." Through his theory of "Scientific Management," Taylor
would redefine the workforce—all for the good of the workers, he
insisted. Taylor described his ideal pig-iron handler as "merely a man
more or less of the type of the ox, heavy both mentally and physically."
Individual insight was an impediment in the Industrial Age.

In the words of historian Steven Diner, Taylorism robbed workers of
"all matters of judgment about their jobs: what tools to use, in what
order tasks should be performed, how many pounds they should lift at
one time, how fast they should work, when they should rest—in short,
every aspect of control over work." Initially, and not surprisingly, this
new system came as a rude awakening to Americans reared in a world of
individual dignity and mastery. Samuel Gompers of the nascent American Federation of Labor complained that the industrial process made
workers nothing but "a veritable machine." Yet he knew he could do little to stem the tide. The men he represented, especially the older ones
who remembered a different past, were less sanguine. One Knight of

Labor told an interviewer, "Men are looked upon as nothing more than parts of the machinery that they work. They are labeled and tagged, as the parts of a machine would be, and are only taken into account as a part of the machinery used for the profit of the manufacturer." When workers in Pittsburgh saw Charlie Chaplin's comedy *Modern Times*, with its image of a man imprisoned in the gears of a monstrous machine, they sat in stony silence. No one laughed.

But as time went on, those who remembered America's original individualism died away. Their children and grandchildren knew only the industrial rules. It was, John Dewey wrote, "a time when mechanical forces and vast impersonal organizations were determining the frame of things." This was true not just on the factory floor, but everywhere Americans worked in an industrial world that transcended industry. By 1890, 381,000 Americans worked in clerical positions. By 1900, that number had about doubled to 708,000. Over the next decade, it would double again to 1,524,000. By 1920, it nearly doubled again to 2,838,000. These men—and many women—might not have been operating heavy machinery, but the outlook of rigid hierarchy and centralized planning that scientific management wrought was just the same. Everywhere one looked, bells and whistles, time clocks and task masters—the instruments of twentieth-century regimentation and control—were evident in one form or another.

As always happens, the ideas that organized the workplace came to govern the political sphere. Ironically, Taylor's biggest booster, the "people's lawyer" Louis Brandeis, would combat the values of regimentation, planning, and paternalism in public life. On the other hand, a rising politician who in 1916 gained a degree of notoriety by banning Taylorism in naval arsenals, Assistant Secretary of the Navy Franklin D. Roosevelt, would eventually introduce those very values into the fabric of American government.

"Frederick Winslow Taylor. Born 1856—Died 1915. Father of Scientific Management," reads the simple epitaph of the gravestone in Chestnut Hill, Pennsylvania. But while Frederick Taylor rested in "piece-rate," the principles he fathered—and the attitude they embodied—

dominated twentieth-century thinking. Taylor had rethought the ways of the workplace so that they worked for the Industrial Age. Like Lucy Ricardo and Ethel Mertz trying to keep up with a conveyer belt of chocolates, industrial workers were controlled by the machines—not the other way around. And the same notions of expert-driven order would be applied to government and community life in the name of the public good. There was little room for individualism in industrial America. Those who understood this were in the driver's seat. Those who did not were left by the side of the road.

THE CARRIAGE-MAKERS OF KOKOMO

In the past, the man was first. In the future, the system must be first.

—*Frederick W. Taylor*

On the Fourth of July 1894, the small crowd of anxious and perplexed onlookers gathered by the Pumpkinvine Pike had no idea what to expect. That day, a man named Elwood Haynes, from a place called Kokomo, Indiana, made the first run of his "horseless-carriage." He drove his contraption 1.5 miles at a speed of 7 miles per hour. Haynes, a field supervisor for a natural gas company who had once been a school principal, had traveled the 130 miles from Kokomo to Chicago to visit the Columbian Exposition the previous year. There he had marveled at the display of Karl Benz's motorized tricycle, and resolved to improve on it. A natural tinkerer with a background in engineering, he worked with two other local men for months on end in order to get his automobile ready for its test run.

Years later, the citizens of Kokomo honored Haynes by placing a stone tablet on the Pumpkinvine Pike that read: "In commemoration of Elwood Haynes of Kokomo, Indiana, the inventor, designer and builder of America's first mechanically successful automobile in the year 1893. This tablet marks the road and starting-place where Elwood Haynes on

July 4th, 1894, sitting in America's first car, made the initial run. Here, too, was the birthplace of a new era of transportation, the nucleus and beginning of the gigantic automobile industry." It was indeed a gigantic industry that would come to define and symbolize the American economy. But it was a gigantic industry that would leave Indiana in the dust.

Haynes' horseless carriage was just that—the handcrafted buggy Americans had known for generations, but powered by a motorized engine instead of a horse. The company Haynes founded was the seed for a large and prosperous Indiana auto industry that at one point numbered 150 manufacturers producing 50 cars a year or more. Yet, by the 1930s, the Indiana auto industry—home to venerable names like Stutz, Auburn, and Dusenberg—had all but disappeared.

While the Indianans continued to build beautiful carriages at prices commensurate with the handicraft this required, their competitors in "Michigan cranked out millions and millions of humdrum cars," according to automotive historian Randy Mason. Michigan's auto industry—and eventually just about all of American manufacturing— would be built on two fundamental insights. The first was Taylor's realization that preset industrial processes had to replace the older ways of individual inventiveness, imagination, and taste. The second was automotive pioneer Henry Ford's realization that automobiles must be mass-produced cars and not finely crafted carriages. He recognized that workers accustomed to the regimented rules of industrial operations had little use for individuality in the products they purchased. By joining Taylor's theories of efficient production processes with his own understanding of Americans' desire for inexpensive products, Ford ushered in the precepts of mass assembly—a system that would define Americans' work lives and worldview for much of the twentieth century.

In 1903, Henry Ford, updating a famous example used by Adam Smith, said that "The way to make an automobile is to make one automobile like another automobile, to make them all alike; just as one pin is like another pin when it comes from a pin factory, or one match is like another match when it comes from a match factory." To accomplish this, creativity was stifled; consistency demanded. At first, Ford, like all other car companies, relied on skilled craftsmen to construct his vehicles. But, as Frederick Taylor's theory of scientific management gained wider exposure, Ford built the first real automotive assembly line. By the early 1920s, machine operators made up almost two-thirds of Ford's employees; craftsmen, only 9 percent.

The careful craftsmanship of Kokomo's carriage-makers won them respect—and failure. In 1913, as Ford was completing his assembly line, Haynes was creating 1,400 automobiles a year. In 1916, Haynes' company built 7,000 automobiles—the most it ever would in one year. That year, Ford built more Model Ts than that every week.

In 1896, in its very first issue, *Horseless Age* magazine predicted that "Streets will be cleaner, jams and blockades less likely to occur, and accidents less frequent, for the horse is not so manageable as a mechanical vehicle." None of this need have been as ludicrous as it now sounds if the number of people with automobiles had remained relatively small. By 1900, there were only 8,000 cars in the United States. And it was just as well. The country had only 150 miles of paved roads. Were it not for Henry Ford and his ilk, the car could have remained like what a helicopter or Lear jet is today—a high-end status symbol that exists for most people only in their fantasies.

At the time, one Ford engineer proudly explained that in looking for assembly line workers, the company has "no use for experience," but instead "desires and prefers machine-tool operators who have nothing to unlearn, who have no theories of correct surface speeds for metal finishing, and will simply do what they are told to do, over and over, from bell-time to bell-time." Frederick Taylor's system was tailor-made for a world where nothing else was. In 1914, when Ford's assembly line was fully operational, he produced 250,000 identical cars per year and sold them for a quarter of their price a decade earlier—and he was the most beloved man in all the land. The popular proverb of the day was plain, flat wrong. The way to induce the world to beat a path to your door was not to build a better mousetrap, but to build more and more mousetraps for less and less—each like the next, without any deviation or human insight. Years later, Ford would run television commercials every few seconds declaring that "At Ford, quality is job one." But, of course, this was after the world had changed.

FIRST STIRRINGS

Then what is it, this principle that will defeat us?

I don't know. The Spirit of Man.

—*George Orwell*, 1984

In March of 1927, 25-year-old Werner Heisenberg submitted a paper entitled "On the Perpetual Content of Quantum Theoretical Kinematics and Mechanics" to a German journal of physics. In his paper, Heisenberg argued that one can never know the velocity of an electron because shining the light needed to see the electron will also alter the electron's velocity. In a larger sense, Heisenberg's uncertainty principle implied that in the process of trying to know the world, we transform it.

Never has this principle held more true than in the case of the 1890 Census. That year's enumeration, in Frederick Jackson Turner's words, "closed the first period of American history" and, through its recognition of the Industrial Age categories of blue- and white-collar labor, marked the beginning of the second period. Yet, in a fateful and striking twist, it also planted the seeds for the third period of American history: the Information Age.

To make possible the tally of the millions upon millions of Americans spread out over the continent—and to satisfy the growing hunger for statistical breakdowns of American phylum—a young Census employee named Herman Hollerith developed a new mechanism for facilitating the count. He invented a system of cards with holes punched in them. Contact brushes were passed over the cards which completed an electrical circuit whenever a hole was present. His system also included a card-punching machine and a sorter that dropped the cards into the appropriate bin based on which holes the electric current had sensed. This system allowed cross-tabulation of the information to give exact numbers on the status of minute subgroups.

In 1896, Hollerith left the Census Department to strike out on his own with his new invention. He started the Computing-Tabulating-Recording Company, which eventually evolved into a company called International Business Machines. Hollerith's cards would come to be known universally as "IBM Cards" and their warning, "Do not fold, spindle, or mutilate," would enter the popular lexicon of the 1950s and 1960s. Even more important, the world of computers had been born. In writing the epitaph for the rural Republic, in painting a portrait of an emerging industrial nation, Herman Hollerith had set in a motion a chain reaction that would lead to the creation of the information democracy that now enters the twenty-first century.

Toward the end of his 1910 work, *The Old Order Changeth*, the great Kansas newspaper editor William Allen White traces the history of humankind from the control of fire by the warrior-priests to the discovery of the wheel to the development of writing to the invention of the printing press and concludes that "the history of man has been a story of the socializing of human institutions . . . distributing the inventions and the blessings they brought among all the people." By the nineteenth century, he recounts, individuals had gained a degree of autonomy and control over their lives. But the rise of the steam engine and Machine Age world it brought with it changed all that:

> It put out the individual fires in a million little forges; it took from the homes and shops of the people millions of little wheels, and gathered to itself all the levers of the world. It was as though, by some strange reversion to the old days, a great pre-Adamite giant had come stalking into the earth gathering unto himself all the fires and their privileges that men had wrested from him in the morning of time, all the wheels and their privileges and all the levers and their special powers that had passed among men in the childhood of the race. The world stood afraid before the steam engine. And to those who controlled it we gave privileges and rights and immunities that we gave of old to the priestly fire-makers, the kingly wheel owners, the royal purveyors of the secrets of the levers.

Today, the forces of technology, communications, and the free flow of knowledge and commerce around the globe have merged to create a new modern behemoth—a jolly, lean giant that is redistributing the wheels and the levers, the powers and the privileges, from the massive to the masses. When it comes to the business world, these forces of the Information Age have led to the birth of the New Economy—new businesses, new ways of doing business, and new goods and services for businesses to provide.

In describing the New Economy, it is perhaps most important to first say what it is not. The New Economy is not about a rising stock market and not about falling inflation. It is not about ISPs or IPOs. Not about strong economic numbers or weak government action. And not just about the clicks of the Internet e-conomy. The New Economy is not found only in the go-go gold rush of Silicon Valley, where it often seems that a fool and his partners are soon moneyed. Rather, the New Economy is as much at home in the Red River Valley, the San Fernando Valley, and Lehigh Valley. What is important in understanding the New Economy is not just the fact that more Americans are working in the computer industry than in the auto industry during its 1950s golden era, but that those who work in the auto industry today are working in the computer industry as well. The auto mechanic who uses advanced diagnostic equipment to fix cars with far more computing power than *Apollo 11*'s lunar landing module is as much a part of the New Economy as the computer nerd tanning by the light of her monitor. The New Economy is the intersection of technology, trade, and the decentralizing power of information. It has only just begun to transform our lives in ways we are only now beginning to understand. Yet this much is already clear: it is putting more individual power into the hands of more individual workers and consumers than ever before in human history.

In 1963, the editors of *Daedalus* magazine wrote, "The day is coming when the 'knowledge industry' will occupy the same role in the American economy that the railroad industry did a hundred years ago." But change in economic structures—and human assumptions—happens very slowly at first.

The late 1960s and early 1970s were the Indian summer of the Industrial Age. America's economy seemed to be invulnerable—to decline and
to change. Not surprisingly, both hit at the same time. In August 1974,
Gerald Ford became president with the announcement that "our long
national nightmare is over." But for some, a different—and longer—
nightmare was just beginning. The following month, Ford traveled to
New York City to address the United Nations General Assembly. There
he delivered a Declaration of Interdependence. "Developing and developed countries," he said, "are all part of one interdependent economic
system." Such pronouncements are common now, tuned out as part of
the buzz of hackneyed political rhetoric. At the time, however, it came
as a shock to many Americans.

If so, the shocks were just beginning. The long lines at the gas pumps
brought about by the Arab oil embargoes of the 1970s were nearly as
powerful a blow to America's self-confidence as the bitter defeat in Vietnam. Yet, despite the strained theories of many traditional-thinking
economists, the oil shocks were a symptom, not a cause, of the weakness
of the American economy throughout much of the 1970s and 1980s.
They were a manifestation of America's growing interdependence with
the international economy—and of the nation's woeful lack of ability to
deal with this new era. In the early 1960s, the United States imported
nearly no manufactured goods. Yet, by 1979, almost a quarter of all
manufactured goods sold in the country were imports. Americans had
gotten used to purchasing lower-priced, more economical foreign goods
during the oil shock—and, having crossed the psychological hurdle,
they never looked back. The oil shocks marked the end of the
post–World War II economic order. But, the new order would take time
to develop.

Three moments can serve as signposts to chart the advent of the New
Economy. The first is the month of January 1984. In Wilkes-Barre,
Pennsylvania, a mother was nursing a broken leg she had received while
being trampled in a crowd of a thousand other shoppers rushing to grab
a Cabbage Patch doll for Christmas. The dolls were a sensation
because—as opposed to previous toys—each one was different, with a

individualized look and name of their own. (While laid up in bed she might have seen the following series of events on television. Mere glimmers, each only relates to the others from the standpoint of a Thursday morning quarterback fifteen years later.) Yet together, they mark the passing of the collective industrial arrangements and the development of the more individualized Information Age—and make January 1984 the first marker on the road to the New Economy.

First, on January 1, a consent decree handed down by Judge Harold Greene in the case of *United States v. AT&T* took effect. *The* phone company was broken apart and the single greatest impediment to the Information Age was demolished. In the age of telecommunications monopoly, it had once been strictly illegal to connect any device to a telephone line—a computer, for instance—that Ma Bell had not approved and supplied. On January 14, Ray Kroc, the genius who built McDonalds and first thought of bringing the assembly line to hamburgers, churning out Big Macs much like Henry Ford built Model Ts, died. "The organization cannot trust the individual," he had believed. "The individual must trust the organization." Thus each hamburger had to consist of a patty that was 3 5/8 inches in diameter topped with a teaspoon of mustard and a tablespoon of ketchup. Hot dogs were not served because Kroc thought that "people were determined to have hot dogs their own way." Three days later, on January 17, the Supreme Court ruled that home videotaping of television programs was not copyright infringement—setting off a wholesale change in Americans' lifestyle and viewing habits and helping create the individualistic concept of "home entertainment."

The final major New Economy event of January 1984 occurred at an unlikely time: during Los Angeles's 38–9 blowout of the Washington Redskins in Super Bowl XVIII. The commercial for Apple computers that aired during the January 22 game nearly didn't happen—but it would have far-reaching repercussions for the gestating New Economy.

The commercial's significance stemmed from the larger context of the computer industry's evolution. Beginning in the late 1950s, IBM—the company spawned by Herman Hollerith's invention—possessed three-quarters of the world's computer business. For all intents and purposes, IBM was computers—and computers were room-sized mechanical monstrosities that were used for complex calculations. IBM's imperious chief, Tom Watson Sr., had once said that he didn't think there was a market for more than five or six computers in the world. While the company would revise that figure upward, computers were still understood to be the province of the few. According to Michael S. Malone, a chronicler of the computer industry, IBM's "big-iron computer guys had built an entire epistemology around mainframe and mini-computers and the MIS departments that ran them. Personal computers in the control of individuals simply didn't fit into this reality." Like the carriage-makers of Kokomo, Big Blue would learn the perils of failing to understand that the technological change they created would come hand in hand with social change.

They saw computers as part of an industrial America built on hierarchy, regimentation, and identical reproduction, instead of an Information Age running on the notion of distributing power and knowledge to individuals. Convinced that the computer was merely a high-tech machine tool, an implement for data factories and assembly lines, IBM ceded the personal computer market in the 1970s to tiny competitors, especially Apple.

Personal computers proved immediately popular among a small, but important, segment of the buying public. In 1980, 724,000 were sold and IBM decided it had to catch up. Partnering with a young, though wily, software developer named Bill Gates, IBM embarked on a crash development project to develop its own personal computer. In 1981, it unveiled the IBM PC. Due to strategic miscues from its Lilliputian competitors and its own strong brand name identification, IBM quickly won significant market share among the 1.4 million personal computers sold that year.

The following year, with 2.8 million computers sold, *Time* magazine decided that it would not pick a "Man of the Year" for 1982. Instead, its editors chose a Machine of the Year: the personal computer. The magazine explained: "The 'information revolution' that futurists have long predicted has arrived, bringing with it the promise of dramatic changes in the way people live and work, perhaps even in the way they think. America will never be the same."

The new computer wars raged on. Ironically, IBM chose, as the mascot for its massive advertising campaign trumpeting its PC, Charlie Chaplin—the same Little Tramp who found himself trapped in the gears of the Industrial Age. By January 1984, the upstart Apple was ready to strike back.

To coincide with the launch of the landmark Macintosh—in many ways the first modern personal computer due to its use of a mouse and on-screen icons—Apple had hired a leading ad agency and *Alien* director Ridley Scott to put together an advertisement to herald the new product. What they produced was a commercial featuring a young woman clad in bright red running shorts running through an auditorium filled with gray Orwellian proles listening to the propaganda of a projected Big Brother figure. She hurls a sledge hammer into the screen, shattering it, and by implication, its totalitarian rule. "On January 24th, Apple Computers will introduce Macintosh," said the words on the screen at the commercial's end, "and you'll see why 1984 won't be like *1984*." The commercial never identified Big Brother as Big Blue. There was no need to.

A few weeks before the kickoff, Apple's board of directors previewed the ad. As it ended, they sat in stunned silence—except for one member who had his head down on the table and was pounding his fist on it in anger. The board universally hated the spot and demanded that it be pulled. However, it was too late. The Super Bowl time had been bought and no other ads existed to fill the slot. So, the ad ran once—and provoked a response that exceeded even Apple's wildest dreams. Apple sold 50 percent more Macintoshes than expected in the computer's first hundred days.

More important, IBM's image as an Industrial Age dinosaur had been amplified. Eventually, both Apple and IBM would fall from power—though both readjusted to the New Economy and came back to life. However, the computer industry would come to be a universe of thousands of companies competing in hardware, software, the Internet, and just about every other niche imaginable. In 1965, IBM had 2,500—mostly piddling—competitors for its markets. In 1999, it had 50,000.

Computers began to capture the imagination of the American public. In its Machine of the Year story, *Time* reported that "the enduring American love affair with the automobile [is] now being transformed into a giddy passion for the personal computer." This same dichotomy was observed elsewhere in those turning years. In *Rocky IV* (1985), Rocky's friend Paulie protested that "I wanted a sportscar for my birthday." Instead, he received a computerized robot. The following year, Ferris Bueller told the audience that "I wanted a car, I got a computer"—and then used the computer to help himself have a day off. If Paulie and Ferris didn't know it before, they were now finding out: computers had displaced cars as symbols of American pride. The Industrial Age was vanishing, the Information Age was slowly awakening.

If January 1984 was the first marker on the road to the New Economy, November 1989 was the second. The fall of the Berlin Wall meant freedom for millions and freedom from fear for billions. The fall, precipitated in part by fax machines smuggled into the hands of Warsaw Pact dissidents and by West German television signals floating into East Berlin living rooms, meant an unleashing of minds and money previously wrapped up in winning a global twilight struggle. In addition, as Peter Schwartz and Peter Leyden wrote in a widely discussed article in *Wired* magazine, the end of the Cold War "cleared the way for the creation of a truly global economy, one integrated market. Not half the world, the free world. Not one large colonial empire. Everyone on the planet in the same economy."

The economic results of the Wall's fall were immediately felt, if not recognized. In 1989, international trade accounted for 17.6 percent of the gross domestic product. By 1996, the combined imports and exports had reached 26 percent—an increase of almost 50 percent. International trade now supports more than one in every four American jobs. Exports from California alone increased by 200 percent between 1987 and 1996. The numbers go beyond traditional trade of manufactured goods to the free flow of ideas and information. Instantaneous communication with the most distant corner of the globe was recently impossible and is now an expectation. Between 1990 and 1995, India, Indonesia, Iran, Pakistan, Vietnam, Morocco, the Philippines, and Thailand doubled their main phone lines. Overall, the number of worldwide installed main telephone lines grew 60 percent between 1990 and 1997. And this number doesn't count the explosion of hundreds of millions of cell phones. Perhaps most startling, humans spent 4 billion minutes talking to people in another country in 1975. In 1996, they spent 70 billion. Globalization has been made possible by technological progress, but it would have been impossible if the world were still wracked by frigid ideological tensions.

The end of the Cold War helped give rise to the wrenching recession of the early 1990s—the third major milestone in the birth of the New Economy. In recent years, conservative propagandists have succeeded in convincing much of the media, and through them the public, that the Bush recession was never so bad—a minor blip in the wave of prosperity unleashed by Reaganomics. This contention flies in the face of the facts concerning one of the worst economic downturns in American history. Between 1989 and 1993, the U.S. economy recorded the slowest growth since the Great Depression. Personal incomes fell and private-sector job growth stopped for the first time since Herbert Hoover, "The Great Engineer," sat in the White House.

The Recession of 1991 was especially powerful because it was a product of more than the normal cycles of boom and bust. It marked the birthing pains of the New Economy. The Department of Commerce tracks business purchases of both the traditional implements of Industrial Age manufacturing, such as turbines and other heavy machinery, as well as Information Age capital spending on computers and telecommunications devices. The spending on Industrial Age purchases has remained more or less level at nearly $110 billion per year since 1982. But Information Age spending has changed dramatically. In 1982, it was $49 billion. In 1987, it was $86 billion. And in 1991, as the economy lurched from the body-blows of recession, it crossed the path of Industrial Age spending and reached $112 billion. It hasn't looked back since. With the benefit of hindsight, the pain and layoffs of the early 1990s recession were the agony of metamorphosis—the shedding of the Machine Age cocoon and the timid first flaps of the New Economy's wings.

Countless breathless tracts and bulky tomes have been written about the New Economy—the corporate competitions, the new economic laws, the inventions, and the inventors. But the force that gave birth to the New Economy—the Information Age—is, itself, far less analyzed and understood. It is not only affecting the economy, but every aspect of people's lives. The values of the Information Age transcend the New Economy and thus need greater analysis. What most affected America in the Industrial Age was not how corporations worked, but how workers worked and how the work they did affected every citizen. In the coming years, it will be this larger effect of the Information Age that will revolutionize community and government by taking power from huge hierarchies and putting it into the hands of individuals.

THE INDIVIDUAL REEMERGES

Whereas at one time the decisive factor of production was the land, and later capital . . . today the decisive factor is increasingly man himself, that is, his knowledge.
—*Pope John Paul II*, Centesimus Annus, *1991*

In 1993, Apple aired its "1984" commercial again in a one-day ad blitz that reached 100 million viewers—in the fifteen nations that once made up the Soviet Union. Apple's avenging angel clad in running shorts was aiming her sledgehammer straight at the hearts of those who had known Big Brother best. After replacing the English voice-over of the original commercial with Russian, the ad ended with an ode to the Information Age, a summary of the spirit of the day: "The right to choose. The right to think. The right to be an individual." Indeed, these three values comprise the new outlook that is defining life in the Information Age.

The first is what I call the Choice Revolution—the growing expectation among consumers that the world be customized to fit their preferences and the growing effort among businesses to meet this expectation of options. The Choice Revolution is by no means limited to the Internet, but it is the Internet where its power and promise are most clearly seen. By the middle of 1999, 52,000 Americans were logging onto the Internet for the first time every day. They entered a cyberworld that increasingly seeks to shape itself around the individual user and that is built on the idea of offering bounteous choices for every service imaginable.

If the forces of the Industrial Revolution were aggregating, if, like the pins in the factory, every car off the assembly line was like every other car, then the forces of the Information Revolution are personalizing. In its Boynton Beach, Florida factory, Motorola makes pagers in 29,000 varieties—in lot sizes as small as one. Greeting cards are made to order on an in-store computer. In 1999, "when the three members of the Beastie Boys sat down to pick the songs that would appear on an upcoming CD retrospective," the Associated Press reported, "they decided to invite a fourth participant—their fans. Devotees of the rap-punk pioneers are being offered a chance, through the Internet, to construct their own custom CD compilation of the band's work that will be mailed to their homes. They can even pick their own title."

On web sites such as Priceline.com, the atmosphere is like that of an old marketplace. In a throwback to the days before price stickers and supermarket scanners, buyers give their best offer and hope the seller will take it. Similarly, the profusion of Internet auction sites is ending the days of one-size-fits-all prices and bringing more of an individual human touch to buying decisions. The era of the Model T—and the world from which it came—is history. The expectation of choices permeates everyday life.

In 1998, Americans spent $3.9 billion on computer sales over the Internet. By 2003, that number is expected to climb to $108 billion. With their zShops initiative, announced in September of 1999, Amazon.com attempted to give individual small entrepreneurs a foothold in the burgeoning electronic commerce marketplace. For a low fee, any merchant can sell their wares at the site—breaking down the physical barriers that once kept all but the biggest businesses from ever venturing outside their locality. In the zShops marketplace consumers can find jam made by Trappist monks and Indian spices sold by a small store. In a story announcing the launch of zShops, the *New York Times* wrote, "Jeff Bezos, Amazon's founder and chief executive, said he wanted to give his consumers what they wanted most: endless choices."

The second Information Age value noted in Apple's Russian Big Brother ad is "the right to think"—new forms of work and new workplaces that rely on employees' skills, abilities, and intelligence to produce innovative, creative, and high-quality products and services. This is upending twentieth-century concepts of what work means. The eminent management guru Peter Drucker was quoted as saying that Frederick Taylor's scientific management is "the most powerful contribution America has made to Western thought since the Federalist Papers." Powerful, certainly. Lasting, less so.

The lion's share of today's workplaces are unlike any those Frederick Taylor or Henry Ford could imagine. In fact, they sometimes seem more like the individualized workshops that Taylor and Ford worked so hard to change. Replacing the behemoth businesses built on assembly lines once found in Detroit, Pittsburgh, and elsewhere, are budding small businesses that are nimble and less hierarchical. The number of people employed by America's biggest industrial corporations dropped by a third between 1979 and 1994. During the explosive job growth of the 1990s, Fortune 500 companies lost more jobs than they created. In the meantime, job growth was concentrated in the small business sectors, especially the fast-growing gazelles (companies with sales growth of at least 20 percent a year for four straight years). Between 1993 and 1996, gazelles accounted for 70 percent of America's phenomenal job growth.

But what really separates today's workplaces from those of Taylor's days is their mind-set rather than their size. Through most of the twentieth century, the work world was defined by the values of its emblematic workplace: the assembly line—hierarchical, structured, regimented, controlled from the top down. Not everyone worked on the assembly line, just as not everyone works in a high-tech start-up today, but the assembly lines' values defined Americans' workdays whether they worked on the factory floor or in the corner office. The emblematic workplaces of today—the high-tech start-ups and small businesses that drove so much of America's economic growth in the 1990s—tell a very different story. There, walls are broken down, power is dispersed, and decision-making authority—and responsibility—are put in the hands of each worker. Workers are thinking for themselves and companies are relying on that thinking. "If Frederick Taylor in effect said, 'Let the experts lead,'" *Fortune* magazine noted in 1997, "today's apothegm is 'We have met the experts, and they are us.'"

In his 1907 classic, *Christianity and Social Crisis*, Walter Rauschenbusch wrote, "Man is treated as a *thing* to produce more things. Men are hired as hands and not as men." Today, most workers are hired to produce *think*, not things. According to calculations by Stanford Professor Stephen R. Barley, the percentage of the American workforce that works chiefly with information was 17 percent in 1900 and 59 percent in 2000. Eighty percent of U.S. workers don't make things, their jobs involve working with people and information. Today, California, always a herald of nationwide change, has more wired workers (those who work with technology and decide for themselves how to do their job) than blue-collar workers.

More important, the distinction between the two is fast becoming meaningless. Even those that still do make things do so in different ways. In the early twentieth century, a thirty-year veteran machinist, a man whose father and grandfather had probably taken great pride in their work as farmers or craftsmen, would half-lament, half-grouse, "You can take a boy fresh from the farm and in three days he can manage a machine as well as I can." In very few of today's factories would that hold true. Knowledge and skills are not seen as infirmities but set the worth of the modern worker. The relentless focus on the bottom-line in the old Ford factories has made way to share room with an emphasis on top-of-the-line products. Today, finally, it is the quality—and not just the quantity—of the mousetraps that matters.

As Europe's Industrial Age gathered steam, Friedrich Engels defined his and Karl Marx's proletariat as "the class of modern wage laborers who, having no means of production of their own, are reduced to selling their labor-power in order to live." In those days, when William Allen White's "pre-Adamite giant" had gathered the wheel and levers of power into the hands of centralization, this was true. Machines were impossible for individuals to purchase, own, or operate by themselves. Yet, the Information Age is driven by neither manpower nor machines, but by minds—and the innovation they produce. Every individual now has "means of production of their own"—they carry it on their own shoulders. The proletariat is dead.

The new workplaces and new jobs of the Information Age have created new workers. When most of Washington's traditional conservatives and liberals imagine a contemporary American worker, they see a big beefy beast of a man more comfortable with Crisco than Cisco; a sweaty, grubby, dim-witted toiler with an unfortunate gap between where his too-small, no-longer-white T-shirt ends and his ill-fitting blue jeans begin. With Frederick Taylor, they imagine an "ox, heavy both mentally and physically."

But in an America where a quarter of workers are wired workers (working with networked computers in a flexible, team-oriented environment) and nearly a third are free agents (working for themselves and from their homes), the old workforce of the twentieth century is but a memory. The new workforce is self-reliant and empowered to do their jobs as they think best. Of course, though there are more and more with each passing month, not everyone is a knowledge worker. Nor will they all ever be. Americans will still bag groceries, still mop floors, still change bedpans. Someone has to operate the forklift at Amazon.com. But as was the case with the assembly line's values, the values of personal power and control that permeate the new workplaces will set the tone for Americans from all walks of life.

The final value in the Russian Apple commercial is central to the Information Age: "the right to be an individual." Everywhere one looks, the individual—whose obituary was being written as the century began—has resurfaced with the confidence of someone who has lived through a near-death experience. With big business ceding economic power to nimble entrepreneurs or behaving with the flexibility of their small competitors, with individuals once again at the center of economic life, Teddy Roosevelt and the rest have been proven wrong. "The day of small things" has returned.

Rarely mentioned, even by famous New Economy gurus, the celebration and empowerment of the individual is the driving force of the modern economy. Some commentators work diligently to obscure this fact. They point to the continued strength of large firms or the merger-mania of the 1990s as an indication that bigness still trumps the little guy. But this looks at the economy through the lens of the way businesses work, not the way people work. Moreover, some of America's biggest corporations now succeed or fail based on their ability to put power in the hands of customers; in many of them, consumers dictate to companies on issues such as price and design, not the other way around. For instance, Industrial Era Ford and present-day AOL-Time-Warner are both huge companies. However, while the first was built on the idea of one-size-fits-all, the second was created to facilitate personalized choices and information. In the economy that matters to people on an everyday basis, the force of change is on the side of giving power to individuals—both as workers and as customers. This driving impetus to the economy is cropping up everywhere one turns.

One randomly chosen, unexceptional magazine from late 1999 exemplifies how deeply notions of personal control and individual power have become embedded in the culture in recent years and how much Americans seem to hunger for them. This was not one of the legion of New Economy booster brochures that now crowd newsstands, but a normal, humdrum edition of *Newsweek*. Raphael's *Vision of Ezekiel* adorned the cover and the headline hyped millennialist misgivings: "Prophecy: What the Bible says about the End of the World." But reading between the bylines on the inside of the magazine, the reader learned much about the birth of the world of the New Economy. Of course, there were the expected ads for cars and credit cards, breakfast cereal and life insurance. But alongside them, in ad after ad for cell phones and software, computers and web pages, came glimmers of the role individual choice plays in driving public attitudes. On page 8 is an advertisement featuring a crowded big city street dotted with people conversing on cell phones—each connected to whomever they want, whenever they want. Page 11 is blank, save for the words "How do you measure success?" The following page pictures a family strolling along the seashore and words, "i prioritize." The ad continues on the next page with men building a house—perhaps through Habitat for Humanity—and the text, "i give back." Next is a page with a photo of a napping man's bare feet propped up on the side of his speedboat. "i sleep well." Finally, this five-page spread concludes by revealing it was an ad for "i choice," Wall Street firm Morgan Stanley Dean Witter's "dramatic new way to invest your money." The text reads, "As an individual, you probably have your own idea of success and how to achieve it. That said, shouldn't you have the opportunity to invest how you want, when you want? With as little or as much assistance as you want?" With this new service, "the point is, you can achieve *your* success, *your* way." Uniting the Information Age's themes of individuality and choice, the ad ends with the words, "**i choice.** In a world where no two people are alike, it's the most individual way yet of achieving success."

Page 22 is selling a printer that allows you to "create your own cards and ornaments" for the holiday season. Page 29 features a home furnishings web page that allows the customer to "express your personal vision for your home." On page 34 a young African-American woman in a computer ad looks at readers to tell them that "My homepage is my castle." Pages 49 and 51 advertise a service offering on-line books that are "ready to read. All the time. Whenever you are." Throughout the magazine's advertisements, the themes are the same, all responding to the attitude modern consumers bring to the marketplace. Page 64 has an ad for an airline's web page that lets customers "buy tickets, check departures, upgrade seats" for themselves. Page 87 offers up a web-based bookseller where "you can instantly compare books by shipping costs, delivery time, and availability from hundreds of online stores." On page 91, an on-line encyclopedia asks, "what's on your mind?" Back on page 61, an ad peddles an "individualized news service that lets you choose what's news." The web page will "bring you all the news you ask for—and none of the news you don't." The web page's name? Individual.com.

Everywhere we turn, we are confronted by the lure of individual choice. In the summer of 1999, a full-page ad in the *New York Times* business section read simply: "Announcing the biggest merger in Wall Street history." Turning the newsprint sheet to the next two-page spread, the ad continued "Merrill Lynch & You," and promoted the brokerage house's new initiative to put more information and choices into the hands of investors. They were not alone. In an advertisement appearing in national magazines near the end of 1999, the Yahoo! web site advertised their service. Below a photograph of a dusty, grimy building built in the shape of a pig, the ad read: "Next time, make your *own* hotel arrangements." At the bottom of the page, the text read: "Take control. Book your flight. Rent a car. Make hotel reservations in like, two minutes. Maybe three." Utility.com said that "Power Just Got Personal." Sonicnet.com's "me music" offered Americans the chance to "create your own radio station" on the Internet. An on-line car market, Autobytel.com, began its TV commercials with the words, "Freedom. Control. What a ride. Just you and your laptop." It was not only the computers that promised new power to the individual. UnitedHealthcare took out a newspaper ad to proclaim that "we believe that no one knows you as well as you know yourself. That's why we are committed to keeping you in control of your own health." An Acura car commercial announced that William Allen White's "pre-Adamite giant" has been felled: "In the name of progress, man has given more and more power to machines. Perhaps its time to take some of it back."

For at least a decade, Americans have been doing just that. In 1960, there were 5,000 installed computers in the United States. In 1997, there were 180 million and counting. Ninety-five percent of these were personal computers, used by individuals in the manner they saw fit. For the first time since Americans traded the country for the city, the farm for the factory, the workbench for the workplace, power is seeping back into the hands of people.

In his excellent work, *Self-Rule*, historian Robert Wiebe shows that the dominant characteristics of twentieth-century American life were centralization and hierarchy. These values were formed in the blinding heat of America's industrial period. Today, that period has ended.

Michael Barone, one of the most astute analysts of American political history, has written that "America today more closely resembles the pre-industrial America that Alexis de Tocqueville described in *Democracy in America* in the 1830s than the industrial America in which most of us grew up."

To some extent, he is right. As in the days when the Republic was taking its first halting steps on young and wobbly legs, the individual is standing tall again. But America has changed and history never retreats. Americans aren't looking for the outlook of the yeoman farmer to replace the centralization and hierarchy Wiebe described. They are increasingly turning to new notions of the market and of meritocracy—and they are waiting for government to follow suit.

The past tells us they will not—and will not have to—wait patiently for this to occur. In the early 1900s, an immigrant worker in Chicago had had enough. She marched up to her boss and demanded better toilet facilities, a demand that must have been met with the incredulous stare Oliver Twist received when he pleaded for "More." Undaunted, she stood her ground. "Old America is gone," she said. "There is new times." As a new century begins, the times have changed once again. Now, as then, politics must respond.

PART II

The Choice Revolution

To-day, when our government has so far passed into the hands of special interests; to-day when the doctrine is implicitly avowed that only select classes have the equipment necessary for carrying on government; to-day, when so many conscientious citizens, smitten with the scene of social wrong and suffering, have fallen victims to the fallacy that benevolent government can be meted out to the people by kind-hearted trustees of prosperity and guardians of the welfare of dutiful employees,—to-day, supremely, does it behoove this nation to remember that a people shall be saved by the power that sleeps in its own deep bosom, or by none.

—*Woodrow Wilson, 1912*

*T*he 1990s saw the resurgence of an old debate about what is foremost in Americans' minds when they think about politics and government. "It's the economy, stupid" read James Carville's famous sign in the Clinton campaign War Room. *Values Matter Most*, especially as seen through major social issues, responded columnist Ben Wattenberg in his 1995 book of that name. And in his 1990 book *Our Country*, Michael Barone argued that Americans have historically divided along "cultural" lines. At any given moment, each of them may be correct. Booms and busts, slavery and civil rights, freemasons and free love have all—over the course of American history—shaped election outcomes.

Yet it is no evasion to say that, in the long run, what forms Americans' beliefs about government are what might be called the "cultural

values of the economy"—the attitudes and outlooks that are engendered
in people by the way they work and live. At times when these cultural
values of the economy are fairly static—when Americans' jobs and stores
are based on notions similar to those of last year or their parents' day—
thinking about government is focused on the means of government
action, be it the spoils system and civil service in the nineteenth century
or taxing and spending more or less in the twentieth. In the past decade,
Republicans and Democrats in Congress and a New Democrat in the
White House have waged an important and long overdue debate over
this question of government's means.

But at times of transformation—when the way the world works is in
the process of changing fundamentally, when the cultural values of the
economy are being replaced by new ones—something more is required:
an examination of government's mission. We live in such a time today,
as we did a century ago. Then, as now, Americans indicated they were
looking for new thinking about government's role. One hundred years
ago, politicians responded by changing the mission of government to
one of using its power to provide for Americans in need; today America
is awaiting a contemporary response that is relevant to our own time.

The fall and rise of the individual in the American economy closely
tracks the historic fall and soon-to-be rise of the idea that government
should put its faith in and disperse its powers to individuals. The goal
of the Choice Revolution is to replace the top-down government of the
age of assembly lines with a bottom-up government that melds the cultural values of today's economy with a field of government endeavor that
has long laid fallow but now is fertile again.

JEFFERSON BOARDS

He was gone, and night her sable curtain drew across the sky;
Gone his soul into all nations, gone to live and not to die.
—*Hezekiah Butterworth,* The Death of Jefferson, *1887*

On the morning of March 4, 1801, Thomas Jefferson awoke in his room
at Mrs. Conrad's Boarding-House in Washington City—the mere

months-old capital of the young United States of America. He made his way downstairs to breakfast and took his usual seat at the long table where meals were served to the boarders—the seat farthest from the fire on this cold winter morning. Someone rose to offer him a better seat. He refused with a smile.

Before noon, he donned his plain Democratic-Republican cloth coat and, with a group of friends and supporters, made his way the one block to the half-finished Capitol. As he strode up the steps and paused to glance at the view, he saw seven or eight boarding houses, a tailor's, a shoemaker's, a printer's, an oyster market, a grocery shop, a stationery store, a dry goods store, a washwoman's home. And nothing else. Just the endless expanse of dense forests and fertile fields that defined America for Jefferson. Washington was a city of three thousand people—an empty capital of an enormous land struggling with its place in the world.

Reaching the rostrum of the tiny Senate chamber, Jefferson faced the assembled senators and representatives and began his Inaugural Address as president of the United States. In a trembling, barely audible voice, this painfully shy man—who would discontinue Washington's and Adams' practice of reporting on the state of the Union in person—set forth a vision of what America was, who Americans were, and what form their government should take. It was a vision that would guide the country through the rest of the nineteenth century.

Jefferson saw before him "a rising nation, spread over a wide and fruitful land," a new Republic demanding "a wise and frugal government" that would provide for the "encouragement of agriculture, and of commerce as its handmaiden." It was surprising to no one that Jefferson saw commerce as the servant of agriculture. "While we have land to labor let us never wish to see our citizens occupied at a work-bench," he wrote on one occasion. "Those who labor in the earth are the chosen people of God," he wrote on another. For these people, the common people of the country, Jefferson was a champion. Jefferson spoke out for the farmers, the "cultivators of the earth"—the 90 percent of the American nation whose muddy moccasins would not be welcome in the front parlors of the fashionable salons of Boston, New York, or Philadelphia.

In his Inaugural Address, Jefferson vowed to govern not just to their advantage, but with their attitude. Far removed from the cities' dense networks of communal relationships, these small farmers relied on themselves. And this faith was the basis of their faith in the nation and its government. Because he recognized that individual self-determination and democratic rule went hand in hand, Jefferson said America had "the strongest government on earth." "Sometimes it is said," Jefferson continued, "that man cannot be trusted with the government of himself. Can he, then, be trusted with the government of others? Or have we found angels, in the form of kings, to govern him? Let history answer this question."

Jefferson's election itself served as history's early returns. For throughout much of the 1790s, as George Washington's presidency guided the infant nation through perilous decisions, Jefferson, his arch-rival Alexander Hamilton, and their respective followers had engaged in a debate over the meaning of America. Their debate has reverberated ever since.

John Adams called Alexander Hamilton the "bastard brat of a Scotch peddler," and Hamilton's life can be seen as an attempt to escape the ignominy of his birth. Born in the Lesser Antilles in the Caribbean, he was the product of a relationship between a Scottish merchant and a beautiful French Huguenot which, though clearly consummated, was never consecrated. Those around him always sensed he was destined for greatness—and if they ever forgot, he was quick to remind them. Amid the swaying palms, he would plow through pages of Plutarch, dreaming of distant lands to conquer. He wrote he would never be satisfied with the "groveling ambition of a clerk." He was 12 years old.

Hamilton's mother died when he was 13, leaving him effectively orphaned. He did resort to work as a clerk in a St. Croix import-export office, but those around him soon shared his belief that he had a higher calling. His obvious talents led impressed elders to send him away to Kings College (now Columbia University) in New York City. After two years, when Hamilton was 19, the Revolutionary War broke out and he thrust himself into its vortex, becoming a valued aide-de-camp to General Washington. With peace he married well and prospered as lawyer, but all the while he nursed his political ambitions—and his worldview.

By the time of the Constitutional Convention, Hamilton was a major power in New York politics and the speech he delivered in Philadelphia was treated with the utmost seriousness. He proposed that presidents and senators be elected for life and that state governors be appointed by the president for life terms. In effect, he sought an American monarchy and nobility. His plan was cast aside, but his words in its support remain as a monument to his ideology. "All communities divide themselves into the few and the many," he told his colleagues gathered at Independence Hall. "The first are the rich and well-born; the other mass of the people . . . turbulent and changing, they seldom judge or determine right. Give therefore to the first class a distinct share of government."

Although unsatisfied with the Constitution, he authored two-thirds of the Federalist Papers written in support of its ratification. Upon Washington's election as the first president, Hamilton, then 34 years old, became secretary of the treasury. It was in this first Olympian cabinet that Hamilton first met the new secretary of state, Thomas Jefferson.

Jefferson was already a legend the world over. In 1776, at the age of 33, at the modest table of a Philadelphia bricklayer, he had written the Declaration of Independence—the most revolutionary statement ever put to paper by human hand. Jefferson's father was a self-made farmer and his mother a member of the blue-blooded Randolph clan. Throughout his life he prided himself on moving freely in both their milieus. While he was quickly accepted into the fox-hunting aristocracy of Williamsburg when he arrived there for college, he grew up among the hardscrabble Western farmers. Virginia's "western counties, then the western frontier, had been populated by Scotch-Irish and Germans—earnest, hard-working, hard-drinking men who wrestled with nature as with their consciences, built churches in the woods, and schoolhouses in the clearing," wrote Claude G. Bowers in his enormously popular 1925 book, *Jefferson and Hamilton*. It was not until he was 18 years old that Thomas Jefferson ever laid eyes on a town.

If Hamilton believed in the wisdom of the few, Jefferson put his faith in the many. Jefferson was convinced that the common people were the repository of goodness and wisdom—and that government's primary role was the protection of their independence. In 1776, he proposed giving every white, adult male in Virginia 50 acres of land—if they did not already own that much. By effectively ending the land requirement for voting and granting each person autonomy, this would have diffused political and economic power into the hands of the many—a horrifying thought for Hamiltonians. "The sheep are happier of themselves," Jefferson would say, "than under the care of the wolves."

As president, Jefferson would demand that Washington's and Adams' tradition of greeting the chief executive with a bow be replaced by a simple handshake, a move that greatly bothered Hamilton's Federalists, who with derision called Jefferson's followers "democrats"—a horrid slander involving fealty to the common people and their common ways. The name stuck.

It was inevitable that Hamilton and Jefferson—the champion of the few and the champion of the many—would clash. Theirs were elemental conflicts that still sunder American politics today. According to Jefferson, the purpose of government was "to secure the greatest degree of happiness possible to the general mass of those associated under it." A few days before he died, Jefferson wrote that "the mass of mankind has not been born with saddles on their backs." Hamilton feared a government that would give in to the inchoate urges and "moral depravity" of the commoners. "Our real disease is *democracy*," he wrote the night before he was struck down by Aaron Burr's bullet.

Hamilton, who began America's first industrial conglomerate, believed that businesses needed government's "interference and aid" through special subsidies. Jefferson, who led the fight to ban primogeniture (the automatic and exclusive right of inheritance of the firstborn) in Virginia, was a dedicated enemy of special privileges.

Hamilton, in the words of one biography, "was born with a reverence for tradition." But his farsighted recognition that manufacturing, industry, and commerce were the tide of the future did more to undermine ancient traditions than he ever knew. On the other hand, it was left to Jefferson—a brilliant scientist and the inventor of the swivel chair—to defend the ways of the old agricultural society in the face of the first glimmers of industrial change.

Perhaps it was odd that their roles were not reversed—that Hamilton from meager beginnings not speak out for the many and Jefferson of the landed gentry not defend the few. Yet, those with the greatest stake in the perpetuation of the status quo are often not the comfortable and wealthy, who have the luxury of striking out against the established order. Many times it is those who exited the womb clutching the short straw and find success who become the primary defenders of the world as it is.

But the conflict between Hamilton and Jefferson was, at its heart, not about personality or even politics. It was an essential struggle about the purposes and premises of American government. This struggle defined the politics of the nineteenth and twentieth centuries. It will very likely come to set the terms of politics in the twenty-first century.

Stripped of the details of debates over agriculture and industry, federalism and states rights, creditors and debtors, finance and France, the philosophies of Jefferson and Hamilton placed in sharp relief two proud strains of thinking. Jefferson believed in breaking apart concentrated power to stifle special privilege and guarantee opportunities for mobility to ordinary people. Hamilton promoted modernization, progress, and prosperity through concentrated government power. The first believed in an America that was run from the bottom up; the second in one ruled from the top down.

It would be bad politics and terrible policy to completely embrace either of these traditions while eschewing the other. No successful leader—not even, it should be noted, Thomas Jefferson and Alexander Hamilton—has ever sought to govern based on only one of these strains. But, since the emphases that they placed and the relative mix of these mind-sets have so characterized American life, they provide an extremely useful prism for considering America's past and its future.

The fact that the divide between Jefferson and Hamilton still has relevance to contemporary questions is a testament to more than their colorful personalities and outsized achievements. The flame of the debate between Jefferson and Hamilton has been kept alive because the vision of each has, at various times, applied more than the other to the demands of American government.

On the occasion of the millennium, *Time* magazine named Thomas Jefferson the Person of the Eighteenth century. This was appropriate enough. His 1776 Declaration of Independence was certainly the defining event of the century, if not the pivot of the last five hundred years. But, for Americans especially, his contribution to the nineteenth century cannot be overlooked. The vision he laid out in that 1801 Inaugural Address—and in his two terms as president—set the tone for much of the next hundred years.

This vision was appropriate for a "rising nation" and its island communities. It governed for the benefit of self-sufficient individuals and with the precepts of individualism. "The party that was gathering about Mr. Jefferson purposed, among other things, the leveling of political privilege. The spirit of the rural nation was against social distinctions. The essential simplicity of its life made pretension ridiculous; the free movement of enterprise throughout its borders made the individual man, with or without property, if only he possessed energy and initiative, the real and only constant unit of power; and the new nation was not long in showing that it wished its government conducted with the economy, simplicity, and plainness of the individual man," wrote Princeton President Woodrow Wilson in his 1902 *A History of the American People.*

Though formed in the eighteenth century, Jefferson's vision formed the nineteenth. Certainly, the Whig Party of Henry Clay sought a greater measure of governmental activism and protection of American industry, but Clay was rejected for the presidency five times. Though he claimed he would "rather be right than be President," the American people saw no danger that he would be either. Though John Quincy Adams was president in the 1820s and various Whigs won the office in the 1840s and 1850s, none appreciably changed the tenor of Americans' views toward government. Though Daniel Webster was the greatest orator of the age, he was unable to sell the Hamiltonian vision to an agrarian America. Though Abraham Lincoln, an avowed follower of Clay, did reach the White House in 1861, he turned out to be the greatest defender of the wisdom of the common people the nation has ever seen.

His greatest legislative achievement—the Homestead Act—was the fulfillment of Jefferson's wish for the dispersal of land, and the power that came with it, to average citizens. Throwing caveats to the wind, the nineteenth century was a Jeffersonian century.

But as that century came to a close, America was transforming. As Turner's frontier gave way to Taylor's Industrial Age, Americans moved from the self-sufficiency of the farm to the stern strictures of the factory. When Jefferson was elected, only 12 percent of Americans had what could be called a "boss." The word did not even enter common usage until the 1830s. By 1860, 40 percent of free Americans had a boss. And by the time Woodrow Wilson left the White House in 1920, fully 87 percent of all wage earners were working for a corporation. The regimented assembly line and its gospel of efficiency would delimit how Americans saw their work lives—and what they expected from government. The slow ways of agricultural life—easygoing if not easy—were replaced by the hustle of time clocks, the bustle of automobiles, the crowded confines of city skyscrapers and autocrats in penthouse suites. Average Americans needed a power on their side in this strange new world—and they would turn toward government. They began longing for programs as hierarchical as the factories, for policies as identical as their products, and for a government as big as the other organizations they encountered every day.

Beginning with Theodore Roosevelt, twentieth-century American leaders cast aside Jefferson in favor of his ancient ideological enemy. "Hamilton's political theories had more validity for the future America than for the simple country with whose common mind and condition Jefferson's ideas agreed," wrote popular historian Samuel Eliot Morison in 1965, as twentieth-century liberalism stood at its high-water mark. "America has outgrown Jefferson's principles." First and foremost among the differences Morison saw between the two men's principles was that "Hamilton wished to concentrate power; Jefferson to diffuse power."

Although they might pledge fealty to the memory of Jefferson, although they were anything but champions of the few against the many, the dominant leaders of the twentieth century—Theodore Roosevelt,

Woodrow Wilson, Franklin Roosevelt, Harry Truman, Lyndon Johnson—built up a strong, central, top-down government to bring progress,
protection, and economic equality to Americans of all walks of life.
Though few leaders would ever admit it, the twentieth century was a
Hamiltonian century.

So what of this new century, the twenty-first? On both sides of the
political spectrum, the obvious predisposition is to keep on keeping on
with Hamiltonianism. This is no surprise. It took the Progressive movement a third of a century to bring Americans to break with the constricting ways of Jeffersonianism at the beginning of the twentieth century. Today, Hamilton would be proud of the Democrats' continued
commitment to a strong centralized government whose expert bureaucrats control the lives of ordinary citizens. He would be thrilled by the
Republicans' worship of the economic elite and their unwavering determination to give those at the top of the economic pyramid the lion's
share of attention. He would be delighted with the subsidies and tax
breaks both parties lavish on the powerful interests who wield the most
political power.

Among the feted thinkers in both political camps, Hamilton's reputation is as strong as ever. In his 1997 book, *Hamilton's Republic*, liberal
commentator Michael Lind defended his hero's principles of a welfare
state at home and *realpolitik* abroad. In a contemporaneous article in the
Washington Post, he wrote that "It is Hamilton who is the ancestor of
what is best in 20th-century liberalism. And it is Hamilton who is the
best guide to a revival of the American center-left in the 21st-century."
On the conservative side, Richard Brookhiser wrote in *U.S. News and
World Report* that "In the '90s, Hamilton is up; Jefferson is down." Conservatives should pay homage to Hamilton as "a great apostle of capital-
ist enterprise as a catalyst for human potential."

The problem is that both conventional Democrats and Republicans,
liberals and conservatives, look at Hamilton from the perspective of
what was, not what is coming to be. What is past need not be prolonged.
The future belongs to Jefferson.

Today, Jefferson's reputation stands at a low ebb. When discussed at all in recent years it is as the hypocritical sire of Sally Hemmings' son or as the distant mastermind in the exploits of explorers Lewis and Clark. Oklahoma City bomber Timothy McVeigh was arrested while wearing a shirt adorned with a Jefferson quotation. Historian Conor Cruise O'Brien wrote that Jefferson's vision is relevant only to "radical, violent, anti-Federal libertarian fanatics." Chief Justice William Rhenquist presided at a mock trial of Jefferson on charges of racism. But the tide is turning, and silently, imperceptibly, Jeffersonianism is lapping up against the shores of the new century.

The twenty-first century won't see a mass return to the farms while tumbleweeds bounce through our cities' streets. Jefferson's world is gone for good. However, Information Age America is returning to some of his values. With the loosening of rigid rules of behavior and the rise of personal technology, Americans are demanding—and receiving—more choices and personal control in the workplace and in the marketplace. The new Choice Generation is emerging shaped by endless options, a distrust of any elites, and a fundamental faith in themselves. Centralized power is being diffused in the economy as consumers have a greater ability to access—and design—the products and prices they desire. Top-down hierarchies are being rooted out and discarded in favor of empowering frontline workers in most every business hoping to find success in the coming years. Jefferson would be so elated he might even forget about the farm; Hamilton would be horrified.

"It is not by consolidation, or concentration of powers, but by their distribution, that good government is effected," Jefferson would write as an old man. Today, as the rest of the world begins to reflect that wisdom, government is almost alone in obdurately refusing to help this process along. The politicians might not know it yet, but the political issue ahead is not the old fight about whether government should do more or less. Rather, the public will increasingly crave a new role for government: a Choice Revolution in government that breaks down concentrated authority, be it private or public, and gives power to and puts faith in the people. It would allow ordinary citizens to make the types of choices for themselves and their families now available only to the wealthy. This new role for government is not bigger or smaller, but different. It is more ambitious than the paltry proposals offered by either party today and more in tune with the contours of life in the new century.

In 1801, Thomas Jefferson was inaugurated and set the course for a century that bore his imprint. In 1901, Theodore Roosevelt became president and eventually guided the country into the arms of a powerful, Hamiltonian government. In 2001, the new president takes office in times that demand the beginning of a new Jeffersonian Age.

On the morning of July 4, 1826—fifty years to the day that his Declaration of Independence was signed—Thomas Jefferson died. Later that same day, hundreds of miles to the north, John Adams expired at sunset. Before he did, he uttered his last words: "Thomas Jefferson still survives." He was right.

BACK TO THE FUTURE

> A lean, bilious-looking fellow, with his pockets full of handbills, was haranguing vehemently about rights of citizens—elections—members of congress—liberty—Bunker's Hill—heroes of seventy-six—and other words which were a perfect Babylonish jargon to the bewildered Van Winkle.
>
> —*Washington Irving,* Rip Van Winkle

Julian West awoke on September 10, 2000, in a world unlike that which he had ever known. After going to sleep on the night of May 30, 1887, he slumbered into an America where there were no stores or banks or money. Everyone was healthy and happy. There were no politicians and no political parties. A powerful government provided security and prosperity for all. It was truly a utopia.

This was the premise of *Looking Backward,* Edward Bellamy's 1888 socialist science fiction story that sold more copies than any other nineteenth-century novel save for *Uncle Tom's Cabin.* Julian West, a rich, educated, and proper Bostonian, sleeps for 113 years, 3 months, 11 days, and awakens in a perfect world. Guided by the kindly Dr. Leete, West is shown and explained the glorious, centrally planned future.

In Bellamy's fantasy, "the industry and commerce of the country [are] intrusted to a single syndicate representing the people, to be conducted in the common interest for the common profit." Under the leadership of the National Party, this central planning authority—"The Great Trust"—decides where people work, what they can buy, what they can learn. Like the gleaming, big machines in the new factories sprouting up everywhere in the 1880s, economic and social life has been standardized in this world of the year 2000 with "the organization of the industry of the nation under single control, so that all its processes interlock."

Like all futurists, Bellamy has a mixed record of success in prediction. He correctly envisioned a future of chain stores and department stores—but was wrong in thinking all Americans would dress and speak alike. He predicted government-required information labels on all food products—but thought tastes in music and furniture would remain static. He realized that women would become part of the workforce—but was overly optimistic in thinking they would get paid at rates equal to those of men. He imagined the radio (he called it a "musical telephone") and even thought there would be televangelists—but expected that Boston's Charles River would look like a clean, clear "blue ribbon." He even anticipated the clock radio—but neglected to mention its most valuable component: the snooze button. Worst of all, from the standpoint of comparison with the real 2000, he imagined a static universe where a centrally planned economy might work—and fell short in realizing the awesome power of technological change in making his vision obsolete. Bellamy's "fairy tale of social felicity" pictured a flawless Industrial Age where top-down regimentation and restrictions are cheerfully accepted by grateful citizens. As 2000 truly turned out, he could not have been more wrong.

Bellamy's book is basically an extended series of turgid Socratic dialogues between West and Dr. Leete explicating every minute detail about the function of this perfect world—with a torpid romance between West and Leete's daughter stapled onto the story. So why was the book so phenomenally successful in its day—a time when bookstores carried such popular authors as Emily Dickinson, Jules Verne, Stephen Crane, Mark Twain, Walt Whitman, Thomas Hardy, Rudyard Kipling, and Robert Louis Stevenson? It is likely that most of the Americans who read his book were less interested in Bellamy's fantastic predictions of the future than they were in his finely tuned descriptions of what was happening in their present.

In the first popularly accessible book to describe the rise of Industrial America, Bellamy—whose cousin Francis composed the "Pledge of Allegiance" in celebration of the 1893 Columbian Exposition—showed his readers that the time when "the individual workman was relatively important and independent in his relations to the employer" had ended. Modern workers had been "reduced to insignificance and powerlessness." There was not "any opportunity whatever for individual enterprise in any important field of industry." Whether or not Bellamy's portrait of the year 2000 rang hollow was immaterial. For many Americans, his picture of their own time rang all too true.

The vision of the future Bellamy put forward planted a seed in the minds of Americans in general—and the impressionable imaginations of young Progressive Generation leaders-to-be in particular—a seed that would come to sprout and bear fruit. Although *Looking Backward's* specifics were never implemented, its spirit helped shape the twentieth century to a greater degree than one might expect. Looking at his own time, Bellamy believed that "the excessive individualism which then prevailed was inconsistent with much public spirit." He believed that this individualism would have to be curtailed by government if social progress were to be achieved. In his mind, the fundamental difference between "the age of individualism and that of concert" was that, in the latter, Americans of the future had learned to harness the forces of bigness to banish poverty and to provide the security of plenty to every American. This became the central dream of twentieth-century liberals. "The movement toward the conduct of business by larger and larger aggregations of capital, the tendency toward monopolies, which had been so desperately and vainly resisted," wrote Bellamy "was recognized at last, in its true significance, as a process which only needed to complete its logical evolution to open a golden future to humanity."

Yet all that lay ahead. A poor graduate student at Johns Hopkins University named Frederick Jackson Turner, unable to afford a ticket home to see his fiancée, spent Christmas immersed in *Looking Backward*. What Americans like Turner knew when they eagerly picked up the book was that their old world was suddenly and steadily giving way to a new one. Bellamy's popularity might have stemmed from the fact that he was the first person to tell Americans what they—silently—already suspected. The ways of individuals and their enterprises were fading away "because they belonged to a day of small things and were totally incompetent to the demands of an age of steam and telegraphs and the gigantic scale of its enterprises. To restore the former order of things, even if possible, would have involved returning to the day of stagecoaches." The world of Julian West would inexorably replace the world of Turner's West.

Frederick Jackson Turner may have declared that the frontier had been settled by 1890, but little else was in those years, as America—then as now—was both affluent and afflux. The 1860s and 1870s, the years of Civil War and Reconstruction, were, like the 1960s and 1970s, discordant years of strife and social unrest. But as was true in the twentieth century, the 1880s and 1890s saw Americans trying to move on with their lives and leaving the divisive social and cultural issues of the previous decades to the politicians who used them for partisan gain. Moreover, the end of the Civil War, like the end of the Cold War, unleashed a long-brewing economic revolution that had been held back by political division and inattention. In the nineteenth century, that meant that Industrial America was being born.

In 1885, a preacher named Josiah Strong published a best-selling book entitled *Our Country* which was notable at the time because it examined America not in terms of its qualities, but its quantities—using the science of statistics to examine American life. Not only was the practice new, but the idea that statistics might have a story to tell—that America was changing—was novel as well. In 1830, 4 years after Jefferson died, one out of 10 Americans lived in cities of more than 2,500 people. Over the next 20 years the number hardly budged. By 1850, a still paltry 3.5 million Americans lived in cities—15 percent of the population in the rural Republic. But by 1890, one out of every 3 lived in the cities of what was becoming an urban, industrial democracy. Ten years later, at the turn of the century, it was 40 percent. On the eve of the 1912 presidential election that would shape American politics for generations, it was slightly under 50 percent. For the hardened Americans living on top of one another in crowded urban cores, the memories of the wide-open spaces of their parents—and the wide-open possibilities they entailed—must have seemed remotely sweet and hopelessly naïve. Change was in the air.

According to the economist Maurice Adelman, in the 1820s somewhere between 75 percent and 80 percent of the American labor force consisted of "independent entrepreneurs"—farmers, shopkeepers, butchers, bakers, candlestick makers who answered only to themselves. But Industrial America pulled—and the changing economy pushed—their children off the farms and into the factories. Between 1860 and 1900, the percentage of the workforce involved in industrial work shot up by nearly two-thirds. Between 1869 and 1919, farm goods dropped from 40 percent of the United States's gross domestic product to 14 percent. Change was in the air.

In the decades after the Civil War, change was in the air everywhere—everywhere except for politics. Then as now, it was fashionable to say that politics had become irrelevant, that true change was brought about in the private sector and not the public arena. John Adams had been president. His son John Quincy Adams was president as well. His son Charles Francis Adams had played a large role in saving the Union as minister to England during the Civil War. His son, Charles Francis Adams Jr., was a railroad executive.

But, then as now, if politics had become irrelevant, it was not because it was unimportant—the changing times made it very important. It was because the thinking of politicians had failed to keep up with the dynamism of a changing world. As Charles Francis Adams Jr. wrote in 1868 about the transcontinental railroad and more generally about the

Industrial Revolution: "Here is an enormous, an incalculable force . . . let loose suddenly upon mankind; exercising all sorts of influences, social, moral, and political; precipitating upon us novel problems which demand immediate solution; banishing the new before the old is half matured to replace it. . . . Perhaps if the existing community would take now and then the trouble to pass in review the changes it has already witnessed . . . it might with more grace accept the inevitable, and cease from useless attempts at making a wholly new world conform itself to the rules and theories of a bygone civilization."

Adams may have been giving politicians too much credit. While many did resolutely stand for the past, many more—just as resolutely—stood for nothing. Commenting on late-nineteenth-century politics in America, the British visitor James Bryce wrote, in words that might well have been written today, that "The Republican and Democratic parties were like two bottles. Each bore a label denoting the kind of liquor it carries, but each was empty." The parties had their ideologies, but no ideas. Like actors in bad dinner theaters who think that the way to convey emotion is by turning up the volume, politicians were saying nothing—louder and louder. Not surprisingly, but all too familiarly, the American people merely walked away. As historian Robert Wiebe wrote, "America in the late nineteenth century was a nation of intense partisanship and massive political indifference."

As America underwent the traumatic convulsions of economic transformation, politicians perfected delay and mutual laceration as ways to avoid having to undertake basic pieces of meaningful legislation. The Senate talked for a decade before it could gather itself to settle on a law regulating the railroads. Between 1877 and 1881, nearly a year and a half of the government's working time was spent in two arguments about who should hold the post of collector of the Port of New York. In the first of these fights, the eventual losing nominee—rejected by the Senate on a vote of 31 to 25—was Theodore Roosevelt Sr., a New York City aristocrat. The strain and worry of the nomination battle led to his physical deterioration and death at age 46, only two months after he was rejected for the job for purely partisan reasons. His son, Harvard sophomore

Theodore Roosevelt Jr., took note. The following year, 1879, another young man looked at government with similar disdain. In the year he graduated from Princeton, 23-year-old Woodrow Wilson dismissed the politics of his day: "no leaders, no principles."

But, in America, public demand is not long left unsatisfied. Americans knew they needed both new leaders and new principles—and the new generation of Theodore Roosevelt and Woodrow Wilson would deliver both. The chord Edward Bellamy had struck came from the transformation that Americans saw all around them. "It was no doubt the common opinion of thoughtful men that society was approaching a critical period which might result in great changes," said Julian West looking backward on the 1880s in *Looking Backward*. "What we did see was that industrially the country was in a very queer way. The relation between the workingman and the employer, between labor and capital, appeared in some unaccountable manner to have become dislocated. The working classes had quite suddenly and very generally become infected with a profound discontent with their condition, and an idea that it could be greatly bettered if they only knew how to go about it." As the 1890s began, Americans were struggling with "how to go about" dealing with the new Industrial Age. In doing so, they began a journey that created the government of the twentieth century.

THE PEOPLE'S PARTING

Election night at midnight:
Boy Bryan's defeat.
Defeat of western silver.
Defeat of the wheat . . .

Defeat of the aspen groves of Colorado valleys,
The blue bells of the Rockies,
And blue bonnets of old Texas,
By Pittsburgh alleys,
Defeat of alfalfa and the Mariposa lily.

Defeat of the Pacific and the long Mississippi.
Defeat of the young by the old and silly.
Defeat of tornadoes by Tubal Cain supreme.
Defeat of my boyhood, defeat of my dream.
— *Vachel Lindsay*, Bryan, Bryan, Bryan, Bryan: The
Campaign of Eighteen Ninety-six as Viewed at the
Time by a Sixteen-Year-Old, *1919*

Two cavemen are huddled in their hole, close to the fire. Outside there is rain and sleet; thunder and lightning. One caveman turns to the other and says, "You know, we never had this crazy weather before we started using bows and arrows."

As the final decade of the nineteenth century began, American farmers could be excused for wondering about the beneficence of the wondrous new technologies being introduced in the rising cities of the East. Something was fundamentally broken in their America; a promise made to their parents and grandparents turned out to be a ruse for their own generation. Their freedom was constrained, their path was blocked, the world was crowding in around them. Farms were failing everywhere. Hundreds of thousands of small farmers were forced into bankruptcy. A life tilling the soil was supposed to be hard, but by 1890 it seemed to be impossible. Everywhere he turned, the farmer was getting the short end of the stick. It wasn't right. After all, wasn't he what America was all about?

It was becoming clear that the answer was: no, not anymore. The free frontier of Frederick Jackson Turner was closing in, the lockstep world of Frederick Winslow Taylor was opening up. Like the caveman in the joke, the farmer blamed the changing world for his plight. Unlike the caveman, he was half right to do so. "Vaguely he felt that his freedom of action, his opportunity to do as he pleased, was being frustrated in ways mysterious in origin and operation, and in their effects most uncomfortable," wrote Mark Sullivan in 1925 in his masterful *Our Times*, "that his economic freedom, as well as his freedom of action, and his capacity to direct his political liberty toward results he desired, was being circumscribed in a tightening ring, the drawing-strings of which, he felt sure, were being pulled by the hands of some invisible power which he ardently desired to see and get at, but could not."

High freight rates on the new railroads, tight money policies promoted by the new Eastern banks, adherence to the constricted gold standard by politicians in the pocket of the new corporations—there was more than a grain of truth in each of these gripes. But even more fundamentally, the farmers' gripe, though they rarely recognized and even less frequently acknowledged it, was against the pace of progress itself. The iron logic of mass production—Taylor's efficiency and Ford's pin factory—had come to the farm. In 1830, it had taken three hours and three minutes of average labor time to produce a bushel of corn. By 1894, with the rise of technological improvements that sped the farming process—the disk harrow, the straddle-row cultivator, Oliver's chilled-steel plow, Marsh's harvester, Hussey's and McCormick's reapers—producing a bushel of corn required only ten minutes. A grim reaper, indeed. For with more and more farmers able to produce more and more crops, prices plunged. In 1870, corn was 43 cents a bushel. By 1889, corn prices fell to 10 cents a bushel—less than it cost to grow it. Farmers who had borrowed to finance their hopes for the age-old American Dream were burrowed under by quickly mounting debts.

One such farmer was Charles Lease, a shy, good-natured, even-tempered, stoic man who is remembered chiefly—in fact, only—as the husband of his wife. Charles and his wife, Mary Elizabeth, a daughter of refugees from the Irish potato famine, tried twice to build a life on the farm in Kansas. They lived first in a dirt dugout with a canvas roof, and later in a sod house with a straw roof and greased paper windows. Despite backbreaking work on both their parts, they failed as farmers and moved to the booming town of Wichita on the green banks of the Arkansas.

There, Mary Elizabeth Lease struggled to keep her growing family's head above water. She taught herself law by tacking up cases on the wall and reading them while she washed the neighbors' dirty clothes for 50 cents a day. Slowly, haltingly, she began to see her efforts as part of a larger struggle. Despite the mealymouthed protestations of her addlepated husband, in 1890 she became involved in politics—the radical politics of Kansas's new party, the Populists.

Pain is always felt more acutely than joy, so it was not surprising that the first political response to the Industrial Age came not from the Americans who were benefiting most, but from those who were hurting most. Moreover, the first widespread political revolt against industrialism came neither in the teeming tenements of New York City nor in the fiery furnaces of Pittsburgh. It came as far from the bright shining centers of the Industrial Age universe as one could possibly get—in the heart of the great American prairie. It was not that the misery was necessarily any greater there, it was that its inhabitants were increasingly on the losing side of history. They may have claimed they were angry about being assailed, but what really steamed them was that they were increasingly being ignored by a culture and a politics focused on the wonders of the cities instead of the charms of the farms. The Populist Party—or the People's Party as it was also called—was the agent of this rural resentment.

It was into this world that Mary Elizabeth Lease stepped out on her own. Finding her own voice, she discovered that it was a roar. From miles around people came to see her; waking the children from their sleep and piling into wagons, they would ride all night and all morning in order to make it to her speeches. Otherwise quiet and well-mannered, something came over them in her presence. For once they didn't feel powerless. Lease made them understand that others shared their fears and failures and made them believe that their world need not necessarily disappear.

"You farmers ought to raise less corn and more hell!" she told them famously. "The West and South are bound and prostrate before the manufacturing East." The newspapers called her "Mary Yellin'." The name stuck and eventually morphed into "Mary Ellen"—the name by which she is still erroneously called in many histories and textbooks.

Like a prairie banshee, she flew around the state giving hundreds of speeches attacking those who did not pay proper fealty to the farmer. In Dodge City, she went after one of her favorite senatorial scapegoats. "He's the errand boy of Wall Street, the silver-tongued champion of special privilege," she charged.

"Give 'em hell, Mary," someone in the audience yelled.

"That's just what I intend to do from one end of the state to the other. When I get through with the silk-hatted Easterners they will know that the Kansas prairies are on fire!" And soon enough, they knew.

In 1892, the Populist Party, buoyed by its successes in Kansas and elsewhere, went national—at least in name. On the Fourth of July in Omaha, Nebraska, 1,776 delegates—including Mary Elizabeth Lease and more than a few members of the "Nationalist" Clubs Edward Bellamy formed around the country—were stirred by the reading of the party's platform. It had largely been written by Ignatius Donnelly, another child of Irish immigrants who had been a successful Minnesota politician. Donnelly claimed to have discovered the Lost City of Atlantis—it was just about the only city he was interested in. The platform's preamble fairly seethed with agrarian anger and made only the faintest feints in the direction of appealing to those in the new industrial urban cores. It was both a growl against progress and a plaintive, furtive prayer that the farmers' dreadful march into darkness might be reversed. In the words of one reporter on the scene:

> When that furious and hysterical arraignment of the present times, that incoherent intermingling of Jeremiah and Bellamy, the platform, was adopted, the cheers and yells which rose like a tornado from four thousand throats and raged without cessation for thirty-four minutes, during which women shrieked and wept, men embraced and kissed their neighbors, locked arms, marched back and forth, and leaped upon tables and chairs in the ecstasy of their delirium,—this dramatic and historical scene must have told every quiet, thoughtful witness that there was something at the back of all this turmoil more than the failure of crops or the scarcity of ready cash.

The Populists nominated former congressman James B. Weaver for president and sent him off and running—often into some rather unfriendly crowds. Mary Elizabeth Lease, who often campaigned with him, said that he was pelted with eggs so often that he "was made a regular walking omelet." But on election day, it was the party's critics who had egg on their face. Although Weaver didn't come close to being elected president, he won 9 percent of the popular vote and 22 electoral votes (Kansas, Colorado, Idaho, Nebraska, and a vote each from North Dakota and Oregon). Throughout the West, the Populists proved more popular than those in "the manufacturing East" would have predicted.

The following year, the Populist governor of Kansas chose Mary Elizabeth Lease as the state's official representative to the Columbian Exposition in Chicago. Though she did not hear Frederick Jackson Turner's lecture, she would not have been shocked by his story. The bright optimism of the Exposition was in marked contrast to the steady decline felt in agrarian America. Soon, however, the rest of America would get a taste of the farmers' pain.

Five days after the Columbian Exposition opened, the Great Panic of 1893 hit with a power unlike that ever felt before in America. Next to the Great Depression, it was the worst economic downturn in American history. Six hundred banks collapsed in 1893—and 1894 was even worse. Tens of thousands of businesses failed. In some respects, it was similar to the recession of the early 1990s. Both were products of the straining and stretching America was undergoing to move from an old economy to a new one. Both also brought to the larger nation a pain that had already been felt in certain regions. In the Recession of 1991, that meant that the heart of the middle class felt a taste of what the factory workers of the Rust Belt had been battered with for most of the 1980s. In the Panic of 1893, it meant that the great-grandparents of those factory workers caught a glimpse of what America's farmers had been feeling for most of the 1880s. One out of five Americans lost their jobs.

In the face of this economic disaster, and in no small measure because of the intellectual incapacitation of the small-minded administration of Grover Cleveland, the Democratic Party all but collapsed in the 1894 midterm elections. It became clear to most Democrats that the party would have to repudiate its own president in order to have any chance of winning the 1896 election and that it would have to ally itself with the ever more popular Populists and their agenda. At the heart of that agenda was the call for the unlimited use of silver in American money.

Since silver was more plentiful than the then-standard gold, it was believed that the coinage of silver money would flood the country with more currency and make it easier for farmers to pay off their debts. It was bad economics, it was foolish policy, but it offered hope—and that was something the embattled farmers didn't have. As the Democrats gathered in Chicago for their 1896 nominating convention, they had all but agreed on a new course—and only awaited a new pilot.

William Jennings Bryan had once lived in Chicago. As a law student, he had spent two miserable years there, separated from his fiancée, watching shivering newsboys hawk their wares on the streets, visiting early railroad factories, avoiding the foul stench of the stockyards. He despised city life and left as soon as he could, making his home in the sparse expanse of Nebraska. In 1896, at the tender age of 36, he returned to Chicago with $100 and a speech that would forever change American politics. He left Chicago, only a few days older, with $40 in his pocket and the Democratic Party's nomination for president.

As a former two-term Nebraska congressman and failed U.S. Senate candidate, Bryan was an unlikely nominee. Yet, he had allies. In Nebraska, he had advocated a partnership between the Democrats and Populists. In 1892, he had campaigned for Weaver against Cleveland. Mary Lease had campaigned for Bryan's election to Congress. Bryan, in turn, would help the Populists take over the party of Jefferson.

On July 9, 1896, Bryan nervously awaited his chance to speak before the Democratic Convention on the issue of free silver. He didn't carry any notes—most every line of the speech he was about to give had been honed before countless country schoolhouse audiences up and down the Missouri River valley. When his turn came, he bounded up the platform steps two at a time. Stretched out before him were ten thousand listeners packed like sardines into the Chicago Coliseum, the largest permanent exhibition building in the world.

Bryan began slowly. He acknowledged his relative inexperience to those who had spoken before him, but insisted that "this is not a contest between persons." Back and forth he alternated between procedural discussions about tabling resolutions and flashes of rhetorical power that began to simmer the crowd. He traced the politics of the silver issue and then began to pick up speed. He turned to the representatives of the East Coast industrial interests and said, "When you come before us and tell us that we are about to disturb your business interests, we reply that *you* have disturbed *our* interests by your course."

Having effectively divided the country into East and West, farmer and factory worker, he began to etch that division ever more deeply. He, of course, had nothing against the people of the East; they were all honorable men. "Ah, my friends, we say not a word against those who live upon the Atlantic Coast, but the hardy pioneers who have braved all the dangers of the wilderness, who have made the desert to blossom as the rose—the pioneers away out there," he lifted his arm and pointed to the West, "who rear their children near to Nature's heart, where they can mingle their voices with the voices of the birds—out there where they have erected schoolhouses for the education of their young, churches where they praise their Creator, and cemeteries where rest the ashes of their dead—these people, we say, are as deserving of the consideration of our party as any people in the country. It is for these that we speak." It was they—and almost only they—who would listen.

As Bryan continued, he gathered up speed and power. "Our war is not a war of conquest; we are fighting in the defense of our homes, our families, and posterity," he continued. Twenty-two-year-old Harold Ickes, a future secretary of the interior, noted that "His wonderful voice filled the auditorium." Lightning bolted forth from his deep-set eyes. "We have petitioned, and our petitions have been scorned; we have entreated, and our entreaties have been disregarded; we have begged, and they have mocked when our calamity came. We beg no longer; we entreat no more; we petition no more. We defy them."

Bryan framed the debate in terms that would be familiar hoary oratory and heartening to Democrats a century later—in the terms of the age-old conflict between Jefferson and Hamilton; between an America that worked bottom up and one that worked top down. "There are two ideas of government," he said, his rich and resonant voice bouncing off the Coliseum's far walls. "There are those who believe that, if you only legislate to make the well-to-do prosperous, their prosperity will leak through on those below. The Democratic idea, however, has been that if you legislate to make the masses prosperous, their prosperity will find its way up through every class that rests upon them."

Following that note, a hopeful basis on which to unite a constituency in all parts of the country, Bryan proceeded to redivide the country— agrarian versus urban, past versus future. "You come to us and tell us that the great cities are in favor of the gold standard; we reply that the great cities rest upon *our* broad and fertile plains," he boomed. "Burn down *your* cities and leave *our* farms, and *your* cities will spring up again as if by magic; but destroy *our* farms and the grass will grow in the streets of every city in the country."

His voice dropped low. The ten thousand leaned forward to hear him. "It is the issue of 1776 over again. Our ancestors, when but three millions in number, had the courage to declare their political independence of every other nation; shall we, their descendants, when we have grown to seventy millions, declare that we are less independent than our forefathers? No, my friends, that will never be the verdict of our people," he said, half-determined, half-vehement, half-sanguine. Now the crowd, cooking for forty minutes, awaited only a push before they boiled over. His voice building, he challenged the party's enemies. "Having behind us the producing masses of this nation and the world, supported by the commercial interests, the laboring interests, and toilers everywhere, we will answer their demand for a gold standard by saying to them," he raised his arms above his head, palms facing one another, "you shall not press down upon the brow of labor this crown of thorns." His hands moved slowly down to his temples, so that the packed galleries could almost see the thorns piercing his skin and the blood trickling down his forehead. "You shall not crucify mankind upon a cross of gold." His hands shot out from his head and he held his arms at a right angle to his body. He stood there for five, full, endless seconds—his head bowed to the ground, his body crucified before them.

He dropped his arms to his side. He looked up. And there was silence. Stillness. Nothing. Devastated, Bryan moved to return to his seat. Not a clap. He left the rostrum. Not a cheer. He walked down the stairs and almost made it to the floor. And then it came. The ten thousand erupted in rapture. For an hour they marched around the Coliseum in an ecstasy of emotion, lifting Bryan up on their shoulders and carrying him to the nomination the following day.

A few weeks later, the Populist Party met at their own convention and joined the Democrats in nominating Bryan for president. James Weaver made the nomination. Ignatius Donnelly and Mary Elizabeth Lease made seconding speeches. The People's Party would disappear soon afterwards. Not that it mattered. The Populist spirit had taken over the body of the Democratic Party.

In August, Bryan set out on the first cross-country speaking tour of any major party candidate for president. Between then and the end of October, he would travel 18,000 miles, sometimes speaking thirty times a day. At first, he couldn't afford a staff or his own railcar. He traveled alone—carrying his suitcase to and from hotels, checking the train schedules when he got to the station, and buying his own tickets. Often, when he couldn't shower, he would use gin as a deodorant. He kept going by consuming massive quantities of food—steaks, sausages, pork chops, dinner rolls, baked potatoes, pies, cakes. He ate tables full of food, five or six times a day.

He not only reached voters all over agrarian America and the West, he reached them in a place where no politician had reached them before. He seemed to understand their daily struggles, their anxiety about a world that no longer made sense to them. He was, wrote Vachel Lindsay, "the one American poet who could sing outdoors." Bryan would speak to 5 million Americans in person by the time the campaign had ended.

Bryan's hard work was not enough. On election day, he won more votes than any previous presidential candidate but still lost to the Republican nominee, William McKinley, by six hundred thousand votes. Bryan had been outspent, perhaps by as much as 50 to 1. Factory bosses had threatened to fire their workers if Bryan won. The economy was beginning to pull out of its trough. But fundamentally, Bryan lost because of the nature of his message—one that turned away as many people as it turned on, one that turned its back on America's future.

As much as Bryan had excited America's farmers, he had scared away factory workers and other urban residents. They, too, had a tough life to bear, but they had hopes for the future and for their children's futures. They didn't want to turn back the tide of industrialism, they wanted to speed it up so that it reached them as well. Ignatius Donnelly would often say that "Jesus was only possible in a barefoot world, and he was crucified by the few who wore shoes." The new urbanites—refugees of the farms and of foreign shores—had come to the cities to find shoes and, hopefully one day, better shoes. They saw no great virtue in bare feet. Moreover, as Bryan's "Cross of Gold" speech, with its "*our* farms" and "*your* cities," made clear, he and the other Populists conveyed the message that the urban toilers were an afterthought in their crusade, if not part of the problem. At the Omaha convention, the best-loved song went, "And the ticket we vote in November / Will be made up of hayseeds like me!"

You get what you pray for. All the hayseeds put together didn't reap a very fertile harvest—and crowded out some more valuable crops. In New York City, the Democratic vote dropped from 59 to 42 percent, in Philadelphia from 42 to 26 percent, in Chicago from 55 to 40 percent. While rural America became more firmly Democratic, places like Pittsburgh marched forthrightly into the Republican column. Democrats had traded the future for the past.

Ironically, perhaps the most articulate critic of Bryan and the Populists came not from Pittsburgh, New York, or Chicago, but from a small town in Kansas itself. In editorial after editorial in his *Emporia Gazette*, 28-year-old William Allen White spoke out stridently against the political fever that was gripping the state. Not surprisingly, this did not make him a top contestant for Emporia's Miss Congeniality. Farmers would march back and forth through the tiny town carrying signs portraying White as a jackass. He was quick enough to understand that it wasn't a compliment, but things didn't really come to a head until one day in mid-August. The temperature had risen to 107 degrees, and the farmers were pretty hot under the collar. A chubby little fellow, White was wad-dling down the street, wearing his best summer suit and a gaudy neck-tie—giving off the appearance of a moving Easter egg. As he returned from the post office, he was beset by a group of older, haggard, shabbily dressed farmers who laid into him about his editorials. They jeered him and poked him with a little stick until White was finally able to break free of them.

Flushed with anger, he rushed back to his office, threw down his mail, and began writing—with the brilliance only haste can bring. He began by noting that while the population of the nation and neighboring states was booming, Kansas had grown by only two thousand during the past year, even though ten thousand babies had born. Families were tripping over themselves to leave the state. "What's the matter with Kansas?" he asked innocently. He answered himself less innocently. In words drip-ping with ire and just maybe a touch of sarcasm, he wrote:

> We all know; yet here we are at it again. We have an old mossback Jack-sonian who snorts and howls because there is a bathtub in the State house; we are running that old jay for governor. . . . We have raked the ash heap of human failure in the state and found an old hoop skirt of a man who has failed as a businessman, who has failed as an editor, who has failed as a preacher, and we are going to run him for congressman-at-large. He will help the looks of the Kansas delegation in Washington. . . . Then, for fear some hint that the state had become respectable might percolate through the civilized portions of the nation, we have decided to send three or four harpies out lecturing, telling the people that Kansas is raising hell and let-ting the corn go to weeds.
>
> Oh, this is a state to be proud of! We are a people who can hold up our heads! What we need here is less money, less capital, fewer white shirts and brains, fewer men with business judgment, and more of these fellows who boast that they are "just ordinary old clodhoppers, but that they know more in a minute about finance than John Sherman" [a senatorial oppo-nent of free silver]. We don't need population, we don't need wealth, we don't need well-dressed men on the streets" [a thrust that might have still been ringing in his ears], we don't need standing in the nation; we don't need cities on these fertile prairies; you bet we don't. . . . we, the people of Kansas, propose to kick; we don't care to build up, we wish to tear down.

He quoted Bryan directly on the subject of the two visions of government he described in the "Cross of Gold" speech, and then answered him. "That's the stuff! Give the prosperous man the dickens! . . . What we need is not the respect of our fellow men, but a chance to get something for nothing." He asked again, "What's the matter with Kansas? Nothing under the shining sun. She is losing wealth, population, and standing. She has got her statesmen, and the money power is afraid of her. Kansas is all right. She has started in to raise hell, as Mrs. Lease advised, and she seems to have an overproduction. But that doesn't matter. Kansas never did believe in diversified crops." White's column fell into the hands of the right people back East and was reprinted innumerable times. He became an overnight sensation and the widely respected voice of middle America for the rest of his illustrious career.

Despite his vitriol, White was right about an essential truth regarding the Populists: they were more interested in attacking the industrial edifice than in reforming it. In one respect, they had little choice. Theirs was a revolt against the force of the oncoming future. They stood in its tracks and hoped to make it stop and turn around. But the force was more powerful than they could ever imagine. They failed to understand that no one can stop the force of history: it hurtles forever forward. The role of a leader is to harness history's power and point it in a positive direction. Falling short of this fundamental test was Bryan and the Populists' greatest failing.

The Populists' downfall came because they sought to deal with new and different issues with ideas straight out of the past. Jefferson's vision of farmers as "the chosen people" warmed them when the rest of politics was leaving them out in the cold, but Jefferson's decentralized, weak government policies were fast becoming a straitjacket. One Populist leader, James "Cyclone" Davis, barnstormed the country, giving speeches while he kept a volume of Jefferson's complete works with him at the podium. When someone asked him a question, be it about free silver or government ownership of railroads, he would open the book and page through it, looking for the answer. The answer wasn't there. Bryan held tight to Jefferson's most anachronistic dogmas, continuing to advocate a government that focused its energies on restraining "the strongest citizen from injuring the weakest citizen." In an Industrial Age, this was no longer enough. He reached out to the downtrodden and brought up issues that would shape politics for years to come, but offered no real solutions. Bryan ushered in twentieth-century American politics; it would fall to others to create a new vision of American government.

The day after Bryan's "Cross of Gold" speech, Illinois' reform governor John Peter Altgeld saw famed attorney Clarence Darrow at the Convention. Darrow had been overjoyed by the speech, figuring it would set up "the greatest battle of modern times." Altgeld wasn't so sure: "I've been thinking over Bryan's speech. What did he say, anyhow?" When it came down to it, Bryan hadn't really said much. His sympathy with American farmers was unmistakable; his strategy for helping them was unsatisfying.

Eighty-eight years later, the Democratic Party met even farther West—by the Golden Gate of San Francisco. There, in 1984, another Convention was inspired by a beautiful speech from a masterful, if little known, orator. While New York's new governor Mario Cuomo addressed himself to the factory economy of Lackawanna and its "thousands of unemployed steel workers," he ignored the oncoming information revolution—though he was just miles away from Silicon Valley, where Apple Computers was changing the world. A few hours later, Arkansas' reform governor Bill Clinton saw his colleague from Colorado, Richard Lamm, at a reception. "What did you think of Cuomo's speech?" Clinton asked Lamm.

"Terrific," Lamm said. "It galvanized the crowd."

"C'mon," Clinton said. "What did it really say about the issues we're trying to raise?"

"Nothing," admitted Lamm.

"Cuomo. Jesse Jackson. Teddy Kennedy. Same speech," said Lamm a couple of days later. "Passionate statements of what used to be. We weren't ready to face the issues of the future . . . so we celebrated the past."

Like Bryan a century ago, most of today's "populist" voices are negative, angry, pessimistic, divisive, and backward-looking. When contemporary politicians grow red in the face arguing for industrial policies to prop up the manufacturing sector, they conjure up the walking ghost of William Jennings Bryan warning the developing urban centers that they must pay homage to the farms or "the grass will grow in the streets of every city in the country." This is, of course, not to say that manufacturing isn't important, or that farming wasn't important in Bryan's day or our own. On the contrary, farmers in the 1890s deserved better than Bryan's chimerical vision of the miracles to come with free silver. Factory workers today deserve more than the populistish Pat Buchanan's promises of a utopia ahead without free trade. Where both—and many others then and now—fell short was in trying to impose outdated ideas on an updated world.

Today, liberals and conservatives alike can rail all they want against mergers, acquisitions, outsourcings, downsizings, and offshorings. The men and women who hear them will, like "the plain people" of the Great Plains a century ago, have the momentary elation that finally someone understands their frustrations. But none of these are the fundamental reason for Americans' dissatisfaction. The world of the twentieth century is fast disappearing—and nothing is going to bring it back. To succeed politically and morally, a new agenda has to be crafted that will appeal to both those who are "left behind" and those who are moving ahead. This is not impossible. In fact, it has been done before. For in the wake of William Jennings Bryan's loss in 1896, the problems he so eloquently elucidated didn't go away. It fell to others to step forward and craft solutions.

Denial isn't just a river in Egypt, defeat isn't just a subject for podiatrists. William Jennings Bryan was an expert on both those areas. In denying that a new Industrial Age had been born, he lashed his party to the rock of defeat. Usually when a major party swallows a minor party, it becomes stronger. The Democrats' digestion of the Populists was a poison pill. They did not find their way back into the White House for the next sixteen years—a time in which Bryan was the nominee three out of four times.

A few minutes after midnight on January 1, 1901, Ignatius Donnelly died in his sleep. He never could face the new century ahead. That was the fate of the Populist movement he had fathered as well. It saw a changed America, but turned away in horror. A new movement would be required to guide America past the perils and toward the promise of the new Industrial Age.

A MADMAN OF DESTINY

A great democracy must be progressive or it will soon cease to be great or a democracy.
—*Theodore Roosevelt, 1910*

The need to address the challenge of industrialization did not die with the end of the Populist movement or the close of the nineteenth century. In fact, both circumstances served only to increase this need. Rising from both the vanquished hopes and relieved fears generated by the defeat of the Populists came a new movement, the Progressives, who did what the People's Party and William Jennings Bryan never really attempted: respond in earnest to the twentieth century, dealing with the world as it had become and not only as it had once been.

The new century dawned with wisps of strangeness all around. At Kitty Hawk, North Carolina, two otherwise sane brothers were conducting silly experiments with a glider. In Cuba, Dr. Walter Reed was investigating a mysterious link between mosquitoes and yellow fever. In New York City, workers were tearing up the city streets to build an underground railroad that would be called a "subway." And if all this weren't strange enough, in Albany, New York, the state's governor, Theodore Roosevelt, was desperately working to avoid a promotion.

Roosevelt was being passed around like a Christmas fruitcake that nobody wanted between Thomas Platt, the Republican "boss" of New York State, and Mark Hanna, President McKinley's political godfather and, in effect, the Republican "boss" of the country. Although Roosevelt had only been governor for a year, he had quickly begun interfering with the nexus of political favors and corporate power that made Platt's political machine run smoothly. Cursing the "damnable alliance between business and politics," Roosevelt signed a workers compensation bill and fired the superintendent of insurance for being in the pocket of the industry he was supposed to be supervising.

Platt knew he had to get rid of Roosevelt before the young governor undermined his entire political operation. The means Platt seized upon was nominating Roosevelt as vice president at that year's Republican Convention. Roosevelt understood the game that was being played, and vowed to have no part in it: "I am doing my best to prevent the corporations and the Machine making [me] the . . . candidate in order to get rid of me here as Governor," he wrote in a letter. If Platt wanted to get Roosevelt out of Albany, Hanna wanted to keep him out of Washington. Roosevelt was, in his mind, a danger to the stability of the Republican Party. As he was quoted saying, over and over again, in this time of peace and prosperity, he wanted the Republicans to "stand pat." Theodore Roosevelt couldn't even stand still.

Born to an old New York Dutch family on his father's side and Southern aristocracy on his mother's, Roosevelt had as a 6-year-old child watched Abraham Lincoln's funeral procession. After she rejected him numerous times, he finally married the dazzling and beautiful Alice Lee whom he had met while studying at Harvard. With his diploma and a new bride, he moved back home to New York. There he attended Columbia Law School in the mornings, secretly wrote his landmark *The Naval War of 1812* in the afternoon, and visited the Jake Hess Republican Club of the 21st Assembly district in the evenings. In entering the grimy world of partisan politics, Roosevelt shocked his upper-crust friends and family. Politics was the province of shysters and hucksters— certainly not the type of people someone of young Theodore's standing should associate with. The path to politics for gentlemen was the pursuit of riches and reputation—and the patience to wait for the state legislature to appoint them to the esteemed U.S. Senate. Getting one's hands dirty was simply not done.

Roosevelt thrust himself into the political world and was soon elected
to the State Assembly—dropping out of law school. By age 24, he was
the minority leader and his name was being bandied about around the
country as a future president. But fate was to step into the path of his
smooth ascent. On February 14, Valentine's Day, two days after the birth
of his first child, his beloved wife died. His mother died the same day.
In the same house. He wrote in his diary, "The light has gone out of my
life." "Like a lion obsessively trying to drag a spear from its flank, Roosevelt set about dislodging Alice Lee from his soul," wrote his biographer Edmund Morris. He would never mention her again, not even in
his *Autobiography* or to his second wife or children.

To free himself from her hold, he headed West—to the harsh and
unforgiving Badlands of the Dakotas. It was in those tough conditions
that the Theodore Roosevelt of history was truly born. The slightly snob-
bish dandy of Manhattan grew both emotionally and physically into an
imposing and determined presence. Returning to New York, he quickly
won third place in the race for mayor of New York, became a U.S. civil
service commissioner, served as New York police commissioner, went to
Washington as assistant secretary of the navy, and—leading his Rough
Riders, a motley crew of Ivy Leaguers and prairie outlaws, all clad in spe-
cially tailored Brooks Brothers uniforms—became a hero of the Span-
ish-American War. He then raced into the governorship of the nation's
largest state—two weeks after he had turned 40. During this time, he
also wrote thirteen books and developed the habit of reading at least
one—and often two or three—books each day. He had such tremen-
dous, unbridled energy that when he was coming to visit the Henry
Cabot Lodges, they would take the advance precaution of clearing space
around his favorite rocking chair because of his habit of rocking so
vigrously that the chair was propelled clear across the room.

Now, Platt wanted to get this man on the move to move on to the vice
presidency. For sixty-four years previously—and for eighty-eight years to
come—the office had been a graveyard of electoral ambitions. No sitting
vice president had been elected to the highest office. So, in the months
before the 1900 Convention, Roosevelt did just about everything he

could to avoid being nominated. But not everything. Warned that if he did not make a firm and airtight disavowal of the draft, his popularity among Western Republicans would sweep him toward the nomination, he poked holes in his stated refusal to accept the nomination. Told that if he went in person to the 1900 Convention he would increase the calls for his nomination, he went. Despite his many protestations that he would much rather remain as governor or even return to private life, the same hand that guided him to the Jake Hess Republic Club two decades earlier was on his shoulder again. The pressure—both public and political—was too much for even a smooth political operator like Mark Hanna. "Do whatever you damn please!" he finally exploded at his associates. "I'm through! Everybody's gone crazy! What's the matter with all of you? Here's this convention going headlong for Roosevelt for Vice President. Don't any of you realize there's only one life between that madman and the Presidency?"

Roosevelt was nominated and took to the hustings, energetically berating William Jennings Bryan, the Democratic renominee for president. McKinley was handily reelected. Upon his inauguration, a congressman expressed pity for the president: "I would not like to be in McKinley's shoes. He has a man of destiny behind him." Roosevelt, however, gave every indication that he did not feel like one. With nothing to do as vice president, he began studying law again, hoping to get a degree and perhaps join a Washington law firm.

Meanwhile, in Chicago, a crazed anarchist named Leon Czolgosz went into a local tailor shop and announced that he had decided to kill a priest. Dismissively, the tailor replied, "Why kill a priest? There are so many priests; they are like flies—a hundred will come to his funeral." Czolgosz considered this for a moment, left the tailor shop, went to Buffalo, New York, and shot the president of the United States.

Roosevelt reached Buffalo shortly after McKinley died. He recited the oath of office in front of a few witnesses and then paused—speechless for once. He asked his longtime mentor, New York corporation lawyer and Secretary of War Elihu Root, if there was anything else he should say. Root whispered in his ear. Roosevelt nodded and said: "I wish to say that it shall be my aim to continue, absolutely unbroken, the policy of President McKinley for the peace, the prosperity, and the honor of our country." It was a promise he would quickly break.

Less than three months after taking office, in his first Annual Message to Congress, Roosevelt would declare that "The old laws, and the old customs which had almost the binding force of law, were once quite sufficient to regulate the accumulation and distribution of wealth. Since the industrial changes which have so enormously increased the productive power of mankind, they are no longer sufficient." If Roosevelt could be a man of action in a rocking chair, the chief executive office of the country—at a time of epic transformation—was not one in which he would refrain from pushing aggressively for change.

In doing so, Roosevelt would encourage—and, even more, would be encouraged by—the new Progressive political movement building up support in the nation. Progressivism was the conviction—at first largely inchoate and then steadily more specific—that government's role needed to be revised for the Industrial Age so that it could confront new problems.

Populism and Progressivism were one in the same—except for the fact that they were opposites. Populists responded to the disappearing agrarian era; Progressives addressed the newborn Industrial Age. Populists appealed largely to the battered farmers; Progressives primarily to the new urban workers. William Allen White would claim that Progressivism *was* Populism—with the hayseeds taken out. But it was more than this. Reformist, positive, modernizing, Progressivism was a sturdier platform for bringing change than the angry, plaintive cry of the Populists. Progressivism could build alliances where the Populists could not. Both William Allen White and William Jennings Bryan would become prominent Progressives. In fact, they would become friends—sitting on White's porch and talking for hours at a time.

Populism and Progressivism had different issues for which they fought, but they fought for similar reasons. They were united as one, perhaps not in their causes, but in their cause—a rapidly changing world that had upended the familiar foundations of American life. The most important difference for government's future was that while, for the most part, Populists wanted to limit the power of government so that it stopped benefiting the powerful, Progressives wanted to expand government's power to protect Americans from the ravages of modern life. Progressives started out by lacking only a means to accomplish this mission. Seeing through the veil of the treasured erudition of their lifetimes, and the nation's history, was no easy task.

So, in the years Roosevelt occupied the White House, Progressivism was mostly agitation without an agenda—an often vague desire for a more powerful government that would address growing social and economic ills. Roosevelt backed up this aspiration with his considerable rhetorical firepower—his "bully pulpit"—but accomplished little in terms of legislation. The modest actions he did take, such as imposing some regulations on the railroads and meat packing industries, were remarkable not for what they accomplished, but for the fact that they were actions at all. After a century that disparaged government activity, Roosevelt made reform respectable and put active government on the side of positive social change as it never had been before. To Americans watching Washington from around the country, this was no small step.

If Bryan had fought to restore America to its glorious past, Roosevelt wanted to connect the nation to a better future. His Country Life Commission, for instance, headed by rural progressive Liberty Hyde Bailey, was animated by the conviction that "it is possible to have the most that is best of the city in the country"; that the country folks' bewildered "how now?" could be answered with the city folks' ordered "know how." By spreading the principles of "scientific farming," Bailey and Roosevelt sought to bring a slice of Taylorism to the countryside. At every turn, this was the Progressive agenda: bringing the values of the Industrial Age to the parts of America that had not felt it—including, eventually, government.

Roosevelt's reputation was strongest for taking on the huge corporate conglomerations known as trusts. His trust-busting had little effect on the overall economy or on average citizens—and Roosevelt disliked the practice immensely—but it began to show that government could be a powerful force and need not be cowed by private interests. This was the heart of Roosevelt's "Square Deal." Trust-busting told Americans that government was able to take affirmative actions when it so chose, that the executive branch could be infused with energy, and that government's power and scope could be expanded to match the bigger, more centralized business of the age—and this began to get their imaginations going.

In a 1999 interview, President Clinton said that Theodore Roosevelt's presidency "was a similar point in the history of America, where we were transforming ourselves from, then an agricultural to an industrial society, now from an industrial to an information-technology-based society." Late at night, with only the thwack of his solitaire cards disturbing the silence, Clinton would ponder his place in history and history's place in his present. Over and over again, he returned to Theodore Roosevelt as a model. "At some points in history," he told an advisor, "we go through change, and no one can stop it." The same advisor later told a reporter, "He knows that Teddy Roosevelt could no more have gotten people back to the farms than we can get people off computers."

Roosevelt's presidency had important parallels to Clinton's. They certainly differed in personality and background, but both governed at times of transformation. Both fought the powerful interests of their party on some issues and found accommodation on others. But most of all, both called into question accepted assumptions about the role of government and prepared Americans for the idea that their government would have to essentially shift if it was to become relevant again. President Theodore Roosevelt did not map out that change (this came later) and neither did Clinton, but both laid the groundwork for the task ahead.

In the years of his presidency, Roosevelt embraced the nation's growing spirit of reform and modernization. But in those years, he, like the early Progressivism of the time, concentrated on dispensing with old notions about the role of government rather than creating new ones. As late as July of 1907, Secretary of War William Howard Taft, angling for the presidency to please his nagging wife, wrote Roosevelt a letter stating that Taft had never met a man "more in favor of small government" than the president. He meant this as a compliment. Roosevelt evidently took it as such—he almost single-handedly gave Taft the Republican nomination the next year. Hanging onto Roosevelt's wave of popularity, Taft was pulled into the White House and Roosevelt made his plans for a departure from Washington.

Moments after Taft had been sworn in, Roosevelt tried to slip out of the Capitol unnoticed through a side door. He failed. He was met by a throng of admirers who escorted him the short walk to Union Station, singing "Auld Lang Syne" as they reached the ordinary Pullman car that would carry the emotional Roosevelt back to New York. He bid them a fond farewell—and many, including most likely him, thought it was his farewell to politics.

It was not to be his final curtain. Soon after he left the White House, Roosevelt embarked on an extended safari to Africa. Softly as it left the docks of Hoboken, New Jersey, Roosevelt's ship carried more than two hundred of his cases, each about 6 by 4 feet. He brought with him rifles and taxidermy equipment. Cans of Boston baked beans and California peaches. He packed more than sixty books, including the Bible and the works of Shakespeare. Homer in Greek and Dante in Italian. Darwin and Dickens. Keats and Cooper. Bacon, Bunyan, and Browning. And, according to historian Matthew Josephson, a new book entitled *The Promise of American Life*.

PROGRESS

We have got to face the fact that such an increase in governmental control is now necessary.

—*Theodore Roosevelt, on the New Nationalism, Osawatomie, Kansas, 1910*

If Teddy Roosevelt, as president, had a hard time sitting still, William Howard Taft had a hard time staying awake. Taft fell asleep in the front row during a funeral. He fell asleep at official White House dinners. He even fell asleep while making an open car campaign tour of crowded

New York City. Taft fell asleep everywhere—including at the wheel of the Progressive movement.

Republican Senator Jonathan Dolliver said that Taft was "a large amiable island surrounded entirely by persons who knew exactly what they wanted." What most of them, particularly autocratic Speaker of the House Joe Cannon, wanted was a return to the status quo stasis of the pre–Roosevelt GOP. Others in the country were less sedate. The Progressive movement, blooming since the beginning of the century, was about to blossom. As the pace of change quickened, so did the depth of the conviction that government needed to change as well. "Progress," cracked George Fitch, "is so rampant that we wake up each morning with a half century of advancing to do and go to bed exhausted at night having covered the half century, and in the meantime having uncovered enough new and vociferous necessities to leave us a whole century behind."

To cure the ills of urban, industrial America and tap its opportunities, the Progressives would turn to the methods of the new society emerging all around them. In the first decade of the twentieth century, schools began to crop up around the nation teaching something that had never before been offered, or even needed: the science of business administration. It was becoming clear that to make modern industrial enterprises move, experts were needed for rational, measured planning. In the assembly lines of Frederick Taylor and Henry Ford, workers weren't allowed to think for themselves. Those who did the thinking for these huge enterprises, who moved all its myriad parts, had to bring stable order to bear. Their means were rules, regulations, regimentation—and a massive number of employees to watch over the individual workers and make sure they didn't step out of the assembly line. Modern bureaucracy was born.

Just as Jefferson had formed his egalitarian, democratic theories of government based on the lifestyle and outlook of the small farmer, Progressives would turn to the new assembly line—and to the experts and bureaucracy that made it run—for their inspiration. Whereas Jeffersonianism fit the world of individual enterprise, the rise of *The Administrative State*,

Dwight Waldo wrote in his book of that title, "mirrored rather faithfully the form and spirit of current business thought on organization and management." Robert Wiebe wrote that the Progressives followed business "in attempts to extend the range and continuity of their power through bureaucratic means. Information would flow upward through the corporate structure, decisions downward." Jefferson was out, Hamilton was in; bottom-up was over, top-down had begun.

No work summed up—and contributed to—this transformation in a more meaningful way than Herbert Croly's *The Promise of American Life*. While a few had expressed Croly's main assertions before, none had put the Progressive movement into the full context of American history and none had nearly as lasting of an impact on the course of American history. Writing in 1959, in the wake of the New Deal and Fair Deal and on the eve of the New Frontier and Great Society, historian Charles Forcey noted, "A half century later the essential philosophy of Herbert Croly's *The Promise of American Life* of 1909 has become the prevailing political faith of most Americans." More than forty years after that statement, Croly's work maintains its grip on the imaginations of most politicians—if no longer most Americans.

The Promise of American Life mentioned agriculture only once. This was a work for the factories of the industrial America of the twentieth century, not the farms of the agrarian nation of the previous century. In many fundamental ways, Herbert Croly picked up where Frederick Turner had left off. In the shadow of the Ferris Wheel, Turner had said that the frontier was the guarantee of opportunity—a means by which every American could have a shot at success. Though Charles and Mary Lease and many before them showed that this shot was a difficult one to make, the very idea of the frontier—that there was a place where ambition and exertion could bring greatness—was an indelible part of America's myth and mystique. Now, with the gateway to Western expansion slammed shut behind the pioneers, some other means would have to be created to guarantee the basic opportunities that defined America's promise. For Croly, this was a big, powerful, centralized government. As Dwight Waldo wrote, "That eminent work of the Progressive period, Herbert Croly's *The Promise of American Life*, may be taken as the symbol of the decision of a considerable number of citizens that we could no longer rely simply upon great natural wealth and complete individual freedom to fulfill the American dream of economic independence." The closing of the frontier—and the opening of the assembly lines— had necessitated the rise of bureaucratic government. A larger and more far-reaching federal government "is the natural consequence of the increasing centralization of American industrial, political, and social life," Croly wrote.

In person, he was bashful. On paper, he was full of bravado. In his Ph.D. dissertation, "Scientific Management and the Progressive Movement," the historian Samuel Haber wrote that Croly's writing sometimes "sounds like Friedrich Nietzche presiding as a YMCA discussion leader." Among his friends, and some enemies, the term bandied about was "Crolier than thou." However, using the power of his pen, he administered a body-blow to the reputation of Thomas Jefferson from which the third president has never recovered.

Croly's parents were immigrants—his father a crusading newspaper editor who waged a war against Boss Tweed, his mother the first full-time newspaperwoman in America. He made his way to Harvard and toiled in the magazine business for years. A creature of the cities, he had no patience for the easy, quiet America that Jefferson envisioned from atop Monticello. As Jefferson's America had disappeared, now his dictums would have to go as well. Croly wrote that "Jefferson sought an essentially equalitarian . . . result by means of an essentially individualistic machinery." This was a machinery entirely unsuited to an America on the move. He believed that Jeffersonianism had been "cant" in the nineteenth century and was entirely dangerous in the twentieth. Political leaders, Croly asserted, should vest government's power in elites capable of wisely directing the nation, not babble on about the wisdom of the masses. At heart, the problem with Jefferson was that he believed "the people were to guide their leaders, not their leaders the people."

Thus, in *The Promise of American Life*, Croly called for a "New Nationalism"—"the rejection of a large part of the Jeffersonian creed, and a renewed attempt to establish in its place the popularity of its Hamiltonian rival." According to him, the New Nationalism's advocates were "committed to a drastic reorganization of the American political and economic system, to the substitution of frank social policy for the individualism of the past, and to the realization of this policy, if necessary, by the use of efficient government instruments." Croly's vision was summed up in a famous phrase, a phrase that defined government for much of the twentieth century: Jeffersonian ends by Hamiltonian means. What did this entail? Hamiltonian means added up to a strong, centralized, top-down government with an inherent distrust in the judgment of the masses. Jeffersonian ends meant government should bring succor and sustenance to all Americans. It was the government that all Americans now know: bureaucratic, expert-driven, paternalistic, offering safety and security to millions who would otherwise be left at risk.

This was government as the dominant power in American life—an often benevolent power, to be sure, but a power that built upon itself. "The program advocated in *The Promise of American Life* amounted to the establishment of a tremendously powerful national state that would regulate corporations, unions, small businesses, and agriculture in the 'national interest,'" wrote Eric Goldman in his 1952 *Rendezvous with Destiny*. Building up such a power, leading America to turn its back on more than a century of established Jeffersonian verities, would not be easy. Despite a rising tide of Progressive thought and commentary, the world is not changed in magazine articles. Such an audacious enterprise would require a leader trusted by millions from all walks of life, someone energetic and courageous, an adventurer who instinctively ran toward danger instead of shrinking from it, a politician of enormous intelligence and a common touch. Such a leader existed. Unfortunately, he was off hunting lions in Africa.

Theodore Roosevelt had sworn off politics and was attempting to ignore developments on the home front while he was away. But the former president, Colonel Roosevelt as he now insisted on being called, was not to be quiet for long. In the words of his eldest daughter, Roosevelt "always wanted to be the corpse at every funeral, the bride at every wedding, and the baby at every christening." If the Progressive movement was going to march forward, it was hard to believe that Roosevelt wouldn't want to be the drum major. For now, however, Roosevelt concentrated on finishing his safari and his whirlwind tour of Africa and Europe. Emerging from the wilderness, TR would lecture to Egyptians in Cairo on "law and order" following the recent assassination of their Coptic Christian premier, Boutros Ghali, by a young Muslim student; get into a verbal tussle with the pope; and join Kaiser Wilhelm in observing the field maneuvers of the German army—an army that would kill his son Quentin only eight years later.

Then, on June 18, 1910, Roosevelt returned home to an enthusiastic reception by a huge crowd. Onboard the cutter *Manhattan*, he made his way into New York harbor (a photo of the day shows that of the more than fifty people who welcomed him onboard the cutter's upper deck, only one had the presence and timing to be smiling broadly into the camera—Theodore's distant cousin Franklin, then a long-shot candidate for the New York State Senate). TR had come back determined to stay out of politics. Politics had a different idea.

It was time for Roosevelt to be not just the leader of the Progressive forces, but to actually lead them. Within a matter of months, he would do just that.

Good politicians can size up their immediate surroundings. Great politicians can look down the road and react to what is coming next. Political genius lies in being able to see around the corner. In 1910, Theodore Roosevelt had just this skill. He saw the industrial America that was rising up, sensed the new demands that it would create in Americans, and envisioned the type of government that would have to be created to respond to these requirements.

In August of that year, he set out on a speaking tour that would take him all over the country. The newspapers were full of speculation about a widening gulf between him and Taft. While he was still away, *Life* magazine wrote:

> Teddy, come home and blow your horn,
> The sheep's in the meadow, the cow's in the corn.
> The boy you left to 'tend the sheep
> Is under the haystack fast asleep.

In fact, Roosevelt was extremely disappointed with his anointed successor's disregard of the Progressives and his deepening alliance with the forces of entrenched Republican conservatism. But what Roosevelt would say on this trip went far beyond any momentary political calculations.

On August 31, 1910, Roosevelt arrived in Osawatomie, Kansas, where he was to dedicate a state park at the site of John Brown's first battle against the Missouri raiders. He used the occasion to announce a new vision for a strong, centralized American government, one that would animate politics for the rest of the century. According to Walter Lippmann, the former president's reading of *The Promise of American Life* had "made articulate for Roosevelt his aspiration to combine the social and political reforms initiated by Bryan . . . with a Hamiltonian affection for a strong national government." Roosevelt was introduced in Osawatomie by a local pooh-bah as "the modern Tom Jefferson." But Roosevelt had come to this dusty Kansas town not to praise Jefferson, but to bury him.

Before a crowd of thirty thousand listeners—many of whom had driven all night through a driving rain to be there—Roosevelt laid out a vision for a government that would not just stop the nefarious activities of the powerful, but that would use its own growing power to lift up the weak. At Osawatomie, the former president made it clear that this vision was broader than that which had animated his presidency. "I stand for the Square Deal," he said. "But when I say that I am for the Square Deal, I mean not merely that I am for fair play under the present rules of the game, but that I stand for having those rules changed."

No longer should Americans try to fight against the inevitably growing Industrial Age, they should master it and use its power. "The citizens of the United States must effectively control the mighty commercial forces which they themselves have called into being," he said. The path to dealing with these new forces was "in completely controlling them in the interests of the public welfare." To do this, individuals would have to give up some of their own power and transfer it to the politicians—"an increase in governmental control is now necessary." "National efficiency"—Frederick Taylor writ large—was Osawatomie's byword. And Roosevelt's new philosophy even had a name, one familiar to readers of *The Promise of American Life*: "The American people are right in demanding that New Nationalism, without which we cannot hope to deal with new problems." Roosevelt had summed up his message two days earlier in Colorado: "Big business has become nationalized and the only effective way of controlling and directing and preventing the abuses in connection with it is by having the people nationalize the government control in order to meet the nationalization of the big business itself."

It was, according to the *New York Evening Post*, "not only the most extreme utterance that he himself ever made previously, but [that of] the most radical man in public life in our time." Eight years earlier, Roosevelt had told the people of Pittsburgh that the growth of collectivized industrial America was like the mighty Mississippi. Now at Osawatomie, Roosevelt told the hardscrabble Kansans that this river of change was washing away the old Jeffersonian ideas of a bottom-up government and carrying the nation to a new, top-down Hamiltonian world. After Osawatomie, Matthew Josephson wrote, Roosevelt was "steering into the full current of his time."

Herbert Croly wrote that Theodore Roosevelt emancipated "American democracy from its Jeffersonian bondage." He freed Americans all over the country to think realistically and creatively about both the perils and possibilities of industrialism. William Allen White, who sat on the platform at Osawatomie, wrote that even in Pittsburgh, the city elders had come to realize that government was "the only thing big enough to counter-balance organized industry and make life sane and normal and beautiful."

Today, a decade short of a hundred years later, life for just about all Americans has become more "sane and normal and beautiful" in large part because of the vision of government Roosevelt revealed at Osawatomie. But that vision was a product of the circumstances of the day. It was intended to be a response to a particular time, not a rule for all times. Nor was it supposed to be the final end-point in the development of American government. Looking forward on the twentieth century that was beginning to unfold before him, William Allen White wrote that "It is reasonable to believe that this century may see an improvement in the condition of the weak and defenseless in our industrial system which the last century saw in the care of the mentally and morally and physically infirm and helpless." He was patronizing, he was paternalistic, but he was right. The twentieth century did see a government that strove to protect those who otherwise would fall victim to the vagaries of life and chance—a marked improvement on the previous century. The question before us now is what unique brand of improvement—different from that of the past and geared toward the specific needs of our time—*this* new century will see.

Unfortunately, as the century begins, neither party seems especially eager to make the kind of clear break with the past that Roosevelt made at Osawatomie. Although the Information Age is bringing changes in almost every aspect of life, most present-day Republican and Democratic politicians seem to be satisfied with only incremental improvements in their own time-tested programs. Democrats want to add a little bit to government here, take away a little bit there. Republicans want to "get government out of the way"—especially when it involves the dispossessed and except for when it involves their own corporate constituencies—and make marginal reductions in the marginal tax rates. Many of the specific programs suggested by both parties are excellent and needed. But few respond to the test of these times. In a world being turned upside-down, they boldly go where everyone has gone before.

Because they claim so much and reach for so exalted a mantle, those who fall farthest short are often those Treadmill Liberals who call themselves New Progressives. Unfortunately, what they offer is, for the most part, neither "new" nor "progress." Self-styled New Progressives such as Cornell West, Alan Brinkley, Senator Paul Wellstone, Congressman David Bonior, and the more than fifty members of the Congressional Progressive Caucus recognize that America is undergoing a transformation similar to that of Theodore Roosevelt's day. Yet, they fall short in their belief that this calls for an expansion of centralized government like that which Roosevelt fought for. This is Progressivism as the defense of the status quo—an outlook that would have been unfamiliar to the men and women of a century ago who fought so hard to change the established policies of the past. The first Progressives didn't bury their heads in the sand and pretend new circumstances didn't really exist, but met the challenge creatively and candidly.

The Progressives of the past changed America's policies so that they would be in line with what was happening in the economy: centralizing decision-making into the hands of the few, elevating the role of experts in policymaking, limiting the freedom of individuals, building up a large bureaucracy. The huge buildings in Washington housing federal agencies and departments, the page after page of regulation and legislation emerging from the federal and state capitals, serve as testament to the enduring success of the original Progressives in bringing about their vision. Perhaps paradoxically, those who would inherit the mantle of Progressivism today must reject those accomplishments as the be-all and end-all of government. They must, instead, embrace the process of the original Progressives and create a government reflecting the economy of our own time: diffusing power into the hands of individuals, giving citizens more choices in every facet of their lives, promoting access to information and knowledge, and personalizing services to fit the contours of each person's life.

The outlook that has defined Progressive politics from the New Deal to the Great Society to the present day has been Herbert Croly's famous "Jeffersonian ends by Hamiltonian means": building up a strong centralized government in order to achieve the goals of security and social equality. As America enters a very different world, politicians must pursue "Hamiltonian ends by Jeffersonian means": relying on a faith in individuals and decentralized government activism to achieve the goals of prosperity and a shared pursuit of common interests.

A century ago, the Progressives focused first and foremost on a clear and widely recognized symptom of the changed economy: the huge consolidated businesses known as trusts. Trusts were a manifestation of institutions that didn't keep pace with a transforming world. Today, there is new evidence showing that modern institutions have once again failed to reflect a changing society. It is *distrust*.

As the economy continues to change, as more and more members of the GI Generation die and the Choice Generation comes to maturity, distrust of the big institutions of American life—especially government—is becoming pervasive and accepted. It doesn't have to be this way. If government and community institutions could be changed to reflect the values of most Americans again, there is evidence that they could win back popular respect. A bipartisan 1997 survey by pollsters Peter Hart and Robert Teeter revealed that 77 percent of Americans felt that "with better management" government could be effective. Only 19 percent said it could not be effective, "no matter what." As a tour through any successful company today will show, management no longer means just balancing the books, making sure everyone has their office supplies, and watching over people's shoulders so that they don't break any rules. Management today is giving decision-making power to people, connecting them to the information they need, and rewarding them for good work. Once again, Progressives must follow the example of the businesses at the forefront of economic change.

One hundred years ago, Progressives sought to improve the nation by breaking apart private monopolies with trust-busting. Today, Progressives should focus on Distrust-Busting—breaking up the public monopolies that stifle innovation, that impede free individual choice, and that rob citizens of the freedom to make basic decisions about their own lives. Whether with new initiatives to let Americans choose the public schools their children attend, choose the doctors they see when they are sick, choose the way they save for their retirement—or countless other ways they interact with government every day—Americans should have the same amount of choice and freedom they have in their interaction with the business world. And this choice and freedom should not be limited to the wealthiest few. By tearing apart one-size-fits-all government programs, contemporary politicians will go a long way in restoring Americans' faith in their own government and its relevance to their lives.

In forming an agenda fit for its times, Distrust-Busting combines the Populists' faith in the people, their disdain for elites, and their antipathy toward concentrated power with the Progressive spirit of modernism, optimism, and reform.

Distrust-Busting requires Americans to expand their basic faith in democracy—in the rule of the common people. Converting this from a common platitude to a real set of policies will not be easy. Politicians of both parties will have to get over the long-held assumption that an active government is necessarily a bureaucratic one.

In 1944, John A. Vieg wrote, in an article entitled "Democracy and Bureaucracy," that "Today no nation lacking a big bureaucracy and a powerful government has the means of insuring either its liberty or its welfare. This proposition is so plain that it should not need to be labored." Around the same time, the great political scientist V. O. Key concluded that "unless our civilization collapses completely this is going to continue to be a bureaucratic world." Today, as the Information Age changes Americans' attitudes, expectations, and experiences, it is possible to have a government that is much more active and far less bureaucratic. With the Internet's ability to put nearly unlimited information into their hands, individuals can make choices for themselves and their families that government bureaucrats now make for them. Government can oversee how and where its funds are being spent, but let individuals spend them as they see fit.

Yet, the advent of the Internet alone does not change government—it only provides an opening. The hard part now, as it was in the Progressive Era, lies in developing an alternative and in confronting and defeating those forces with a vested interest in the status quo; those who feed off of and depend on outdated assumptions for their livelihood and their comfort—both physical and mental.

The goal of Distrust-Busting relies on the means of the Choice Revolution to strip apart the century-old assumptions and institutions of bureaucratic administration and give power, choices, and decision-making ability to average citizens. Anybody who has even set foot in Washington, D.C.—or for that matter most state capitals—knows that this is an awesome assignment. The present order and its defenders have developed deep roots in the soil of public life. The idea of trained experts making decisions for ordinary citizens is not only ingrained into the nation's psyche, it has its own infrastructure.

In his 1994 State of the Union Address, President Clinton said, "After years of leaders whose rhetoric attacked bureaucracy but whose actions expanded it, we will actually reduce it by 252,000 people over the next five years. By the time we have finished, the federal bureaucracy will be at its lowest point in 30 years." This was met with cheers by a nation tiring of the old-style top-down machinery. At Harvard's Kennedy School of Government, it was met with hisses and boos. The assembled bureaucrats-in-training, watching the address on a big screen TV, were only a quarter joking. Clinton's words not only threatened their future job prospects, they were an affront to their view of America. The students at the Kennedy School, and thousands of others at similar schools around the country, often see themselves as an expert elite who have the scientific calculators and quantitative knowledge to figure out what is best for ordinary Americans. The attitude conveyed in their classrooms is often, "Governing is not for everybody. Ladies and gentlemen, we are trained professionals—don't try this at home."

For those who believe that the Information Age necessitates that citizens have a greater say in their own lives, the task ahead is likely to be what it was for Teddy Roosevelt and the original Progressives: a generation-long crusade to remake and reimagine government.

To find inspiration, Americans can turn back to a fork in the road nine decades ago—when Jeffersonianism had its last stand. "We've stumbled along for a while, trying to run a new civilization in old ways, but we got to start to make this world over," Thomas Edison wrote to Henry Ford in 1912. The Wizard of Menlo Park felt that civilization was "out of gear." But in that year, Americans would begin to shift into a new gear and set out on the road we continue on today.

The need for this new direction was becoming evident to an increasing number of Americans. Confronted with the problems and uncertainties of an industrialized America that had already robbed them of their independence as workers, they were willing to exchange their individualized freedoms as citizens for bureaucratic control. Everywhere power was flowing out of the hands of people and into the palms of experts. In 1908, in Staunton, Virginia, the electorate gave up its power to America's first expert city manager. Four years later, Staunton's hometown hero would run for president to give Americans their powers back.

AN ECHO OF A CHOICE

When I look back on the process of history, when I survey the genesis of America, I see this written over every page: that the nations are renewed from the bottom, not the top; that the genius which springs from the ranks of unknown men is the genius which renews the youth and energy of the people.
                    —*Woodrow Wilson,* The New Freedom, *1912*

In his magisterial work, *Diplomacy,* Henry Kissinger described the difference in the foreign policy philosophies of Theodore Roosevelt and Woodrow Wilson as "the hinge"—a choice of two fundamentally different international views. The former was an exemplary practitioner of "global balance of power" politics; the latter believed that "America's international role was messianic." Today, the career of Woodrow Wilson is discussed almost entirely from the perspective of World War I, his Fourteen Points, his League of Nations, his obstinate inability to compromise on the Treaty of Versailles. This is as it should be. But there is another part of the Woodrow Wilson story—a story of what *might* have been. In 1912, Wilson and Theodore Roosevelt met at another "hinge"—not in America's foreign policy, but in its domestic policies. In that year, Wilson and Roosevelt waged a vigorous campaign for the White House. More important, they engaged in a monumental struggle to define government's mission in the Industrial Age. Roosevelt continued to speak out for the Hamilton–Croly vision of a benevolent and bureaucratic government. Wilson proposed a twentieth-century Jeffersonianism: an activist government geared toward dispersing power to individuals. In 1912, Woodrow Wilson won the election-year battle; Teddy Roosevelt won the larger war—and the path of the twentieth century was set.

Thomas Woodrow Wilson was born to a Presbyterian minister in Staunton, Virginia, in December 1856. He was, from a young age, convinced that destiny had tapped him for greatness as a statesman—and set out to build himself into a leader worthy of such an honor. After graduating from Princeton, he attended law school and then struggled to eke out an interest in the practice of law. Unable to defeat his boredom, he returned to the academy and received his doctorate in the young field of political science at Johns Hopkins University. After teaching at Bryn Mawr and Wesleyan colleges, Wilson returned to Princeton—first as a popular professor, then as president. Throughout this time, he, like Roosevelt, was a well-known author of books on politics and history. His political career had not caught flame as he once had hoped, but its pilot light still burned steadily.

Woodrow Wilson is remembered as a stern and dour figure—serious and proud. He believed that there were two sides to every issue, "the right and the wrong." His austere Calvinism and his faith in his preordained place on the planet did not endear him to many of those he met. During the 1912 presidential contest, a Maryland ward boss confided to his bartender, "He gives me the creeps. The time I met him, he said something to me, and I didn't know whether God or him was talking." When placed alongside a figure of the vibrancy and vigor of Theodore Roosevelt, as he was in 1912, Wilson's colors seemed all the more muted. In December 1905, the Army–Navy football game was played at Princeton. At half-time, the two presidents—of the United States and of Princeton—walked across the field together, as one faculty member described "Roosevelt exuberant, smiling, delighted, waving his hat, acknowledging the plaudits of the multitude and tugging along the dignified university professor who followed 'with conscious step of purity and pride,' if not reluctant, at least not equally ebullient."

Yet, there was more to Woodrow Wilson. He carried with him more than a touch of whimsy—he was an expert composer of hilarious limericks. Furthermore, Wilson's personality contained a spark and sparkle that, when revealed, proved infectious. From his very early years, something set Wilson apart and made him noticed by all. "Dr. Wilson is here, homely, solemn, young, glum, but with fir in his face and eye that means that its possessor is not of the common crowd," was the description of his professor which Johns Hopkins graduate student Frederick Jackson Turner sent to his fiancée back home in 1889.

Wilson's cool demeanor came about because he was an emotional person, not because he wasn't one. Like politicians from a young Bobby

Kennedy to an old Bob Dole who were likewise accused of being cold and aloof, his reserve was a cover on a bubbling kettle. He told his first wife that he always felt the need to "guard my emotions from painful overflow."

His uncompromising, disciplined, honorable outlook—which would prove so devastating to him politically in the aftermath of World War I— lifted him from a private citizen and first-time political candidate to the president-elect of the United States in only 658 days. Had he not spent a lifetime preparing for the moment, he would not have remade American government as he did.

In 1910, when New Jersey's corrupt and disgraced political bosses came to him and asked him to be their candidate for governor, it was generally understood by everyone that he was to serve as the high-minded, respectable window dressing in their campaign to keep their hand in the public till. Everyone understood this except for Wilson himself. He said he could not commit to propping up their power. What the bosses did not comprehend was that he meant it. Before he even took office, Wilson made his stand against their demands—and defeated an attempted power grab. The headlines reverberated throughout the country and made him an immediate contender for the Democratic presidential nomination in 1912.

Meanwhile, on the other side of the political aisle, the force of the explosive speech Theodore Roosevelt had given at Osawatomie was propelling him toward a final break with President Taft. Roosevelt's political ambitions, and Taft's impolitic moves toward his former boss and mentor, impelled the colonel to announce, in February 1912, that "My hat is in the ring! The fight is on and I am stripped to the buff!" He would challenge his protégé—the incumbent president of the United States—for the nomination of the Grand Old Party. As Roosevelt continued to lay out his New Nationalism program, it became clear that his battle for the Republican nomination was more than a mere naked grab for power. His was a battle to remake the Republican Party forever in the Progressive image he had cultivated.

Roosevelt won nine presidential primaries against the incumbent president—even winning in the tubby Taft's native Ohio. But it was meaningless; at the time, primaries were not even of secondary importance in picking presidents. Political chieftains beholden to business interests controlled the process from beginning to end—and they would be damned if the cowboy with radical ideas would be allowed to win. Taft's men ran the convention—and handed him a nomination they knew would be useless. Everyone, including Taft himself, understood that he would go down to defeat in November. But better to lose with Taft, the party bigwigs figured, than to allow the Republican Party to become infected with Progressivism.

The sombrero-topped Roosevelt would not take defeat sitting down. With the rump of his supporters, he organized a new Progressive Party to carry his message into the fall campaign. At the Progressive Party Convention, in August of 1912, the forces of reform converged in an army dedicated to defeating the last vestiges of old thinking and building a new, modern America. To the tune of the "Battle Hymn of the Republic," the delegates sang:

> The moose has left the wooded hill; his call rings through the land.
> It's a summons to the young and strong to join with willing hand:
> To fight for right and country; to strike down a robber band,
> And we'll go marching on.

The convention's keynoter, Senator Albert Beveridge, quenched the delegates' thirst for purity and goodness: "The people vote for one party and find their hopes turned to ashes on 'their lips,' and then, to punish that party, they vote for the other party. So it is that partisan victories have come to be merely the people's vengeance; and always the secret powers have played the game." A scholar-politician, like both Roosevelt and Wilson, Beveridge summed up the Progressives' spirit: "The Progressive motto is 'Pass Prosperity Around.'" The old Jeffersonian idea of free and unfettered opportunity was shelved in favor of redistribution of wealth.

It was, of course, Roosevelt himself who summed up his party's message best. Before the cheering multitudes, he delivered "A Confession of

Faith," which summed up his New Nationalism. After the obligatory throat-clearing of introduction, Roosevelt laid out the guts of his case: "The prime need to-day is to face the fact that we are now in the midst of a great economic evolution." In response to that evolution, Roosevelt laid out the Progressive platform. The trust-busting that once had been centrally associated with his brand of Progressivism was now dismissed as "futile madness." Instead, Roosevelt called for a government that would increase its powers to meet the powers of the big businesses—that would not try to break apart the modern economic system, but instead harness it for the general welfare. The Progressive Party brought to the fore a new set of ideas in American politics: regulation of factory conditions, government subsidies to agriculture, a progressive income tax, environmental protection, a minimum wage, national health insurance, and other social welfare legislation. These ideas came to define and delimit government activism for the rest of the century.

If his Confession of Faith was not radical enough "then," Roosevelt would later say, "I do not know what radicalism is." His platform would not be radical for long. By the 1930s, with cousin Franklin in the White House, it would become part of the fabric of American government. But before it became as much a part of Washington as columns and calumny, the Progressive vision of Theodore Roosevelt faced a final challenge—from Woodrow Wilson and his now-forgotten strand of Jeffersonian Progressive thought.

As 1912 dawned, the Democrats had held the White House for only eight of the previous fifty years. They wanted to win—and no candidate shined with more luster than the Progressive governor of New Jersey. One month before the Progressive Party nominated Roosevelt, a tumultuous Democratic Convention had finally agreed on Woodrow Wilson as their nominee, setting up a three-way battle for the presidency unlike any seen before or since. Here were presidents—past, present, and future—fighting it out with one another. Together, the three men running for the highest office in the land in 1912 held that office among them continuously from 1901 to 1921. Most remarkable, the incumbent president of the United States was—as he quickly recognized—

effectively out of the running and consigned to third place. Realizing that his time as president was coming to an end, Taft eschewed active campaigning and spent most of the rest of his term concentrating on the issue of his golf game. The campaign fast boiled down to the combat between Roosevelt and Wilson—the peripatetic hunter and the hubristic professor—as John Milton Cooper called them, "the warrior and the priest." But as both would come to insist, the choice between them was not just about personality—it was about the path of Progressivism and the path of American government in the twentieth century.

By 1912, the most sophisticated political thinkers of the age had accepted the need for a powerful, Hamiltonian government. Yet, the individualist, Jeffersonian spirit still had deep resonance with average Americans who refused to accept the demise of the individual in American life; who still struggled to break free of this iron law of the age of steel. It was only Americans who couldn't read who were "thruc to th' principa's iv Jefferson an' Jackson," said Finley Peter Dunne's fictional Irish saloon keeper, Mr. Dooley.

Wilson himself had once looked down his Roman nose at the quaint faith of Jefferson. As a law student at the University of Virginia in Charlottesville, he had not even bothered to make the short trip to visit Monticello. But, buffeted by the shifting winds of the early twentieth century, Wilson would make a philosophical pilgrimage to the mind of the "Philosopher of Democracy."

The campaign began slowly, as campaigns did back then. In the weeks after his nomination, Wilson sat in his home at Sea Girt, New Jersey, opening the mail himself, scrutinizing campaign contributions for any nefarious connections, and greeting the growing stream of visitors who found their way to his front porch. When the gathering flood of good wishes and well-wishers became too taxing, Wilson would cross the Hudson to visit New York; walking the crowded streets of Manhattan, alone and anonymous. His name was universally recognized as that of the front-runner for president of the United States, but his face was entirely unrecognized on the bustling streets of its premier metropolis.

At the same time, Wilson began to consider the platform on which he would wage the campaign. Both he and Roosevelt had struggled to get where they were intellectually by 1912. In a 1904 speech to expat Virginians in New York, Wilson had said that the Democrats should be a "party of conservative reform." In 1908 comments to a British journalist, Roosevelt had said that Republicans should be a "party of progressive conservatism." But both had been swept up in the flow of Progressivism—even if they claimed different streams.

Wilson responded instinctively to Jefferson's faith in individual initiative and free competition, but—unlike the Populists—he knew better than to adopt Jefferson's Agricultural Age policy prescriptions. "Big things are happening in the development of this country," gushed the editors of *Harpers* in 1912. As Wilson strolled alone through the streets of New York that summer, America's future was clear. Above him the Woolworth Building was nearing completion—it would be the tallest building in the world until well into the Great Depression. Half of Americans lived in cities, and more were moving there every day. Only 16 percent of Americans lived in households with electricity, but more light bulbs were turning on all the time. In April of that year, the world's largest luxury liner went down in the icy waters of the North Atlantic, but the band of bigness was playing on; the force of technological progress was still king of the world.

America was clearly changing and Wilson was second to none in acknowledging this. Jefferson's pronouncements on limited government belonged to "a time which was without railways and telegraph lines." So, Wilson did not merely repeat the stale nostrums of Jeffersonianism, he sought to update them for this "very different age." His New Freedom, Wilson said, was "the application of Jefferson's principles to our present-day America." Unlike Roosevelt and Croly, he refused to concede that the force of the industrial economy would not allow the individual to take center-stage regardless of government actions. He was "confident that if Jefferson were living in our day he would see what we see: that the individual is caught in a great confused nexus of all sorts of complicated circumstances, and to let him alone is to leave him helpless as against the obstacles with which he has to contend; and, therefore, law in our day must come to the assistance of the individual."

If Roosevelt's New Nationalism had been inspired—in great part—

by the influence of Herbert Croly's *The Promise of American Life*, Wilson's New Freedom tenets had been crystallized in a three-hour August meeting at Sea Girt with the neo-Jeffersonian Louis Brandeis, the "People's Lawyer" and future Supreme Court justice. Like Croly, Brandeis was a child of immigrants. His parents had fled Bohemia during the tumult of the Revolutions of 1848 and had imparted the radical democratic promise of those uprisings to their son. Although he would come to be associated with the Boston which he so loved, Brandeis grew up in Louisville, Kentucky—a city that, if no longer part of the frontier, was far too Western to be taken by the settled establishments of the East. Growing up Jewish in this community gave Brandeis experience in standing apart from the crowd and holding firm in his beliefs—training that would prove invaluable when the Progressive movement was stampeding toward Roosevelt in 1912.

Both Roosevelt and Wilson confronted the newfound centralization of business power and the denigration of individual initiative with a new role for government—but each did so in different ways. Roosevelt brought the top-down Hamiltonian spirit to bear on the problems of industrialism. His New Nationalism argued that bigness must counter bigness. To protect the "forgotten man," he wanted to regulate business with a powerful government. In a world where massive forces checked one another, none would become too strong to harm the common person. Under Brandeis' influence, Wilson sought to update Jefferson for a new century by breaking down power, whether it was vested in business monopolies or political machines, and returning decision-making authority to the individual.

At the time, some failed to see the crucial difference between these two points of view. "Between the New Nationalism and the New Freedom was that fantastic imaginary gulf that always has existed between tweedle-dum and tweedle-dee," wrote William Allen White. Time has shown the gulf to be bigger. "In opposition to Roosevelt's embryonic vision of a protective welfare state, Wilson painted a countervision of a state that promoted social and economic mobility," wrote historian John Milton Cooper. Historian George Mowry described the "deep and significant ideological rift . . . between the two wings of progressivism" this way: Wilson "cherished the competitive system with its individual values and feared the powerful state," while Roosevelt "welcomed concentrated power whether in industry or politics, looked to a paternalistic state staffed by an educated elite for leadership, and deprecated individualism." Both men confronted a world of behemoth powers that had undermined individual initiative; the world of William Allen White's "pre-Adamite giant." Roosevelt wanted to employ Goliath, Wilson wanted to arm David.

In the fall campaign of 1912, Roosevelt and Wilson touched the hearts and excited the minds of Americans as no two opposing candidates for president have since. They treated Americans to the rare delight of two presidential candidates who spoke to the nation that was coming to be, not to that which once was. Across the country, Americans debated the merits of their divergent brands of reform. For his part, Roosevelt vigorously pounded away at his idea of a more powerful government that would channel the forces of industrialism toward social justice. He sought to create powerful government commissions that would oversee the monopolies and ensure that they were acting on behalf of the social welfare. He believed that "the only effective way of controlling and directing" the new big business lay in "having the people nationalize the governmental control in order to meet the nationalization of the big business itself." Roosevelt, in effect, wanted to create Bellamy's "Great Trust."

Together with his running mate, California's fighting Progressive Governor Hiram Johnson, Roosevelt attacked Wilson as a hidebound exponent of obsolescent approaches. "He is against using the power of the government to help the people to whom the government belongs," Roosevelt said of Wilson. "We take flat issue with him. We propose to use the government as the most efficient instrument for the uplift of our people as a whole; we propose to give a fair chance to the worker and strengthen their rights. We propose to use the whole power of the government to protect those who, under Mr. Wilson's *laissez-faire* system, are trodden down in the ferocious, scrambling rush of an unregulated and purely individualistic industrialism." There it was—the call for a more powerful government that would watch over citizens and protect them from other big powers. This was the newborn cry of twentieth-century government.

While Wilson's vision was certainly not laissez-faire, he campaigned with a diametrically opposing view of how government's power should be expanded. He argued that government should actively seek to break apart the trusts and other large powers that were standing in the way of individual ambition and upward mobility. He wanted government to ensure free enterprise at home and free trade abroad. Under the tutelage of Brandeis—who had done more than anyone else to publicize the views of Frederick Winslow Taylor—Wilson argued against the political implications of Taylor's views. While Roosevelt and most Progressives wanted to subjugate the individual to an "efficient" and benevolent system, Wilson insisted on a policy of promoting competition and small entrepreneurship that would prevent organized powers and regimentation from gaining an unbreakable stranglehold on individual ingenuity.

With a growing passion and an eloquence never again equaled in the annals of American presidential campaigns, Wilson spoke out in opposition to Roosevelt's vision of a dispassionate and educated corps of experts who would minister to the needs of passive "clients." Addressing TR's proposal for a government powerful enough to control and regulate huge corporations, Wilson said, "I say, then, the proposition is this: that there shall be two masters, the great corporation and over it the government of the United States. . . . I don't care how benevolent the master is going to be. I will not live under a master. That is not what America was created for. America was created in order that every man should have the same chance with every other man to exercise mastery over his own fortunes." It was a grand idea, but as Wilson acknowledged, he was "swimming against the stream."

Although Wilson's policies attempted to respond to the Industrial Age, Wilson's vision was a romantic faith in the individual; a memory of the America that existed before the clang, clatter, and constraints of steel machines. On the morning of October 4, 1912, Woodrow Wilson spoke to a crowd of thousands from a platform by the local courthouse in Kokomo, Indiana—Elwood Haynes' hometown. There he praised the town's "locally owned and locally controlled" small businesses and promised that "in all that I may do in public affairs in the United States, I am going to think of towns like Kokomo in Indiana, towns of the old American pattern. And my thought is going to be bent upon the multiplication of towns of that kind." That same year, in Michigan, far away from the carriage-makers of Kokomo and their carefully crafted handiwork, Henry Ford told his distributors that "Any customer can have a car painted any color he wants—so long as it is black." The New Freedom never had a chance.

With a divided Republican Party, Wilson won the election in 1912 and was narrowly reelected in 1916. But the reign of the New Freedom was short-lived. Roosevelt could have predicted this—indeed, he did predict it throughout the campaign. Even back in 1911, he had written to a friend that the Progressive movement was divided between the Wilson–Brandeis view, which was "representative of a kind of rural toryism, which wishes to attempt the impossible task of returning to the economic conditions which obtained sixty years ago," and the mainline Progressive desire "to go forward along the proper lines, that is, to recognize the inevitableness and the necessity of combinations in business, and meet it by a corresponding increase in government power over big business." In his *Autobiography*, he would write, "the men who saw the evils and who tried to remedy them attempted to work in two wholly different ways, and the great majority of them in a way that offered little promise of real betterment. They tried to bolster up an individualism already proved to be both futile and mischievous." The futility of individualism, the inevitability of big business and big government—these were the bedrock truths of the Industrial Age. They might easily be glossed over on the campaign trail with the sun at your back and a crowd of thousands before you hungering for the reassurance that the world of their childhood need not have vanished forever. But Roosevelt had sat behind the desk in the West Wing. He knew that there was no running from facts when it came time to decide the fate of a nation. Because he was wise and honorable, Woodrow Wilson would learn this same truth very quickly.

The historian Richard Abrams wrote in *Burdens of Progress* that the failure of the New Freedom was a "failure of nerve." This misses the mark. The New Freedom's failure came because it was out of step with the twentieth century. Upon first taking office, Wilson made several thrusts at breaking down organized private power and opening paths for the energy of individual Americans. But, as the admiring historian David Steigerwald admits, "Wilson's solutions to the great problem of concentrated power amounted to nothing more than tame reforms that lowered the tariff, brought some coherence to the banking system through the Federal Reserve Board, and clarified anti-trust law." Wilson soon jettisoned his New Freedom agenda—not because he lacked courage, but because he realized that Roosevelt had been basically correct. "Facing the actual conditions of 1913, matters seemed a good deal more complicated," than they had in the campaign, and Wilson, according to historian August Heckscher, "accepted ultimately a Rooseveltian solution." Historian William Leuchtenberg maintained that, "Before he had ended his first term of office he had jettisoned almost every one of the New Freedom doctrines." By 1916, wrote historian Arthur Link, Wilson had adopted the New Nationalism "lock, stock, and barrel." A historian named Woodrow Wilson agreed with them all. He bragged in 1916 about enacting the Progressive Party platform. His conversion was more than election-year politics. In a 1918 letter he wrote, "The world is going to change radically, and I am satisfied that governments will have to do many things which are now left to individuals and corporations." Roosevelt had won. Not that this surprised the colonel for a second. In 1912, TR confided to a friend that because of his campaign, even if was not successful, "the cause of liberal government would be advanced fifty years." Roosevelt—whose career was marked by "bully," bluster, and bombast—for once, sold himself short. His vision was relevant to America for most of the rest of the century.

Contrary to popular perception, it was the Progressive Era of Teddy Roosevelt and Woodrow Wilson—more than Franklin Roosevelt's New

Deal, Harry Truman's Fair Deal, or Lyndon Johnson's Great Society—
that built the support and structure of the modern big government we
know and sometimes love. In the fifty years between 1871 and 1921, the
year when Wilson left the White House, the number of federal civilian
employees increased by 1,097 percent. Over the next fifty years, between
1921 and 1971, the number of employees increased far more in actual
numbers, but far less in percentage terms: a mere 435 percent jump.
When it came to America's acceptance of the idea of big government, it
was the Progressives who did the deed.

As befit someone who had grown up in the America of the Industrial
Age, nobody was harder on Wilson in his New Freedom phase than a
brash young man named Walter Lippmann. In his 1914 book, *Drift and
Mastery*, a 25-year-old Lippmann, mustering all the self-assurance and
cocky certitude that only someone of his age could command, mocked
Wilson as an out-of-step old-fogey who had tied himself to a bygone
world. "The political economy of his generation was based on competition and free trade," Lippmann wrote. "The Democratic Party is by tradition opposed to a strong central government and that opposition
applies equally well to strong national business—it is a party attached to
local rights, to village patriotism, to humble but ambitious enterprise; its
temper has always been hostile to specialization and expert knowledge,
because it admires a very primitive man-to-man democracy." Today, the
public values Lippmann scorned—such as competition, free trade,
decentralization, community concern, support of small business enterprises, trust in the people to make their own decisions, and a belief in
grassroots democracy—are roaring back into style. Lippmann's disdainful words would now be taken as a compliment. As Will Marshall and
Fred Siegel wrote in their landmark article, "Liberalism's Lost Tradition,"
Wilson's "emphasis on citizens rather than clients, markets rather than
managers, is far better suited to the dispersal of power in the Information
Age than the New Deal nostrums that once served us so well."

In 1912, Wilson wrote to his friend Mary Hulbert that "I was saying
to-day that I wished I had been born 20 years later, so that I could have
20 years more of this exhilarating century upon which we have entered."

It turns out that Wilson was born a full century too early. According to E. J. Dionne, "The Croly/Roosevelt doctrine was thus more 'advanced' than Wilson's, being closer to the spirit of social democracy." Today, however, the forces which impelled this doctrine are, if not in retreat, at least "advancing" in the opposite direction. Today, businesses of all sorts—large and small—thrive to the extent they can take their power and pass it back to their customers. Today, the public cares less and less about the sainted words from experts in Washington, and trusts its own judgment more than ever. Today, it is fast becoming clear: Teddy Roosevelt was right for his day, Woodrow Wilson is right for ours.

A century ago, the Progressives reached back and dusted off the decaying corpus of Alexander Hamilton. Today, we should exhume the spirit of Woodrow Wilson. Naturally, this does not mean following his every precept, but it does mean embracing his vision. "America was created to break every kind of monopoly, and to set men free, upon a footing of equality, upon a footing of opportunity, to match their brains and their energies," said Woodrow Wilson in 1912. The battle against overlords and their monopolies is a useful lens for viewing America's principal eras of reform. In 1776, Americans "fired a shot heard round the world." In declaring their independence from their English overlords, they overthrew a monopoly of political power. In 1912, as the Progressive movement reached its heights, Americans voted overwhelmingly for government action in the face of the new economic overlords and their monopoly of industrial power. And how goes the battle against monopoly today? Today, Americans are demanding an end to the rule of the expert overlords. In the way they work and shop and live, Americans are finding more and more freedom to make choices of their own. Americans are looking for a new bottom-up idea that would overthrow the monopolies of decision-making power, be they in big business or bureaucratic government.

In a world that is at least much "safer" for democracy, where self-determination shows itself to be a still awesomely powerful force, where international cooperation grows ever deeper, Woodrow Wilson's vision of the world is becoming vindicated. In the aftermath of 1989, Daniel

Patrick Moynihan asked George Kennan, the realist exhorter of the policy of containment, what the collapse of the Soviet bloc meant to "the Wilsonian project." Kennan explained that while he "was long skeptical about Wilson's vision," recent events led him "to think that Wilson was way ahead of his time."

The same is true for Wilson's vision for America. Today, private monopolies have receded as a major campaign issue. Even with the present wave of mega-mergers, consumers have more and more power to shop around for bargains, value, and quality than they ever did before. However, the monopolies of public power permeate Americans' lives. The major issue of our time, as it was in Roosevelt and Wilson's, is how government will change its role to respond to new circumstances. If history is any guide at all, this question will come to dominate political debate.

Confronted with this question, Treadmill Liberals, like the Republican "stand-pat" conservatives of the Progressive Era, try to bring about some modest changes, but mostly try to change the subject. If the status quo conservatives who supported Taft saw nothing wrong with concentrated corporate power, the Treadmillers see no problem with a coercive bureaucracy—especially if it accomplishes what they know is in the best interests of the American people. Iowa Senator Tom Harkin once said he would gladly run on the 1892 Populist Party platform. Most contemporary liberals would just as gladly campaign on the basis of the 1912 Progressive Party platform—it is the extent of their ambitions and a point beyond which they can look no farther.

On the other hand, the Blockhead Conservatives reflect Theodore Roosevelt's Progressives in their vision of eliminating bureaucratic power. As Wilson criticized Roosevelt for wanting to grant corporations "power given out in a lump," the Blockheads want to take power out of Washington and turn it over, in large lumps, to the state governments. This dismantles the federal programs of the previous century, but does nothing to give individuals more choices and decision-making power. It merely substitutes top-down solutions at the state level for top-down solutions at the national level. In the meantime, it eviscerates the federal guarantees that Americans have come to depend on while offering nothing tangible in their place. Nevertheless, many Republicans continue to peddle the idea that getting government programs out of Washington will magically transform their character. In a 1996 book entitled, ironically, *Power to the People*, Wisconsin's Republican Governor Tommy Thompson offered what he called "A New Progressive Idea." It was this: "transferring authority and decision-making from Washington to the state and local level." In that election year, resigned from the Senate but not yet resigned to defeat, Bob Dole carried a beat-up copy of the Tenth Amendment in his pocket. Oftentimes, to rile up an otherwise listless crowd, Dole would read aloud the twenty eight words of the amendment: "The powers not delegated to the United States by the Constitution, nor prohibited by it to the states, are reserved to the states respectively, or to the people." He might as well have left out the last part.

There is a third option which neither party has fully explored. It is the alternative put forward by Woodrow Wilson in 1912: transferring power to the American people themselves. By emphasizing the last three words of the Tenth Amendment—the final words of the Bill of Rights—today's leaders could push forward on the work of the Founders. They could revitalize the democratic process. They could respond to the spirit of the age and build on the progress of the past. "To the people" need not be only a slogan. It can transform government—letting Americans make choices on education, health care, child care, retirement, and so on that are now prescribed for them by the regulations of government programs and the decisions of the bureaucrats that administer them.

The year 1912 is a cobweb-draped moment in America's past. But the vision Woodrow Wilson outlined then—radically democratic, disdainful of encroaching power whatever its source, trusting of the common people, committed to truly free competition, assuring open avenues to individual achievement for all—could serve as the model for a new politics for the twenty-first century. This is the politics of the Choice Revolution. On the occasion of Wilson's death in 1925, William Allen White published a poem in his *Emporia Gazette:*

God gave him a great vision.
The devil gave him an imperious heart.
The proud heart is still.
The vision lives.

NOT IN KANSAS ANYMORE

Somewhere over the rainbow
Skies are blue.
And the dreams that you dare to dream
Really do come true.
                    —*Edward "Yip" Harburg,* Over the Rainbow

The quarter century in which Bryan, Roosevelt, and Wilson dominated
American politics saw Americans move from farms to factories and from
the country to the city. It saw Americans turn aside the old Jeffersonian
faith for the strictures of Hamilton. It saw massive changes in every facet
of American life. By 1920, after the terrible horrors of the Great War,
after two decades of Progressive agitation that had transformed the
nation's government, Americans were ready for an end to allegro notes
and a return to normalcy. Or, in the words of 1920 Republican presidential candidate Warren G. Harding, "a return to normalty." Harding
assumed all Americans adored alliteration as much as he did. So the
small-town newspaper editor turned senator used it at every turn. He
summed up his opposition to the Progressives this way: "Progression is
not proclamation nor palaver. It is not pretense nor play on prejudice.
It is not of personal pronouns nor perennial pronouncement. It is not
the perturbation of a people passion-wrought nor a promise proposed."
If that was not clear enough, he explained his passive vision for America in a May 1920 speech in Boston. "America's present need," he
informed an eager audience, "is not heroics but healing, not nostrums
but normalty, not revolution but restoration, not agitation but adjust-
ment, not surgery but serenity, not the dramatic but the dispassionate,
not experiment but equipoise, not submergence in internationality but

sustainment in triumphant nationality." His speech text, of course, did not have the word "normalty," but "normality." Reporters covering the speech tried to cover up for the friendly candidate and transcribed his remarks as "normalcy." With the slogans of "A Return to Normalcy" and "Down with Wilson," Harding and the Republicans waged their campaign to recapture the White House.

Harding was smart enough to realize his dimness, but it did not make his life any easier. "Jud," he would once exclaim to a White House aide, "you have a college education, haven't you? I don't know what to do or where to turn in this taxation matter. Somewhere there must be a book that tells all about it, where I could go to straighten it out in my mind. But I don't know where the book is, and maybe I couldn't read it if I found it! And there must be a man in the country somewhere who could weigh both sides and know the truth. Probably he is in some college or other. But I don't know where to find him. I don't know who he is, and I don't know how to get him. My God, this is a hell of a place for a man like me to be!" To oppose him in 1920, Democrats had nominated James Cox, the Progressive governor of Ohio, and, as his running-mate, Assistant Secretary of the Navy Franklin Roosevelt. Cox and Roosevelt traveled thousands of miles exhorting the country to stay with Progressivism—at home and abroad. Harding sat on his front porch and delivered prewritten speeches to professionally assembled crowds. In the middle of one such speech, he stumbled over his words, paused, looked up at the crowd, and said, "Well, I never saw this before. I didn't write this speech and don't believe what I just read." He had a beautiful smile. He wouldn't lead America on any grand crusades in the faraway fields of Flanders or in the arena of government activism at home. He was elected with a record-breaking majority—more than 60 percent of the vote.

When Inauguration Day came, Wilson—a shell of a man, rendered doddering and decrepit by a nearly incapacitating stroke—struggled to make the journey to the Capitol to perform the courtesy of watching Harding take his place. The Secret Service had counted that it would require 526 steps for Wilson to make it to his seat on the inaugural platform—far more than he was capable of. But he would make the ride to the Capitol together with Harding. The feeble Wilson made it to the car and it took off. Wilson sat there, joined by Harding, Philander Knox (once McKinley's attorney general), and former House Speaker Joe Cannon. It was as if the Progressives had never risen to wring out the vestiges of the rural past and ring in a new era of governmental involvement. With his jovial manner and great hair, the amiable Harding waved triumphantly as the car moved through the assembled crowds. Wilson was hardly able to move. Harding charged into a bizarre discussion of how he had always wanted an elephant as a pet and then launched into an inane story about an elephant that would gently hug its trainer. He looked over at the still-president. Hot tears were streaming down Wilson's cheek.

Wilson was not the only Progressive devastated by the return of the old guard in the 1920s. For Progressives, the decade was a period of self-doubt and a crisis in self-confidence. America had seemingly rejected the Progressive dream—leaving the dreamers to wonder whether they had been right in the first place. After Harding—the champion of "rugged individualism"—was elected, Herbert Croly refused to see anyone for three days. On the fourth, he summoned the editors of *The New Republic*—the magazine he had founded together with Walter Lippmann and Walter Weyl in order to promote the centralized, collectivized New Nationalism. He announced to them that "From now on we must work for the redemption of the individual."

As if the genie of big, paternalistic government would agree to return to its bottle. Both the Progressives and the status quo conservatives were wrong in thinking that Harding's crowd would be able to turn back the clock on Roosevelt's and Wilson's achievements. The idea Croly and others had done so much to promote—the subjugation of individual choice to collective undertaking, an idea that so clearly grew out of its Machine Age incubator—was here to stay. As the Progressives had been arguing all along, centralized government was not an idea they had pulled out of thin air, it was a response to the economic conditions of the time. This was as much true when conservatives were in power as it was when Progressives ruled. Every administration in the twentieth century acknowledged the importance and centrality of big government power—the differences came only in how they used it. Like the Reagan and Bush administration of the 1980s, the Republicans in the 1920s did not turn back the Progressive achievements, they merely transferred the use of the bureaucracy to help their own constituencies.

Harding's secretary of commerce, Herbert Hoover, was committed to using the powers of government to prop up the nation's large corporations, arguing that "the changed economic situation of the world demands that the functions of government in aid to commerce and industry be given more concentration and wider scope." During his tenure, the Commerce Department's magazine—*System: The Magazine of Business*—ran a monthly feature entitled "What Washington Offers Business This Month." As president, Hoover called for "a new era of national action, in which the federal government forms an alliance with the great trade associations and the powerful corporations." He followed through. "In 1920 only an estimated dozen trade associations were functioning," Eric Goldman wrote. "When Hoover left the White House, more than two thousand were in existence and many of them had worked out codes of close co-operation which virtually ignored the anti-trust laws."

For the Progressives, it was a case of being careful what you wish for: the collusion of big government with big business turned out to be a force that could stifle reform as easily as it could support it. The Progressives, once so full of confidence in the powerful government they were constructing, lost their faith as government's power was turned against everything they held dear.

It is no wonder that, confronted with the monster he had helped create, Croly finally decided to pursue the course of individual empowerment. But he, of all people, should have realized that it was the march of history and technology, not the easily reversed agitation of Progressive reformers, that had given rise to the big collective government. The Progressives had fought to speed up the process of change, but no one would be able to stop it. Nevertheless, Croly became undone. He took up yoga and fad diets and fell under the influence of a Russian mystic named Gustave Gurdjieff. He died three years before the New Deal redeemed his vision.

Confronted with a conservative brand of centralized government using its power on behalf of big corporations and the wealthiest Americans, Democrats backtracked from Wilson's presidential embrace of top-down Hamiltonianism. In 1928, they selected Claude Bowers to be the keynote speaker at their National Convention—for the sole reason that he was the author of a popular biography of Thomas Jefferson; the only book Franklin D. Roosevelt ever agreed to review. The Democratic Party "has mobilized today to wage a war of extermination against privilege and pillage," Bowers thundered. "We prime our guns against autocracy and bureaucracy. We march against that centralization which threatens the liberties of the people. We fight for the republic of the fathers."

It all rang a little hollow. "We practice Hamilton from January 1 to July 3 every year. On July 4 we hurrah like mad for Jefferson. The next day we quietly take up Hamilton again for the rest of the year as we go about our business," wrote historian James Truslow Adams. Surveying the scene at that 1928 Convention, Will Rogers—as usual—got to the heart of the matter: "I have heard so much at this convention about getting back to the old Jeffersonian principles that being an amateur, I am in doubt as to why they *left them* in the first place." They had left them, because they had realized that Jefferson's America was gone. They would come to realize it again, but now—far from the responsibility of power—there was no rush. One convention speaker after another promised to turn back the encroachments of centralized governmental power and bureaucracy. "Hamiltons we have today. Is there a Jefferson on the horizon?" asked former assistant secretary of the navy Franklin Delano Roosevelt.

The answer to that question lay beyond the opaque curtain of the future. For now, Progressives wandered in the bewilderedness. Democrats were so lost that William Jennings Bryan became the closest thing they had to a prophet of the future. In the 1920s, he would propose such modern, forward-thinking ideas as legal aid for poor people, better highways, campaign spending limits, cabinet departments for health and education. He was, however, the party's Jacob Marley—torturing them with reminders of a happier past, highlighting the sadness of their present, beseeching them to think of what was to come. His dark mane had turned to gray; his receding hairline had receded. Wilson and Roosevelt were gone, but he—their political forbearer—remained depressingly alive. At a 1924 Democratic National Committee meeting, one observer wrote of Bryan, that "most of the time he was wandering about the lobby of the hotel, attracting no attention," during sessions he was merely "a spectator pressed against the back wall of the meeting-room, wedged between a fat woman and a cub reporter." The mixture of ignominy and anonymity with which he was greeted reflected the broader public attitude toward the Progressive movement he had helped bring about.

In 1925, Bryan made one last run at the modern world. In his participation in the Scopes Monkey Trial, he ended up only bringing trouble to his own house. He called his battle against evolution "a duel to the death." He died six days after a merciless grilling by Clarence Darrow.

Two months before he died, Bryan visited Monticello. On departing, he was unrepentant. "To my mind, Thomas Jefferson was the greatest statesman our country produced—then or since." As the 1920s came to a close, it seemed that the Progressive hope for a powerful, bureaucratic, centralized government that would guard the welfare of ordinary Americans was out of reach; a murky memory of a brief interlude in more youthful days.

They were all dying—and with them their dream. Bryan was dead. Wilson was dead. Roosevelt was dead. Croly was dead. And what of Mary Elizabeth Lease—"the Kansas Pythoness," Joan of the Arkansas? She gave up on raising both corn *and* hell. Mary Elizabeth Lease moved to Brooklyn.

THE FLIGHT OF THE BLUE EAGLE

> Once I built a railroad, made it run,
> Made it race against time.
> Once I built a railroad,
> Now it's done.
> Brother, can you spare a dime?
>
> —*Edward "Yip" Harburg,*
> Brother Can You Spare a Dime?

As 1932 dawned, America lay prostrate. Strong men stood about peddling pencils in the street—sellers without any buyers. They could think
of nothing else to do. Mothers cried all day long. Their children alternated days eating. A quarter of the nation was unemployed. The warn-
ings of the Progressives had come to pass: a government without the full
means to guard the people's welfare had been unable to cope with the
vagaries of the industrial economy. At long last, the nation was looking
for a return to the Progressive spirit, for "bold, persistent experimentation"—and New York Governor Franklin Roosevelt was promising to
bring just that.

He was called "the Democratic Roosevelt," and in 1932, the open
question was whether he was more of a Democrat or more of a Roosevelt. FDR had been an early supporter of Woodrow Wilson and served
as his assistant secretary of the navy. With his offices in the huge gray
building across West Executive Avenue from the White House, FDR lit-
erally looked down on Wilson's Oval Office and was a very active member of the administration. In the years after Wilson left the presidency,
Roosevelt defended his former boss's record while campaigning for vice
president and began a foundation dedicated to advancing his principles.
On the other hand, he was, of course, Theodore Roosevelt's distant
cousin and had modeled himself after the Rough Rider. From service in
the New York state legislature to the assistant secretary post in the Navy
Department to the governor's office in Albany, FDR had sought to follow TR's path to the White House. He even modeled his speech patterns
and attire after Teddy's. Where Theodore Roosevelt was formed by the
terrible Valentine's Day in which he lost his wife and mother and his subsequent escape to the Badlands, Franklin Roosevelt might not have had
the strength to lead America through two of its most desperate hours
were it not for his cruel war of attrition against polio. When, in the
depths of a trying moment as president, he was asked whether he ever
worried, he replied simply, "If you had spent two years in bed trying to
wiggle your big toe, after that anything else would seem easy!" Since he
owed so much to both Teddy Roosevelt and Woodrow Wilson, it does
not come as a surprise that his pre-presidential career saw him alternating between espousal of the New Nationalism and the New Freedom.

In 1912, as a state senator and backer of Woodrow Wilson's campaign for the Democratic nomination, FDR described his views in ways more compatible with Teddy Roosevelt's Osawatomie than Wilson's Sea Girt. He believed that the new "conditions of civilization" had brought up new "questions that mere individual liberty cannot solve." Government policies should assist in the "struggle for liberty of the community rather than the liberty of the individual." Shortly thereafter, he became a leading exponent of the New Freedom. Throughout the 1920s and early 1930s, he shifted back and forth—at times criticizing Jeffersonians who believed "we should have *less* governing from Washington with a decrease in the existing functions of the national government"; at other times attacking Hamiltonians for being "committed to the idea that we ought to centralize everything in Washington as rapidly as possible."

Yet, Roosevelt's basic instincts were Jeffersonian—and it was primarily as Wilson's heir that he waged his 1932 campaign. In one of his first major speeches as a candidate, he took to the radio—as he would so profitably for the next thirteen years—and in a booming, confident voice called for economic plans "that build from the bottom-up and not the top-down, that put their faith once more in the forgotten man at the bottom of the economic pyramid." Somewhere, Jefferson and Wilson smiled. But many others did not. In a Democratic Party that was almost as beholden to the privileged powers as the Republicans, such talk was not welcome. Al Smith—once of First Avenue and the Fulton Fish Market, now of Fifth Avenue and the president of the Empire State Building—would have none of this: "I protest against the endeavor to delude the poor people of this country to their ruin by trying to make them believe that they can get employment before the people who would ordinarily employ them are also restored to conditions of normal prosperity."

In the central address of his campaign, before California's Commonwealth Club, Roosevelt summed up his views on the present crisis and his view of America's past, by telling the following story: After the American Revolution there "began, in American political life, the new day, the day of the individual against the system, the day in which individualism was made the great watchword of American life. The happiest of economic conditions made that day long and splendid. On the Western frontier, land was substantially free. No one, who did not shirk the task of earning a living, was entirely without opportunity to do so. . . . It was in the middle of the nineteenth century that a new force was released and a new dream created. The force was what is called the Industrial Revolution, the advance of steam and machinery and the rise of the forerunners of the modern industrial plant. The dream was the dream of an economic machine, able to raise the standard of living for everyone; to bring luxury within the reach of the humblest. . . . It was to be expected that this would necessarily affect government. Heretofore, government had merely been called upon to produce conditions within which people could live happily, labor peacefully, and rest secure. Now it was called upon to aid in the consummation of this new dream. . . . Our task now is not the discovery or exploitation of natural resources. . . . It is the soberer, less dramatic business of administering resources . . . of distributing wealth and products more equitably, of adapting existing economic organizations to the service of the people. The day of enlightened administration has come." In this "day of enlightened administration," Roosevelt would finally fulfill the Progressive dream and build an American government with institutions capable of harnessing "the new force" and using its power. This idea was the very heart of his New Deal.

Like Wilson, FDR ran on a platform of Jeffersonian idealism. He advocated breaking up centralized power and called for a balanced budget. In the book he wrote in the long, desperate months between his election and his inauguration, and which was released shortly after he took office, Roosevelt affirmed that "Good government should maintain the balance where every individual may have a place if he will take it, where every individual may find safety if he wishes it, where every individual may attain such power as his ability permits, consistent with his responsibility." Here was the old language of equal opportunity, of a hardworking government that would help those who worked hard, of the rejection of something for nothing. The book's title was *Looking Forward*.

However, like Wilson two decades earlier, Roosevelt in office would run into the solid, cold realities of the Machine Age. His "Brain Trust"—

the wise academic experts whom Roosevelt made his advisors and on whom he relied to formulate his agenda—understood this from the very beginning. According to Raymond Moley, the chief of the Brain Trusters, he and his colleagues wanted to end "the thoughtlessness and aimlessness of free competition." His words dripping with condescension, Moley said the group was unanimous in their resolute "rejection of the traditional Wilson–Brandeis philosophy that if America could once more become a nation of small proprietors, or corner grocers and smithies under spreading chestnut trees, we should have solved the problems of American life."

The centralized power of industrial America, its dependency on efficient planning, its hierarchical, assembly line thinking did not mesh with Jeffersonian ideas about faith in the person "at the bottom of the economic pyramid" and helping each individual to choose their own course. Once Roosevelt considered the magnitude of both the trauma with which the American people were living and the industrial transformation in American life, the Brain Trusters did not have great difficulty in convincing him of the necessity of augmenting government's power over that of individuals. "It is the inherent duty of the Federal Government to keep its citizens from starvation," he said. He would do whatever it took to accomplish that—especially if it meant rejecting a theory that had proven shop-worn anyway.

In his National Recovery Administration, Roosevelt picked up the idea that government must expand its power over private enterprise. Those businesses that accepted Washington control were allowed to put up a placard with a blue eagle in their window. The poster read: "We do our part." As FDR prepared to deliver his Fireside Chat unveiling the National Recovery Administration, Moley asked him whether he felt comfortable with the "enormous step" being taken in the speech toward the New Nationalism's philosophy of centralized planning and away from the New Freedom's promotion of free enterprise. Roosevelt pondered the matter for a moment and blithely replied, "I never felt surer of anything in my life than I do of the soundness of this passage."

Throughout the New Deal, in all of its incarnations, FDR sometimes employed the New Freedom's rhetoric, but never its outlook. When he did strike a blow for real competition and against corporate attempts to lock in their power, as he sometimes did during what historians term "the second New Deal," it was usually only a stick to impel big businesses to act in responsible ways—not an attempt to actually break down concentrated power and remake the economy. The dream of Osawatomie would be fulfilled in the New Deal. For the rest of the twentieth century, American government—under Democrats and Republicans alike—would function under the idea that a big government was needed to stand up to the other big powers in the country and stand up for "the forgotten man" without a champion.

In *The Next American Nation,* his 1995 tome arguing for a Democratic embrace of the mind-set of Hamilton, Croly, and Theodore Roosevelt, Michael Lind complains that "Hamilton is missing from the American pantheon, a victim of the rather devious effort of New Deal propagandists in the thirties and forties to paint FDR as an heir to the Jefferson-Jackson Southern Democrats and disguise the actual roots of New Deal statism in the Federalist-Whig-Republican-Progressive tradition." On this, Lind is right. Writing thirty-five years earlier, historian Merrill Peterson concurred: "In many respects, the New Deal's prophet was Herbert Croly. Its administrative theory and practice, its fiscal apparatus, its political economy were Hamiltonian." When it came to policy and not just politics, works and not just words, the New Deal owed more to Hamilton than Jefferson, more to Teddy Roosevelt than Woodrow Wilson, more to Croly than Brandeis. Up to a few years ago, the same could be said of American society. The same can still be said of American government.

When the Jefferson Memorial was completed, Franklin Roosevelt had a clump of trees near the Tidal Basin torn down so that he and every future president would have a clear view of the memorial and a constant reminder of its meaning. But the memorial was more a mausoleum than a monument. FDR had shut the door on the old Jeffersonian Republic—seemingly forever. In 1960, Merrill Perterson could write, "The New Deal killed the Jeffersonian philosophy as a recognizable and usable tradition in American government and politics." Neither Democrats nor Republicans would feel comfortable with its tropes and tenets for more than two generations to come.

Like the last crinkly leaf on a barren, wintered tree, Louis Brandeis remained in Washington as a reminder of the Progressive Spring from which the New Deal flowed. He was a sainted, but far from central, figure to the New Dealers. Roosevelt referred to him as "Old Isaiah" *("I said, 'Here am I, here am I,' to a nation that did not call on my name")*. He looked askance at the cocky and gallant New Deal reformers. "As for your young men," he complained to Tommy Corcoran, the ringleader of the brash New Dealers who had come to the capital to better America, "you call them together and tell them to get out of Washington— tell them to go home." It was there, Brandeis said, "where they must do their work." But Brandeis and his ilk were living in the past *("Remember not the former things, nor consider the things of old")*. "Democrats, Democrats, why Thomas Jefferson would not speak to these people," muttered the ancient Carter Glass. Yet, Jefferson was long, long gone— and Roosevelt took his place in defining the role of government in America. Even after he too left, his spirit would live on as long as his America lived on. Every year of his presidency, on April 13—Jefferson's birthday—FDR had a funeral wreath placed by Jefferson's tomb at Monticello. The last one was placed there on April 13, 1945—as the train carrying FDR's dead body rolled through Virginia. In 1995, his memorial would be built right next to Jefferson's *("Who has announced from of old the things to come? Let them tell us what is yet to be")*.

Franklin Roosevelt closed the loop. The New Deal fulfilled the Progressives' dream by fully replacing Jefferson's government with one that responded to the circumstances of industrial America. In the age of Jefferson, when individuals had power all their own, the paths to opportunity were found in the land. "It followed from the lack of organized political life, from the atomic conditions of the backwoods society, that the individual was exalted and given fair play. The West was another name for opportunity," wrote Frederick Jackson Turner. But Jefferson's day had come to an end in Chicago in 1893. Turner mourned the loss of "the democracy of free land, strong in . . . individualism, intolerant of administrative experience." In its place, according to his biographer, Ray Allen Billington, the New Deal brought a conviction that "the federal government must supply Americans with the opportunity and security formerly provided by free land." The government would, in the words of one of FDR's heirs, create a "New Frontier."

Where the air is so pure, the zephyrs so free,
The breezes so balmy and light,
That I would not exchange my home on the range,
For all the cities so bright.

Roosevelt might claim—as he did—that this song, "Home on the Range," was his favorite, but like two-thirds of Americans he felt more at home in the cities; more comfortable with automobiles than antelopes. His New Deal completed the transformation, begun by Theodore Roosevelt and Woodrow Wilson, of America's government from one suited for an agrarian Republic to one built for an industrial democracy. The work of Frederick Turner and Frederick Taylor had come together at last. "Equality of opportunity as we have known it no longer exists," Roosevelt told the Commonwealth Club in 1932. "Our last frontier has been reached, and there is no more free land. More than half of our people do not live on the farms or on lands and cannot derive a living by cultivating their own property. There is no safety valve in the form of a Western prairie to which those thrown out of work by the Eastern economic machines can go for a new start." It was now up to a centralized, bureaucratized, hierarchical, massive government to give Americans that "opportunity," that "new start." Impersonal, regimented government programs would have to take the place of the "Western prairie." Frederick Jackson Turner died in 1932.

THE OLD DEAL

Each age is a dream that is dying, or one that is coming to birth.
—*Franklin Delano Roosevelt, Second Inaugural Address*

In the years after the Republican victory of 1994, the partisan atmosphere in Congress boiled over with bitterness. Most members of both parties concentrated on attacking the failures of their opposite numbers and defending their party's maxims from assault. Few new ideas were proposed. Rather, the angry exchanges marked the dying gasps of the New Deal debate. In 1999, during a debate over raising the minimum wage by a tiny amount, Democratic Representative Major Owens of Brooklyn said, "The only thing we can do in America that is worse than ethnic cleansing in Yugoslavia is to abolish the minimum wage." Unfortunately, he wasn't joking.

Republican Representative William Goodling gave Owens the opportunity to retract his remark and gently reminded him that "I think we can all agree that if you're being ethnically cleansed, there is nothing worse than that."

Owens snapped back, "That's your opinion."

Owens' words were remarkable not because of their harsh tenor, which was all but routine, but rather because of the stakes involved: they came in defense of a proposal to raise the minimum wage by 50 cents in each of the following two years. A wise and needed idea to be sure, but the extension of an idea that Teddy Roosevelt had proposed ninety years earlier—and one that was in circulation for many years prior to that. Its age alone does not make it archaic, but it would be nice if politicians like Owens felt as passionately about some new ideas as they do about TR's and FDR's old ones. Seventy years after Franklin Roosevelt defined the New Deal as "bold, persistent experimentation," its parameters have long been set: a top-down bureaucracy that sees to it that Americans in need are taken care of and protected from the sometimes brutal vicissitudes of life. While its values are in the right place, its policies are now in the wrong century—a better source of bumper stickers than of progress.

The New Deal idea of government was a landmark achievement of the American Century. Where once a stroke of bad luck—a lost job, a broken arm—could plunge a family into utter destitution, the "safety net" of government programs brought a sense of security to millions who otherwise would have lived on the edge or plunged over the side. Were it not for Social Security, the elderly in America would still disproportionately live in poverty. Were it not for federal home loans, the great post–World War II economic boom might not have lifted as many as it did into the life of the middle class. To walk away from this progress, as many Republicans would have America do, is folly. To be satisfied with it, as many Democrats would have us do, is a disgrace to all those who struggled against the established order to bring about these changes in the first place.

"Everyone has met the man who approached life eagerly and tapered off to a middle age where the effort is over, his opinions formed, his habits immutable, with nothing to do but live in the house he has built, and sip what he has brewed," wrote Walter Lippmann in *Drift and Mastery* in 1914. This is the story of twentieth-century liberalism: a rush of effort and exertion in the Progressive Era, a final victory in the New Deal, a consolidation through the 1960s, a lazy life in the easy chair—feet up, shoulders slouched, eyes resting—ever since. Throughout the century, conservatives either opposed or colluded with the New Deal government expansionists, but never succeeded in putting into practice an alternative vision of government. So, the lazy liberalism—the off-spring of Progressive and New Deal activism—still shapes Americans' understanding of government.

For all its virtues, the New Deal paradigm cannot be the end of the line for the development of American government. One of the most thoughtful of modern liberals, Professor Theda Skocpol, wrote in a 1997 book entitled *The New Majority* that the modern-day "progressives" wanted to achieve "the dream of many Progressives and New Dealers, not to mention the hope of farsighted black and white leaders during the 1960s"—"a more seamless and complete system of social insurance and family support." There is nothing wrong with such an idea, and many of her proposals are valid, but—in a time of epic change—mere, measly extensions of the New Deal are both too little and too late.

Just as a hundred years ago, the changing population of America, the evolving needs of Americans, and the failure of both parties to address those changes will combine to spark a new Progressive impulse that is likely to overthrow the established order of government. But it will not be merely the effort to revise and extend the work of the original

Progressives. This new task will mean doing in our day what they did in theirs: rethinking old notions to respond to the new nation.

As before, this will not occur without opposition. In the early 1800s, "General Ned Ludd" and his band of eponymous followers emerged from Sherwood Forest and the areas around Nottingham to attack and destroy the knitting frames that had marked the beginnings of the Industrial Revolution. They stole from the future to give to the past. Today, economic Luddites have receded from the mainstream of political debate. But both political parties are burdened with political Luddites— so in love with what once was that they protest what is coming to be at every turn. What will curtail their power in the end, however, is the same force that shut out those fighting change, be they the Populists or the "Stand-Patters," in the beginning of the twentieth century: the desires of citizens who are accustomed to changed circumstances.

Once these new voters were the assembly line workers of the factories in Pittsburgh and everywhere else Industrial America was ascendant. Today they are knowledge workers who deal with information and ideas on a daily basis; the wired workers who function in a networked, team-oriented workplace; the free agents who work for themselves; the millions and millions of Americans who work in jobs where hierarchies have been flattened, decision-making decentralized, and results made the true test of performance. Together, these new workers constitute a majority of Americans eager and ready for a new form of government.

A politics that reflects the values of the new knowledge workers and a government that is suited for the Information Age does not mean the abandonment of industrial workers or their work. It only means that they be looked at through the prism of the present. "Railroad, machinery, and scientific advances opened more farmland in the last third of the century than in the nation's previous history," wrote Robert Wiebe in *The Search for Order*. In 1860, 173 million bushels of wheat were produced. By 1890—as Industrial America was growing by leaps and bounds and the farms were being denigrated in the minds of the Populists—449 million bushels were produced. The same processes that brought science and order to the factories brought them to the farms.

So, too, the New Economy does not mean the end of American manufacturing—it merely transforms it for a new time. Only about 5 percent of today's jobs involve work on a traditional assembly line. Yet, since
1970, factory output is up 109 percent. In the past twenty-five years,
textiles are up 62 percent, coal mining up 59 percent, apparel up 55
percent, and steel up 15 percent. While the Information Age does not
mean the end of the factory—and does not, for that matter, mean the
end of the farm—it does mean that the character and values of our age
are no longer defined by industrialization. All Americans, wherever they
may work, experience the values of the Choice Revolution every day.
They will not long understand why their government must forever lag
behind.

The drive to empower individual consumers—driven by leaps in
technology and responsible for so much of America's recent prosperity—
has yet to seep its way into the nation's political agenda. While the way
most Americans live is being dramatically rearranged, contemporary
political debates have failed to understand this transformation of citizens' expectations. If George Mowry was right in noting that, before
Teddy Roosevelt and Woodrow Wilson, the solutions proposed by
politicians to the "problems spawned by the great industrial, urban, and
population changes of the late nineteenth century were essentially rural
answers to urban problems," then today's politicians are still proposing
industrial answers to Information Age problems.

Instead of rethinking government policies and bringing changes commensurate with the transformation the nation is undergoing, the nation's
leading politicians in both parties are largely divided into two unsavory
camps. The first is that of the ideological fantasists—blithely pretending
they still live in a bygone world. These are the type of politicians whom
William Allen White described as leaders "who look forward to the time
when the country will go back to the Good Old Days." Like sailors' wives
lingering by the docks until their husbands return from the sea, they bide
their time waiting for the moment when top-down government programs or top-down tax cuts come back into fashion. They refuse to consider—and reach a boiling fury at any suggestion—that an increasingly

mobile and self-reliant public has less desire for such policies and that a globalized economy makes them less viable.

The second major species in the bipartisan political taxonomy are the timid moderates—attempting to shore up Machine Age institutions while upsetting neither the status quo nor its defenders. On the Democratic side, they take a Hippocratic Oath: first, do no harm. Unfortunately, this is their second and third policy as well. The mirror-image Republicans are even worse. They swear by a Hypocritcal Oath: steal traditional Democratic language of giving power back to individual people, but never do more than make rhetorical thrusts in the direction of giving average people the same choices that the well-to-do have.

The problem lies in the fact that Republicans love individualism—it's individuals that they're less crazy about. Meanwhile, though Democrats shower benevolence on individuals in need, the notion of individualism is anathema to most of them. The gaping hole in American politics—a hollow growing larger as the Information Age heats up—is a set of policies that help individuals succeed as individuals, that marries individual abilities with individual needs.

This bottom-up vision of a Choice Revolution in government is fundamentally at odds with the outlook of the committed traditionalists in both parties who put their faith in an educated expert elite in the upper echelons of either government or corporations. They are satisfied with showering tax breaks or government benefits on their constituencies, but are unwilling to look at what ordinary Americans are increasingly coming to demand: not a redistribution of wealth, but a redistribution of power. This means taking personal decision-making ability out of the hands of distant governments and disinterested businesses and putting it into the hands of individuals.

According to Eric Goldman, the history of political progress in America can be divided into three periods. The nineteenth century consolidated Jefferson's vision of individual liberty. The politicians of the Progressive Era fought to keep open the pathways of equal opportunity. The New Dealers picked up where this crusade left off and added the drive for economic security. None turned their back on what came before.

None was satisfied with the progress of the previous era. Today, government has, once again, failed to keep pace with a changing America. If government is to re-earn Americans' trust in this new century, it must reinvent itself again and make its policies relevant to the world we are entering. Perhaps paradoxically, the way to do this is to reanimate the forgotten fighting faith of the twentieth century's dawning years, Progressivism's path not taken: the individualist, empowering philosophy of Woodrow Wilson's New Freedom. The time has come to add a fourth value to liberty, opportunity, and security—the value of choice.

Some will criticize a politics that looks toward America's Information Age future as elitist—the same charge Bryan made against the politics that paid attention to the cities and factories. In fact, the real elitism is a politics that neglects to look at the new circumstances Americans are dealing with—that allows only the lucky to share in the possibilities of the New Economy. Woodrow Wilson, as president of Princeton, said automobiles "are a picture of arrogance of wealth, with all its independence and carelessness." A few years later, he became the first president of the United States to ride in a car to his inauguration. By then, of course, Ford had sold five hundred thousand Model Ts—and the car was no longer a symbol of elitism. Today, the charge of harnessing technology and the Internet in the arena of public policy might be criticized for leaving out the millions who do not have access to these innovations. But with the amazing speed of their diffusion—and the wise government and business actions that are making this process even faster—practically every American will soon have access to the Internet and its opportunities. The last excuses for the Choice Revolution will begin to disappear and American politics will be transformed.

One of the primary ideas that ties together two centuries of progressive and reform thought in American history is the belief in equality. Throughout American history that has been grounded in the notion of equality of opportunity—the day when all Americans can rise as far and as fast as their talents and drive can take them; when the impediments to mobility will be eliminated; and when those who work the hardest can claim their fair share of the nation's bounty. Yet, other forms of equality have stepped to the fore with the times. The nineteenth century introduced the idea of equality of suffrage; the twentieth century added a concern for equality of wealth. The Choice Revolution is a new means of achieving equality of opportunity. However, it would also add to the political debate a new type of equality: equality of power—the idea that the wealthy and esteemed are not the only ones who should be allowed to rule themselves, but that all Americans should be entitled to the choices and decision-making abilities that those at the top of the pyramid take for granted.

In another age of change, Walter Weyl wrote that "Our hand is stayed by ancient political ideas which still cumber our modern brains; by political heirlooms of revered—but dead—ancestors." As much as we might revere Theodore Roosevelt's and Franklin Roosevelt's top-down Hamiltonian vision of a government big enough and strong enough to counter the forces of centralized industrialization, it no longer fits our times. But old habits die hard. In September of 1999, presidential candidate Bill Bradley told the Democratic National Committee that his was "the party that knows that, if we don't hang together, we will hang separately, and *we know that that's the only way we can counter the large power in this country.*" There once was, of course, another way to fight the privileges of large power: breaking down that power and returning it to the people— an idea that has not been actively presented to the American people in ninety years, an idea never really tried. Somewhere, however, we remember it. A month after that speech, in his first debate with Vice President Gore, Bradley was asked to name his heroes. He picked three: Jimmy Carter, Mikhail Gorbachev—and Woodrow Wilson.

BEGGING TO BE CHOOSERS

With in-demand movies on digital cable, you rule.
—*Radio advertisement, 2000*

A 20-something young man looks earnestly into the camera and declares, "We're not relying on the government." Another Choice Generation cohort follows up with, "We're not relying on the company." Moments later, this television commercial for Suretrade.com concludes with a crimson-haired young woman ending this haiku of choice, individualism, and self-reliance by announcing that "We're betting on ourselves."

And so it goes. When a commercial for Homeloan.com—an Internet service that allows one to bypass traditional financial institutions in hunting for a mortgage—ends with the words "Bureaucracy Beware," it is clear that those meant to be tremulous are found manning the window at the end of the long lines in both the Motor Vehicle departments and the mega-merged banks. "Believe in yourself" urges Ameritrade. The tagline for still another television commercial—for DiscoverBrokerage.com on-line trading—sums up the spirit of the age: "Power to the People."

The Choice Revolution has already begun to transform the business world. What does the Choice Revolution really mean for government? How would it work? As a general rule and wherever possible, government power and funds should go directly to citizens—and only rarely to institutions. Americans should have personal control over the money that government spends on their behalf, thereby putting decisions about the direction of government programs into their hands instead of those of bureaucrats. For instance, parents should decide which public school their children attend and have the funds follow the children to the schools that deserve them; unemployed workers should decide how to spend their job training benefits and choose the services they feel would be most beneficial to them; young people should decide where to invest a portion of their Social Security retirement funds and accept a greater share of both the risk and reward. Suddenly, government would become the engine of fulfilling one's own individual aspirations, not just an out-of-date, out-of-control, and out-of-touch annoyance that is ignored and avoided when at all possible.

In 1914, 24-year-old Benjamin Parke De Witt wrote that the disparate strands of Progressive thought could be woven together into three basic goals: extending the role of government, rooting out the power of privileged interests, and widening democracy. The Choice Revolution is made up of these same three goals.

This first part of the Choice Revolution is extending the role of government. Like Progressivism, the New Deal, and the New Frontier, the Choice Revolution is more an attitude, an outlook, and a set of principles than a line-by-line agenda. Its central impulse is replacing one-size-fits-all programs with programs that offer a range of options and give Americans the ability to make personal decisions for themselves. Some Americans are already blessed with such a freedom. Those who have achieved a measure of wealth—be it through luck or pluck—have the chance to choose their children's schools, their family's doctors, their own way of saving for retirement, and so forth. Once this disparity did not seem to bother many Americans. As America built a safety net in the twentieth century, Americans were willing to forgo individual choices in exchange for freedom from fear. Their own workplaces were built less on individual initiative than on collective solidarity. But Americans are no longer satisfied with this trade-off. In a 1998 poll, 12 percent of Americans said that the "proper role" of government was to "solve problems and protect people from adversity," while 35 percent said "government should stay out of people's lives so they can solve their problems without interference or regulation"—the opposing alternatives of politics' New Deal imprisonment. However, fully 50 percent said "government should help people equip themselves to solve their own problems." The nation is no longer willing to endure half powerful and half powerless. Americans want to be masters of their own destiny again. And they need a government that is much more active, energetic, and aggressive in helping them reach this goal.

The Choice Revolution's force should be felt in every aspect of government action. But four big areas—education, retirement savings, job training, and health care—best illustrate why the Choice Revolution is needed and how it would specifically work.

A central plank of the Choice Revolution is giving every parent the right and responsibility to choose—from a large menu of good options—which public school their children attend. In an Information Age where knowledge, creativity, and critical thinking define success, a high-quality education is more important than ever. But nowhere does government fall farther short than in the public school system—America's greatest, and worst, public monopoly. Paging through most any high school textbook of American history, one will run across a photograph—perhaps taken by Lewis Hine or Margaret Bourke-White—of a young child at work in a mine or factory. Their small stunted frame is so at odds with the dreary lifeless eyes which plainly knew too little of the laughter of childhood and too much of the sorrow of life for someone that age. Serenely and smugly, we shake our heads at our misguided ancestors and snicker at them for allowing such a cruel travesty to go on for so long. Yet, the chances are that this history textbook is in use in a school that—in this Information Age—does nearly as much harm to today's children's future chance of success as a youth of drudgery did to the opportunities of yesterday's children.

Nearly two decades after *A Nation at Risk* sounded the alarm on the need for education reform, changes in the public school system have inched ahead—at best. Some schools are abysmal; others provide education that is far, far worse than it should be. By now, the dismal performance of American students is legendary. In the most recent round of tests in the Third International Math and Science Study, U.S. twelfth graders placed nineteenth out of twenty-one nations in math and sixteenth out of twenty-one in science. The highest scoring American students did the worst—scoring dead last in physics when compared to the highest scoring students in other countries. The longer students stay in American public schools, the farther they fall behind the rest of the world. By twelfth grade, U.S. students are behind 95 percent of the schoolchildren tested globally. Thirty percent of freshmen entering college need remedial courses. According to U.S. businesses, 60 percent of 17-year-olds do not have the reading skills to hold down a manufacturing job. Eight out of 10 employers say that high school graduates' spelling and grammar is "poor" or "fair." One out of seven students leave high school unable to read. When asked to grade the schools, in a 1999 poll, only 9 percent of Americans gave their local schools an "A."

As these statistics and numbers show, despite the near universal rhetoric emanating from politicians and policy wonks in both political camps, the crisis in public education is not one confined to the inner cities. These ivory tower leaders see an America with public school systems divided between the urban war zones of *Stand and Deliver* or the *Beverly Hills 90210*-like high schools that are found in their own tony suburbs. Yet, between the schools with gang warfare in the cafeteria and those with Jaguars in the parking lot, are the vast majority of middle-class American public schools. If the poor urban schools furnish a clear and present danger to the lives and livelihood of our children, the vast mediocrity of most of the rest of the public schools is not just a barrier to the dream of equal opportunity but—in the New Economy—a fundamental strategic challenge to our national prosperity. Long after modern-day Henry Fords and Frederick Winslow Taylors gave up on assembly line thinking in the car business, public schools still rely on a top-down, regimented "one-size-fits-hardly-anyone" model that strangles innovation and excellence.

In confronting this basic challenge to the American Dream, the old thinking politicians of both parties have played true to form. The Treadmill Liberals want to do more of the same: build more schools, hire more teachers, put more money into the Industrial Age system in the hope that its ever more fundamental failings will be papered over with cold hard cash. As is often the case with their goals, much of what they propose is good and right, but not nearly enough. Over the past twenty years, America has doubled the amount of money it has spent on education—without an appreciable improvement in our students' performance. In certain areas, more investment is needed—but total, systemic change is needed even more.

The Blockhead Conservatives play their part in this debate beautifully as well. As usual, they seek to devolve responsibility without devolving real power—throwing their hands up in despair and giving up on public endeavor. They appropriate the Wilsonian Democratic rhetoric of choice and competition with the mirage promise of private school vouchers—a cruel hoax to play on parents who lie awake at night wishing for a better life for their children. The biggest problem with vouchers is not that they are too radical, but that they are not radical enough.

While draining funds from the public schools and giving them to private academies, these vouchers would, under most serious proposals, only go to a select small number of the poorest children and would not be nearly enough to get them out of deteriorating local schools. Under George W. Bush's plan, for instance, these vouchers would be worth only somewhere between $500 and $1,500 dollars—nowhere near the tuition of most private schools. These vouchers would be a leaky lifeboat for a lucky few that would worsen the plight of all other children. They would sacrifice America's greatest unifying institution, put public money into private hands without any accountability, and have little impact on the vast majority of schools and schoolchildren.

Both ideas are Industrial Age responses to the Information Age's first crisis. The worst part of both camps is that, faced with an urgent emergency that calls into question both America's global future and the central promise of our historic past, both are satisfied with small ambition—propping up a failing system or bringing choice and competition to a narrow few. By giving choices to every parent and bringing competition to every school, the Choice Revolution offers a better way—a bigger idea that can bring salvation to each and every child in the public school system.

Although such a plan has never been fully attempted before, it builds on charter schools, a public innovation sweeping the nation. In relying on such an innovation for inspiration, the Choice Revolution would be embracing a proud tradition. Geologists have long known that household pets can sense an upcoming earthquake before it happens. So, too, one can receive a clue of coming political realignments by observing the innovations occurring at the nation's grass roots. Those closest to the ground have a much better sense of the shifting tectonic plates of American life than those who live inside Beltways and high up in ivory towers. Before Theodore Roosevelt and the Progressives remade American politics, hundreds of men and women in disparate communities around the nation were building the psychic and physical infrastructure for the modern safety net and welfare state. These social service providers laid the groundwork for twentieth-century American government.

In 1889, long before the Progressive movement was born, Jane

Addams established Hull House at the corner of Polk and Halsted streets in Chicago's Near West Side. For its needy and immigrant clients, Hull House provided Chicago's first public baths, first public playground, and an employment bureau.

Addams' work captured the spirit of the age. In 1891, two years after Hull House opened its doors, there were six settlement houses in the nation. By 1897, there were seventy-four. In 1910, there were four hundred. Addams wrote that these settlement houses—the building blocks of modern bureaucratic government—were "an experimental effort to aid in the solution of the social and industrial problems which are engendered by modern conditions of life." Her efforts captured the imagination of Americans looking for answers to these new questions. Young people—especially young women, including William Jennings Bryan's daughter, Ruth—flocked to join her crusade. It proved a short leap from the special efforts of these social workers to the belief that government should step in on their side with similar means. Frederic C. Howe, the great early-twentieth-century urban reformer, wrote: "That the private activities of to-day will become the public ones of to-morrow is inevitable. The creche, kindergarten, settlement, playgrounds, public baths, lodging houses, hospitals were inspired by private philanthropy. They are slowly passing under public control."

By 1912, when Addams rose to second the Progressive Party's nomination of Theodore Roosevelt for president, she called the party "the exponent of that great American movement which is seeking the betterment of social conditions." That movement—and the settlement houses which embodied it—would come to be described as "spearheads for reform" by Allen F. Davis in a book by the same title. They set the parameters for the form and function of the New Deal thinking that would come to guide American government.

A century later, the building blocks of the Choice Revolution are being developed at the local level with new "experimental efforts" to address the "modern conditions of life." Yet, tellingly, instead of social services provided to help clients, today's innovators see their work as providing choices to their "customers." These men and women are, in their own way, defining the next wave of governmental activism just as surely as Jane Addams and her colleagues did in the last century. By offering Americans more choices in their most basic decisions, they are setting the outline for a new era of reform.

If settlement houses were the paradigmatic public innovation of the beginnings of the Industrial Age and the Progressive Era, then charter schools are the definitive institution of the start of the Information Age and the Choice Revolution. In 1992, the City Academy—the first charter school in the nation—opened in St. Paul, Minnesota. In 2000, there are nearly three thousand.

Yvonne Chan, the principal of the Vaughn Next Century Learning Center in Los Angeles's San Fernando Valley, is a modern Jane Addams. A tiny woman with an outsized personality, she inherited an elementary school that, in the early 1990s, was in disastrous condition. Drug deals took place on school property, a dead body was found one morning on the school's front steps. The student test scores were the lowest in the area. In 1993, under Chan's leadership, Vaughn became a charter school—a self-governing public school that is allowed to innovate by being freed from burdensome bureaucracies and regulations, but is held strictly accountable for its results. Charter schools are publicly authorized and funded schools that set their own rules and hire their own employees, but cannot discriminate, charge admission, or fall behind achievement benchmarks set down in its charter (or contract). Vaughn traded in the accepted one-size-fits-all model for rigorous goals and standards but wide flexibility as to how they are met. Today, the school's test scores are 20 points above those of neighboring schools.

In Houston, Michael Feinberg and David Levin established the public Knowledge is Power Program (KIPP) Academy. Their charter school is a stereotypical child's worst nightmare. School runs from 7:00 A.M. to 5:00 P.M. Monday through Friday in addition to class on Saturday and mandatory summer school. Kids who fail to do their homework stay after school until it is done—no matter how late. Yet, they have brought results—in both the first KIPP school in Houston's southwest Gulfton area and a spinoff academy in the South Bronx. In both areas, the students have thrived and reached the upper echelons of academic performance. "It's not all children *can* learn," says Feinberg. "At KIPP, it's all children *will* learn."

Charter schools have begun to revolutionize the public school system—not just for those students who attend them, but for all children in the community. As an article in the *Wall Street Journal* in 1999 on charter schools put it, "It's the stuffed-crust pizza theory: faced with defections in their customer base, the schools will deliver a better product to regain their market share." But a world with a limited number of charter schools also takes pressure off the rest of the school system by giving the parents who care the most an out and reducing the need to fire terrible teachers or bring up math scores. Children who remain in the regular school system are often stuck with the rankest of the rank-and-file. Charter schools have become oases of innovation in a larger desert of monopolistic cookie-cutter schools. Yet, this can no longer satisfy us. It is time to bring life to the entire desert.

Every single public school in the country should be made a charter school—by giving each school a contract that grants the freedom to innovate and experiment and freedom from restrictive red tape in exchange for a firm demand for high-end results. Children would attend the public school their parents feel is best for them, instead of the specific government-run school the bureaucracy assigns them to. By giving parents the ability to select their children's school and actual options from which to pick, the Choice Revolution would offer them two things they do not have in the public school system today: choice and choices.

This would strap the money to the backs of children instead of giving it to the schools, forcing public schools to compete against one another for students and the funds they bring with them. This force of competition would compel all schools to get better. The decision would be simple: improve or perish. Greater choice would create greater accountability.

In addition, it would give parents control over their children's education. Some parents will choose a "back to basics" school, others will choose a liberal arts school. Some parents will choose a school focused on phonics, others a school focused on foreign languages. Some will choose a school centered on "Great Books," others a school emphasizing multicultural education. Some will choose "alternative" programs, such as Sobriety High in Marin, California, others will choose schools run by religious groups or even corporations. As long as the schools live up to the standards agreed to in their contracts, each school should be allowed to choose its own course—to hire and fire principals, teachers, and janitors; to set budgets and curriculums. A given school would rise or fall based on whether parents want their children there. And parents would be required to choose wisely for their children—this new freedom would bring with it a New Responsibility that they cannot shirk.

Some parents, perhaps the top 20 percent or so of households, already have these kinds of choices. They can send their children to a private school of their choice. They can pick up and move to a different neighborhood with schools more to their liking. But the vast majority of parents are stuck with the schools in their neighborhood. They are not any less able to make decisions about their children's schooling. Their children don't deserve a lower-quality education. These parents should have the right to make choices for their kids as well.

Some will claim that such a plan—and other such ideas in the Choice Revolution—swings the balance from justice to liberty; giving parents more freedom while undermining a sense of equality in the public schools. The fact is that justice is an increasingly rare quality in the current public school system. In 1999, administrators of the Los Angeles Unified School District announced they were shelving their plan to stop "social promotion"—the practice whereby children are moved on to the next grade level even if they have not learned the skills required in the grade they are presently in. They had found that they would be required to flunk nearly half of the students in the nation's second largest school district—and nearly two-thirds of its eighth graders. These are not stupid children. They are not lazy. They are trapped in a system that is robbing them of their basic rights as Americans—a system that dares to hide from calls for reform behind the tattered skirt of justice. In the past two decades, more than 10 million Americans have reached twelfth grade without knowing how to read. Twenty million have reached twelfth grade without the ability to do the most basic math. A poor excuse for justice. As the twenty-first century dawns, it increasingly appears that, when it comes to American schools, quality need not be in conflict with equality and that liberty may be justice's last hope.

The need for the Choice Revolution is driven not only by grassroots innovation such as charter schools. The real engine for this new political outlook is the growing trust Americans have in themselves—a trust built by working in nonhierarchical, empowering businesses; living in a networked, choice-based economy; and witnessing the demographic changes that are remaking the face of American life. One example of this newfound self-confidence is the explosion in the number of Americans investing in the stock market. This, in turn, is why the Choice Revolution includes a call to allow Americans to decide how to save for their retirement—namely, to control a portion of their Social Security funds.

In *Looking Backward*, Edward Bellamy wrote of a year 2000 where people would say that investing was an "art now happily lost." In the real year 2000 more Americans are investing than ever before. In 1980, 6 million families owned mutual funds. By 1998, 44 million did. In 1965, 10 percent of American adults owned stocks. This number rose slowly and steadily—during booms and busts, expansions and contractions—to 19 percent in 1983 and to 21 percent by 1990. But during the 1990s, America turned over a new leaf when it came to investing. By 1997, 43 percent of American households owned stocks. Two years later, the number was 48 percent.

This eruption of interest in investment is not merely a product of faith in the growing stock market, but a by-product of Americans' growing faith in themselves. They are not just buying securities, they are buying into the notion that true security in the Information Age comes in the form of personal decision-making ability. This fundamental faith will likely last through any lean years that will come when the bear market awakes from its hibernation.

To be a stockholder, wrote Walter Lippmann in *Drift and Mastery*, "all I have to do is to choose some well-known stockbroker and put myself in his hands. . . . I know I can't have any foresight. I don't understand the inner workings of the business world. I'm not allowed to know. That is reserved for specialists like stock brokers and private bankers. In the modern world investing has become a highly skilled profession, altogether beyond the capacities of the ordinary shareholder. The great mass of people who saved a little money can no more deal with their prosperity on their own initiative than they can deal with disease or war on their own initiative. They have to act through representatives. Just as they need physicians and organized armies, so they have to have stock brokers, financial experts, public service commissions and the rest." This basic belief that Americans were not bright enough to understand the workings of a complex world provided the background for the Progressives' and the New Dealers' suspicion of investing when it came to the "great mass of people." The common folk were held to be simply unable to navigate their way through the thickets of ticker tape.

The Great Depression certainly did not help matters. In *Looking Forward*, Franklin Roosevelt wrote, "I believe that after the experience of the last three years, the average citizen would rather receive a smaller return upon his savings in return for greater security for the principal, than to experience for a moment the thrill or the prospect of being a millionaire only to find the next moment that his fortune, actual or expected, has withered in his hand because the economic machine has again broken down." The assumption of New Deal programs, like Social Security, was that Americans preferred the "security" of sustenance to "the thrill" of finding success. For many years, this was true.

Today, Walter Lippmann's admonition that Americans can only "act through representatives" seems a foreign concept. Franklin Roosevelt's belief that Americans preferred government-insured "security" to the security of personal control is increasingly out-of-date. In 2000, T. Rowe Price marketed their "Retirement Income Manager" investment account with footage of Roosevelt signing the Social Security Act. "In 1935, FDR introduced Social Security so millions of Americans could retire with *less worry*. Today, we're *picking up* where he left off," read their print ads. As more individualized power and individual responsibility is put into their hands at home and at work, Americans are coming to feel more confident about their own ability to decide their economic fate. This self-confidence is not just limited to the upper-income brackets. Today, half of all stock owners earn less than $60,000 a year. With this confidence comes a growing demand that they be allowed to exercise control over their own retirement savings—the Social Security funds that are a sacred trust between the American people and their government.

Part of this demand comes from a perception that Social Security is fiscally unstable and unsound. In an infamous early 1990s poll, more young people believed in UFOs than believed that Social Security would be there for them when they retired. This, however, might say more about the number of young adults who believe in little green men (46 percent) than it does about the long-term stability of America's premier entitlement program. While the actuarial tables and changing age demographics point toward a need for reform, Social Security will not run out of money for generations to come. The budget surplus means that Social Security reform can be dodged if balancing the books is the only question.

For most in Washington, this is good enough. However, for more and more Americans, the status quo is no longer satisfying. Social Security's initial goal of lifting elderly Americans out of poverty has been largely met. But increasingly Americans are looking for something else from the system—the same choices they have in other aspects of their lives; the same choices the wealthy have when it comes to their retirement today. This is especially true of the Choice Generation, for whom Social Security's impersonal regimentation is more alien than any flying saucer. In the huge increase in the number of Americans owning stock, nowhere has there been a bigger jump than among young people. In fact, while only 27 percent of Americans over 75 own stocks, 42 percent of American adults under 35 have made these investments.

Driving both the generational and the general dissatisfaction with Social Security is the impetus of technologies that put more and more power into the hands of individuals. In one 1997 survey, 51 percent of the "Super-Connected"—the fast-growing segment of the population that lives in a world with cell phones, laptops, pagers, and home computers—thought Social Security "needs truly major reform." When it came to the dwindling number of Americans left out of this world, only 33 percent concurred. The cry for more choice in Social Security is not about the system being bankrupt, but about change in Americans' lifestyles and expectations. Just like the Kansas farmers of the Populist Era, some Americans have yet to experience this new world. But, in the years ahead, most every American will—metaphorically—move to Brooklyn. When they do, the plea for more personal control over their retirement dollars will only grow.

However, when it comes to Americans' retirement years, all that glitters is not best for the old. The avoidance of total risk is a hallmark of Social Security that should not be sacrificed. The Blockhead Conservatives peddle the idea of a complete privatization that would leave Americans totally in the lurch in the event of an economic catastrophe. This would undermine the very spirit of the system.

On the other hand, Treadmill Liberal opponents of Social Security choice see a stupid and callous country where Americans are too soft-headed to manage their own money and too hard-hearted to help the less fortunate unless they are tethered to them through a huge and antiquated Ponzi scheme. Instead, Americans should—for the first time— be guaranteed a minimum Social Security benefit, come what may. This should be coupled with the freedom to choose to invest a portion of their Social Security payroll taxes as they see fit. In the 1990s bull run on Wall Street, the wealthiest 10 percent of American households received nearly 90 percent of the profits. All Americans should have a greater chance to share this prosperity—and a greater choice in how to achieve it.

In a 1998 survey, Americans were given three choices as to the future of Social Security. Seventeen percent chose to "leave the system as it is and make changes such as reducing benefits to make the trust fund last longer." Fifteen percent wanted to "privatize the entire Social Security system." But, 61 percent chose to "leave much of the Social Security system as it is, but make it easier for individuals to invest a portion of their payroll taxes in personal savings accounts." Most important, 55 percent held on to the belief in private accounts even when confronted with the

specter of a market downturn where "individuals could be left with little retirement savings." It is very possible that these poll numbers are not
just brave talk in the midst of a booming stock market, but reflective of
the ethos of the age. In a recent television commercial for E* Trade, a
balding middle-aged-to-be man is sitting in his cubicle, trading stocks
on-line. His stock goes through the roof and he prances through his
office's hallways, kissing colleagues and knocking over stacks of papers.
He marches past the receptionist into the lair of his boss—a Mr.
Dinky—and announces that he quits. But by the time he returns to his
desk, his stock has plummeted back to Earth. What is remarkable is that
the "Mr. Dinky" commercial is for, not against, on-line trading. Individual responsibility and acceptance of risk is an understood trade-off
for increased personal choice.

Americans' greater participation in the stock market has implications
even beyond attitudes toward Social Security. It is another reason they
are coming to reject the stock answers of the political past. While many
conservatives look at the rising number of investors and salivate at the
prospect that Americans will come to see themselves more as tax-cut
seeking Wall Street capitalists than government program-dependent
Main Street workers, the real outcome is probably neither of these two
dated, twentieth-century outlooks. As the *Los Angeles Times'* Ron Brown-
stein, perhaps the nation's most farsighted political commentator, put it,
Americans investing in the market "are likely to demand reforms that
give them more choices: innovations such as charter schools and individually controlled investment accounts that would supplement, not
replace, Social Security. The millions of investors plunging into the market are mostly hunting for a better return, but they are also displaying a
desire for personal control that is likely to be a hallmark of politics in
the next century."

Where else will this personal control come to be exercised? The
increasingly important world of job training is another natural arena for
the Choice Revolution. In 1994, President Clinton called for a consolidation of hundreds of different job training programs into a single
voucher that displaced employees could use in a number of different

ways. Republicans in Congress responded by passing the buck and sending the money to the fifty states. Thus it is now up to the states to give working Americans the freedom to choose which way to manage their own transition to the New Economy. In a world of big businesses bleeding jobs and growing numbers of workers displaced by technology and globalization, job training is a fundamental imperative for the nation's prosperity and for the job prospects of millions of Americans. Lifelong learning is now a necessity, not a luxury.

According to Peter Plastrik, formerly an economic development official in Michigan, job training vouchers would allow workers to "buy the job search, skill assessment, job placement, career counseling, education, and training services of *their* choice, instead of the choice of some government employee." The intrinsic value of this goes beyond both Distrust-Busting and the demands of a rising Choice Generation: "Putting displaced workers in the driver's seat with vouchers would reap a number of benefits. First, workers would take charge of their careers, making better decisions than bureaucrats. Second, competition among private and public service providers would create a market dynamic likely to lead to innovations and improvements. Third, competition would create accountability for performance—dissatisfied customers could 'vote with their feet,' taking their business to more effective providers. And fourth, the bureaucracies that lord over the current program would be reduced." Workers would be able to use these vouchers with headhunters and temp firms, at for-profit training institutes and nonprofit organizations, at community colleges and—of course—at government agencies. Most important, workers themselves would be in the driver's seat—making the final decision for themselves about what advice, services, and skills they want and need.

The health care arena is another area desperately in need of the transfer of power inherent in the Choice Revolution. Unfortunately, health care reform during the 1990s highlighted the limitations of the options presented by both parties. Republicans either ignored the issue or presented small ideas such as tax breaks for Medical Savings Accounts—health care plans featuring low premiums and high deductibles. Democrats began the decade with an attempt to create a centralized, bureaucratized national health care system and ended it by proclaiming their satisfaction with "small steps."

The current rage in Washington is the bitter fight over a "Patient's Bill of Rights"—consumer protections in dealing with health insurance organizations. It would put more power into the hands of government regulators and trial lawyers in order to clamp down on abuses. There is nothing objectionable about the idea. In fact, it is good and necessary, but it is not nearly enough. If more Americans had choices about their health plan—and didn't have to take whatever was chosen for them by their employer or the government—they would have more bargaining power, would have more say in their own health care, and would get better service from doctors, hospitals, and insurers. The Choice Revolution would give Americans the right to pick their own health plan from a range of choices, putting power in their hands and taking it out of those of bureaucrats in government agencies or HMOs.

Instead of giving up on universal health care, the Choice Revolution would achieve it by putting power and responsibility in the hands of individual Americans. Just as all Americans must send their kids to school and save for their retirement, every American should be required to have health insurance—either on the job or individually. To make this possible, a system of tax credits and grants should be put in place to help those who cannot afford to purchase coverage. The tens of millions of Americans without health insurance present not only a moral crisis, they represent a threat to public and fiscal health. Because they do not have access to preventive care and do not see a doctor until they absolutely have to, they often end up in the emergency room far sicker than they would be otherwise. Because they are not turned away from care, Americans who do have health insurance end up footing the bill in the most expensive possible way.

This system of universal coverage for all would ensure Americans not only better health, but more power. If Americans chose which health plan they wanted instead of relying on their employer, they would have more decision-making power about their health care and more bargaining power with their health plan. Under the Choice Revolution, the two big issues of health care in the 1990s—access and quality—would be handled together in an Information Age reform far more ambitious than anything offered by the two parties today.

As befits an Information Age political ideology, the Choice Revolution is contingent on providing Americans with the information they need to make wise decisions for themselves. In the world of Walter Lippmann, information was a scarce commodity. His cry of "I'm not allowed to know" was not limited to the stock market. This was another reason Americans had to rely on experts and "specialists" to make decisions for them. However, today Americans are swimming in facts just about everywhere they turn. They can compare the prices of a hundred different camcorders with a few mouse clicks and compare the quality of a dozen different cell phones with a few more clicks. In some years, *TV Guide* makes a larger profit than the four television networks combined. But if Americans are to make decisions for themselves as promised by the Choice Revolution, they will need access to even more information. That means tests in schools that allow parents to compare students, teachers, and schools against national and international benchmarks. It means rating health care plans, hospitals, and doctors. It means detailed, useful, and useable information on the history and results rendered by every provider of every service that Americans will be able to choose from.

Education, retirement, job training, health care—these are just some of the areas where the Choice Revolution would give every American decisions to make and the power to make them. Areas such as child care, after-school care, and pensions are also ripe targets, and many more areas will become apparent as America continues to change.

Over the past decade, those who have thought about the impact of the Information Age on government have, almost universally, taken an extremely narrow view. They have sought to use the implements of the Information Age (computers and the Internet) but not its impetus (decentralization of power and the desire for personal choices). For instance, with the "IowAccess Network," Iowans can renew their driver's licenses, register their cars, apply for hunting and fishing licenses, and reserve campsites on-line. States around the nation—and slowly the federal government—are joining in the push to make more and more of their services accessible over the Internet. As computer access becomes ever more widely distributed, this will become increasingly important. By going on-line, Americans can spend less time waiting in line. However, it is not enough to put the same old "one-size-fits-all" services on the Internet. People dealing with bureaucracy are not frustrated just because of the long wait to get to the right window. They are dissatisfied with the services they receive once they get there. The promise of the Information Age's impact on government is not just limited to paying parket tickets on the Internet. Americans want choices and control—as well as convenience.

The Choice Revolution applies not just to those who receive government services, but to those that provide them. Putting power into the hands of individuals breaks the stranglehold bureaucracies and government contractors have on service delivery. With the Choice Revolution, the new person with new ideas—the public entrepreneur with a new way of teaching that produces better results for children, with a new method of job training that provides workers with better skills—will be able to quickly put their ideas out where people can have access to them. Today, the bureaucracy and expertocracy prevent innovation—or at least delay it for years in order to protect themselves and their way of doing things. When people can reach new ideas without impediments, failed programs will have a shorter shelf-life.

By transferring power to the people, the Choice Revolution would end bureaucracy as we know it. The bureaucracies that would still remain in areas of government transformed by the Choice Revolution would largely focus on facilitating the ability of individuals to make choices and monitoring the competing institutions (such as schools or health care plans) to make sure they live up to set standards and to their commitments.

Neither party is entirely comfortable with the parameters of this proposed Choice Revolution. Though they place a high value on the idea of diversity, many Democrats shy away from reforming government programs so that they reflect the diverse desires of those that use them. Too many Democrats believe that mechanisms which allow Americans more choice and control are not as important as continuing to expand government protections; that such instruments are, in the words of Robert Kuttner of *The American Prospect*, a "second order question." Perhaps they once were. But, in this Information Age, the demand for personal decision-making ability is a question of the first order—one not just about government's form, but about its function.

The Republican Party is usually far worse. Most of its leading politicians exhibit an icy indifference to the real effects of their drive to dismantle government and replace the hand-holding of the New Deal with the invisible hand's raw deal. Instead of the Choice Revolution's plan to raise the performance of government by introducing the market forces of choice and competition into the public sector, the unrequited Republican revolutionaries want to raze government itself—unlearning the twentieth century's lessons about government's role in providing for equal opportunities, civil rights, and a sturdy safety net.

Despite a shared premise that big bureaucracies are not the answer to twenty-first-century challenges, the Choice Revolution could not be further from Republican orthodoxy. It would not discard government's powers, but would disperse them into the hands of individuals. It would give Americans the actual ability to make decisions for themselves—not just an abstract liberty to do so. It offers an activist government that uses government power to give average Americans choices and decision-making power—the options that the wealthy elite already enjoys. The Choice Revolution builds on the progress the Progressive movement bequeathed to America in the past century. As E. J. Dionne has written, "The difference between this era's conservatives and the American progressive tradition lies in the distinction between two phrases, 'freedom from' and 'freedom to.'" Conservatives still focus on freedom from taxes, freedom from regulations, freedom from government. Americans in the twentieth century came to demand freedom to be healthy, freedom to get an education, freedom to work without fear. Now, those who believe

in both progress and the modern world need to add a new freedom—
the freedom to choose, the freedom to set one's own course.

Most fundamentally, the Choice Revolution is at odds with the inside
Washington crowd's view of America and is an insult to their view of
themselves. The fact is that many of those who run our government love
the "for the people" part—it's the "of the" and "by the" that they're less
sure about. The governing class in both parties simply doesn't trust
Americans to make the most basic decisions about their own lives. And
it believes that by virtue of its education and righteousness it is better
able to make those decisions than the people themselves.

"If I thought that the American people were reckless, were ignorant,
were vindictive, I might shrink from putting government in their
hands," said Woodrow Wilson in 1912. Unless we think this about
Americans today, we should not shrink from putting decision-making
power over their own lives in their own hands. Unfortunately, too much
of America's educated elite believes just this. They look out on the country and see a bunch of Jerry Springer-watching, Dorito-munching, flip-
flop-wearing, Yoo-Hoo-drinking yahoos. This has been the price of a
century of industrial progress that relied on rigid regimentation and
strict hierarchies. In an Information Age that relies on the skills of each
and the inherent genius of all, this is a price we can no longer afford to
pay. Ordinary Americans do not love their children any less than the
wealthy, but the elite does not trust them to decide where they send their
kids to school. Ordinary Americans do not care any less about their
golden years, but the elite does not believe they have the intelligence or
responsibility to plan for their future. Ordinary Americans want good
jobs that will help them provide for their families, but the elite does not
think they understand the economy well enough to decide what kind of
training they need. Once this sanctimonious sympathy could define
government's worldview. That time has passed. "I'm a Democrat," said
Nebraska Senator Bob Kerrey in 1998, "because I believe in the dignity,
not the density of every American. I'm a Democrat because I believe
Americans need a partner not a parent. I'm a Democrat because I believe
in the people and because I believe in the people more than I believe in

the individuals that walk before me and say they've got good opinions because they have the letters P. H. and D. after their name. Or anybody else whose bank account is sufficiently large that they can handle their affairs on their own."

Today, Americans' freedom of choice is imprisoned. Someone is going to free the average citizen, someone is going to break the public trusts and the public's distrust, someone is going to give decision-making power to those who most need it. The only question is who and how soon. Fifty years ago, in *The Vital Center*, Arthur Schlesinger wrote that "Most men prefer to flee choice, flee anxiety, flee freedom." Today, those words could not be more false. Over the past two decades, all around the world, people have put their lives at risk in order to join the rush toward freedom. The dustjacket of the first edition of *The Vital Center* said the book contained "the main outlines of a 'new radical program'—a militant liberalism which would once more make freedom a faith worth fighting for." Today, with freedom ascendant around the world, a muscular, modern, reform progressivism must bring the battle home and build on Americans' faith in their own freedom. That is the faith of the Choice Revolution.

NEVER WAS SO MUCH OWED
BY SO FEW TO SO MANY

Every monopoly and all exclusive privileges are granted at the expense of the public. . . . It is to be regretted that the rich and powerful too often bend the acts of government to their selfish purposes. . . . Every man is equally entitled to protection by law; but when the laws undertake to add to these natural and just advantages artificial distinctions, to grant titles, gratuities, and exclusive privileges, to make the rich richer and the potent more powerful, the humble members of society—the farmers, mechanics, and laborers—who have neither the time nor the means of securing like favors to themselves, have a right to complain of the injustice of their Government.

—*Andrew Jackson*, Bank Veto Message, *1832*

A decade ago, any pundit worth her or his saltiness would have proclaimed that Americans just didn't care about the issues of budget deficits and national debt. But when Americans were probed deeper on the question, it turned out Americans cared about these issues very deeply—not because of an imbalance in the accounting tables, but because of the fundamental imbalance of values inherent in a government with the arrogance to spend more than it had. Today, unchastened, these same pundits maintain that Americans don't really care about campaign finance reform and the influence of money in politics. Once again, it all depends on the question asked. Americans may not get exercised about soft-money or spending caps, but they are increasingly angered by the expanding influence of powerful special interests who game the political system to their own ends. They are fuming at a government that allows the privileged few to overpower the quiet voice of Main Street interests and mainstream values. They have every right to be angry.

The second plank of Progressivism was removing what Benjamin Parke De Witt called the "corrupt influence in government." The Choice Revolution would pick up that fallen standard. New means of cleaning up the political system form the second part of the Choice Revolution.

Americans might be surprised to find that the influence of special interests in government is both smaller and larger than they might suppose. On one hand, contrary to the public's suspicions, the quid pro quo—the furtive handshake and the briefcase bulging with crisp hundred dollar bills—almost never happens. On the other, the actual influence of moneyed powers is more pervasive and more insidious than they might suspect. The daily, omnipresent contact with individuals of great wealth warps the process by pushing their particular voices and peculiar concerns into the forefront of the politicians' attentions. Politicians' attempts to curry the favor of the powerful are necessarily funded by all the American people. In most every policy decision that politicians make, one of the—if not *the*—first questions they ask themselves is where the relevant interest groups come down on the matter.

They rarely have to wonder for long. In the past generation, political lobbying has become a major industry. In the 1980s, Democrats in Congress revolutionized politics by making the shakedown common practice—selling out their values and their votes for campaign contributions. In 1994, Republicans promised to get the lobbyists out of the corridors of Congress. In power they kept that promise—by bringing them into the committee rooms and having them write legislation themselves.

The influence and power of special interests and their mercenaries grew significantly in the late 1990s. With the collapse of both parties' governing ideologies, there is less resistance to the demands of the influence peddlers. Without an agenda to say "yes" to, politicians have little incentive to say "no" to the special favors demanded by the powerful interests. In September of 1997, the month after the balanced budget was signed on the White House lawn, 14,969 lobbyists were registered with the Senate Office of Public Records. By June of 1999, that number had swelled by a shocking 37 percent to more than 20,000 lobbyists. In 1998, special interests spent $1.42 billion lobbying Congress, the White House, and the federal bureaucracy—up by 13 percent in only one year. This number does not include the lobbying in 50 state capitals, in cities, and in counties across the country. It does not include the "grassroots" lobbying efforts that manufacture evidence of public sentiments and flood congressional offices with carbon-copy outraged postcards. It does not include the campaign contributions that give the lobbyists entree to the feeding frenzy and are the politicians' favorite entree at the feast. The numbers do serve as a reminder of what happens when leaders are lost and the public disgusted. Without a path forward, Washington insiders have concentrated their energies on doling out government favors and budgetary beneficence to big corporations in the form of tax breaks and special subsidies. America has been left with a government of the bureaucrats, by the lobbyists, for the special interests.

A century ago, attacking political corruption meant fighting political machines that were interested almost solely in protecting their own partisan power. Today, the threat to clean campaigns and good government comes less from political bosses than it does from the corporate chieftains who insist on special favors from the politicians they support. In the beginning of the twentieth century, Senator Nelson Aldrich of

Rhode Island led the "Railway Senators"—who owed their careers and their livelihoods to the railroads that owned their votes—in preventing any legislation to regulate the railroads' power. Today, politicians are no longer on corporate payrolls, but the need to feed at the corporate campaign trough impels many to railroad through legislation granting special favors to powerful interests. For instance, the nonpartisan General Accounting Office estimates that taxpayers spend $60 billion a year to subsidize the Florida sugar-growing empire of the Fanjul family. The cost to Americans is even higher than that. It comes in the environmental degradation of the Florida Everglades, the abysmal treatment of migrant farmworkers processing raw sugar, and sugar prices that are more than twice as high as in the rest of the world. But all this is far less surprising when it is learned that of the four Fanjul brothers, one served as the co-chair of Bill Clinton's 1992 Florida campaign and another was Bob Dole's national finance vice chair in 1996. The family donates major dollars and they get their money's worth.

The most appalling corruption in politics today is not the kind found on the television news magazines during sweeps month—the hidden camera, the wad of bills, the celebratory cigar. The corruption that cameras cannot catch is the corruption of the ideals of both parties. For Democrats, corporations become just one more interest group to appease and buy off—even if it means taking taxes from those who shop at the Price Club to enrich those who lounge at the country club. Some of those who call themselves "pro-business" Democrats are among the worst offenders—trying to prove their economic credentials by lavishing largess on those who need it the least. For Republicans, their commitment to special favors for the rich and powerful lays bare the fact that their commitment to the free market often applies only to the weak and defenseless. When it comes to their golf buddies' interests, the "invisible hand" is easily handcuffed.

Unfortunately, these subsidies and tax breaks do not come without a cost. They are harmful for three reasons: they weaken the economy, they weaken the budget, and they breed distrust. Special interest subsidies and corporate tax breaks hurt the economy by stifling innovation, inhibiting competition, and transferring hard-earned money from the weak to the strong. Especially in a global economy, giveaways to corporations mean Americans' tax dollars flow into the eager hands of corporate fat cats in Kuala Lumpur or Amsterdam.

In 1938, the Commissioner of Inland Revenue (the predecessor agency of the IRS) received this note: "I am enclosing my income tax return for the calendar year 1937, together with my check for $15,000. I am wholly unable to figure out the amount of the tax." The epistle came from President Franklin Delano Roosevelt at a time when the tax code was a mere shadow of its present size. The original tax code was 14 pages long. Today, it is 17,000 pages thick. Its length and complexity—contrary to the rhetoric of Steve Forbes and other flat taxers—does not come from deductions encouraging charitable donations or reducing student loans. It comes from the myriad of special exemptions for the wealthy and powerful, hidden from all but the most sophisticated accountants.

The tax system today is not one of "progressive" taxation as much as it is one of "protective" taxation—shielding corporations from the need to innovate, from the demand that they lower their prices and raise their quality, from struggling competitors trying to break through. When well-connected pressure groups buy a tax code larded with loopholes and a budget bursting with tailor-made subsidies, they are able to block new enterprises and entrepreneurs. When the "Bigtime Widget Producers" company gets a subsidy to do their work, they can effectively prevent anyone else from entering their market even without having to produce a better product. When the "Association of Kansan Surfing Instructors" gets a tax break for their members, their neighbors in Nebraska can't compete in the same business. The budgetary lottery has picked the winners. If too much of big labor seeks protectionism abroad, then too much of big business fights for protectionism at home—and too few in either party are willing to say no to both on behalf of average citizens.

Second, special subsidies and tax breaks harm the budget. In his fascinating yet ultimately sadly pessimistic book, *Government's End*, Jonathan Rauch describes a process he calls "demosclerosis"—the steady,

unremitting blockage of the arteries of our democracy with special interest provisions that inhibit the flow of public action. Even in this era of
bulging surpluses, government is constrained by a seeming straitjacket
that prevents any actions with a modicum of monetary ambition. More
and more of government's money has been accounted for; less and less
is left to the discretion of contemporary leaders. By some accounts, over
$100 billion a year is allocated to special subsidies and tax breaks. When
the "public-private partnerships" that give bragging rights to all involved
end up funding activities businesses ought to do themselves, they simply add to a budget that is increasingly the purview of special interests.
Year after year, these subsidies stay in place—untouchable, unquestion-
able, and unnecessary.

Third, the certitude that the powerful are gaming the system to their
own ends breeds public distrust of government. A May 1999 political
cartoon ran with the title: "Corporate Welfare: The Cycle of Dependency." It featured a father in a gray business suit and red tie sitting down
next to his young son, in baseball cap and jeans, on the couch and telling
him: "My father wrote everything off, I write everything off, and soon
you too will be writing everything off." The same public anger which
built up for a generation against a welfare system that transferred money
from those who worked hard to those who refused to do their own share
is building against big businesses which milk their power to ease their
way with government handouts.

One hundred years ago, big corporations had a different boondoggle:
it was called the tariff and it was a political hot button for generations.
Visiting America in 1889, Rudyard Kipling noticed that Americans felt
extremely strongly about the tariff—especially if they were Democrats
and especially if they were drunk. Barroom boozers argued about the tariff not because of a deeply held Ricardian faith in free trade, but because
of a central conviction that the tariff was fundamentally unfair to the
interests of ordinary working people. It guarded the fortunes of the elite
while raising prices for everyone else.

Today, the public has a similar certitude when it comes to the tax
code. What most infuriates them is not whether they are taxed at 28 per-

cent or whether the capital gains tax is indexed, but the knowledge that those who can afford an army of lawyers and lobbyists are able to shirk their obligations while everyone else is stuck holding their bill.

Americans don't hate successful businesses or the wealthy—these are basic elements of the American Dream. What they despise is basic unfairness—when cheaters seek to play by their own rules. "Big business is not dangerous because it is big, but because its bigness is an unwholesome inflation created by privileges and exemptions which it ought not to enjoy," said Woodrow Wilson accepting the Democratic nomination in 1912. When Americans see tax dollars flowing from the pocketbooks of the many into the pockets of the few; when they hear about budgetary boondoggles that insulate the powerful from the same struggles endured by everyone else, they come to feel that government is the private playground of the powerful—and they are outside the fence, looking in.

With politicians pledging to take on special interests in campaign after campaign, the presumption is that nothing can be done. But if the economy is to lose its shackles, if entrepreneurs are to have a clear path to innovation, and if Americans are to trust that government is looking after their interests and not the special interests, then something must be done to stay the greedy hand of the powerful. If the Choice Revolution is to succeed, the powerful cannot be allowed to use government to prop up their outdated ways or to block Americans' abilities to make their own decisions.

The first step is for erstwhile campaign finance reformers to take a broader view on the problem of money in politics. Campaign finance reform, while necessary and important, attacks the symptoms and not the cause: the pervasive influence of powerful special interests in the political system. Some reformers concentrate on stemming the demand of politicians for campaign funds. Others focus on limiting the flow of money into campaign coffers. But all too few reformers pour their energies into cutting off the rotten relationship between public and private power that is the spring from which campaign cash flows.

Limitations and restrictions on campaign funds should certainly be enacted, but they are not enough. Although some individuals and interest groups give to politicians on the basis of shared beliefs and common causes, many corporations and pressure groups give to candidates on the basis of expected results. For powerful interests concerned with the bottom line, donations are not tendered out of the kindness of their hearts; for them, it's an investment in a government with the power to make or break their business success. Private funds will always find a way to affect the political process—if they can secure a beneficial outcome. The task for reformers should be to limit not only the funds, but the reason for the funds in the first place. By getting rid of the subsidies and the tax breaks, and by limiting politicians' abilities to put them back in place, reformers will give the powerful less incentive to play games with the political system.

There is no magic way to do this in the absence of political leadership willing to stand up to special interest power. And political backbone is rarely found outside the presence of public backup. The American people will have to demand that politicians stop doing the bidding of powerful corporations and interest groups. Fortunately, the Y2Kampaign featured more discussion of campaign finance reform than ever before in recent history.

In the end, however, relying on the politicians to do right and the people to pay attention is a time-tested way to avoid to real reform. As with the Progressives, the Choice Revolution has to build in real checks on the power of the corrupt. One way to do this has been proposed by Robert Shapiro, formerly of the Progressive Policy Institute, and introduced as legislation by Senators John McCain and Joseph Lieberman. It would break the stranglehold of the special interests by establishing a Corporate Subsidy Reform Commission. This would be modeled on the Military Base Closing Commission—which was established when the political process proved incapable of deciding which installations should be shut down after the end of the Cold War. Then, each politician defended the military base in their community at all costs, much as politicians guard the subsidies for their favored—and favoring—interest group. The Corporate Subsidy Reform Commission would systematically evaluate all industry- and firm-specific programs and recommend to Congress and the president the repeal or reform of those tax breaks or giveaways that serve no overriding social or national purpose. Congress would then have to take the Commission's recommendations and vote them up or down—with no amendments.

However, limiting the power of the privileged few by bypassing the democratic process is a clever dodge, not a real solution. True reform won't come unless the power of democracy is strengthened as well. The special interests are able to exert their influence not because democracy doesn't work, but because it has been perverted—with political power concentrated in the hands of Washington legislators, lobbyists, and bureaucrats. If the Choice Revolution were to return that power to ordinary people, the will of the special interests would be stymied.

As Jonathan Rauch points out, taking decision-making power out of Washington and giving it to citizens would greatly limit the ability of the special interests to use government to end-run the competitive market. No longer would government subsidies be able to block off their competitors and shut off their need to compete. When Americans have choices in issues like education, health care, and retirement, then these decisions and others will get made on the basis of what works best for them, not which corporation is able to get government's blessing for their product. Instead of lobbying a few hundred members of Congress and bureaucrats, firms that want the public to use their services would have to try to win the allegiance of hundreds of millions of Americans. And wouldn't that be a pleasant change of pace?

HEAR THE PEOPLE RULE

Go tell your master that here the People rule!
—*Mirabeau, answering Louis XVI's messenger's call*
for an adjournment of the Estates General, 1789

America is a nation built on a notion: that we are all created equal and endowed with equal rights. The story of the nation's history can easily be

seen as an attempt to be worthy of—and live up to—this original Jeffersonian faith. "The arc of history is long," wrote Reinhold Niebuhr, "but
it curves towards justice." We rarely get it right at first and never get it
right always, but in the long view, we grow progressively more just. In
America, the arc is long as well—but, in the end, it curves, most of all,
toward democracy. In our saddest moments, we have turned away from
this struggle and have failed to live up to the faith of the Founders—a
faith they never fully lived up to either. However, the role of the most farsighted leaders in American life has been to speed the curve, to tighten
the arc, to bring a richer and fuller democracy to ever more Americans.
Woodrow Wilson said democracy was "always a-making," a process of
progress, a goal never quite reached.

The greatest generations in American history have endeavored to
expand democracy—in both its scope and its institutions. In the time
of Jefferson and Jackson, the ability to vote and elect leaders was transferred from the tight grip of the wealthy landowners into the hands of
the common farmers and laborers. At the same time, the old "King's
Caucus," which vested power in the hands of the politicians, was
replaced by political conventions and other elements of a participatory
democracy that bound Americans together.

In Lincoln's era, Americans fought a war over whether people of a different skin tone could be counted as full citizens—even as full humans.
Moreover, his generation saw an era of expanding connection between
people and politicians—not just the Lincoln–Douglas debates, but
lyceum addresses and handbills that appealed to a more literate voting
public.

In the Progressive Era, the widening of democracy was one of three
themes identified by Benjamin Parke De Witt. Direct election of senators,
the merit system for government jobs, the secret ballot, the initiative, and
the referendum all made government more responsive to citizens and
increased their power. Concurrently, this period saw the woman's suffrage
movement finally succeed with the Nineteenth Amendment to the Constitution, guaranteeing women the right to vote.

The 1960s saw the flowering of political primaries that brought the
nominating process out of the back rooms and into the ballot box, the

final destruction of the old-time political machines, the one-person-one-vote rule, and the elimination of the poll tax. Together with this came the civil rights movement and the elimination of the last barriers keeping Americans from the right to vote.

The Choice Revolution would expand the institutions and the scope of democracy as well. In his 1915 testimony before the U.S. Commission on Industrial Relations, Louis Brandeis said that "It is absolutely essential in order that men may develop that they be properly fed and properly housed, and that they have proper opportunities of education and recreation. We cannot reach our goal without those things. But we may have all those things and have a nation of slaves." Today, we are still struggling toward the goal of seeing that all Americans are properly fed and housed, that they have opportunities of education and recreation. This struggle will continue. But as Brandeis said so long ago, in words that were ignored then and now, it is not enough. We must expand the scope of our democracy as well.

Brandeis was right when, discussing the centralized structures of the Industrial Age, he said that "As long as there is such concentration of power no effort of the workingman to secure democratization will be effective." During the twentieth century, Americans had to content themselves with perfecting and providing access to one form of democracy—the ability of citizens to vote for their leaders. But democracy can be much more than this. The Information Age is fundamentally about democratization—about power to the people. We have witnessed a democratization of the workplace as more employers are giving their workers the freedom to make their own decisions on the job. We have witnessed a democratization in the marketplace as consumers have more decisions to make and more ability to shape what they buy. The challenge of the twenty-first century is to make political democracy come alive; to make democracy what John Dewey wanted it to be, not just a form of government, but a "way of life"; to make democracy mean more than elections, to make it real self-rule.

The first step in accomplishing this is to finish the job of the Progressives. One of their signature projects was the statewide initiative. After nearly a hundred years of trial on the state level, it is time to declare the initiative a success. For big-eyed ideologues and bitter partisans, such a statement is shocking. In California, where the initiative process has become a way of political life, the extremes of both parties have come to rue a process that upsets their control over the political agenda. But for voters in the middle, initiatives have become a way of getting their voice through to a political class uncomfortable with outside sentiments. Whether it was issues like environmental protection, insurance reform, illegal immigration, education, crime, and property taxes, Californians have been able to use initiatives to bring about results in areas where the politicians refused to act. Ordinary citizens understand this clearly. In a December 1998 survey of the state by the Public Policy Institute of California—taken at the close of a decade featuring year after year of expensive, emotionally wrenching initiative contests—75 percent of Californians said they thought that ballot initiatives were "the best way to address the most important problems facing" the state, as opposed to 21 percent who preferred to vest power in the governor and legislature. (In fact, Latinos were even more strongly in favor of the initiative process than the rest of the population). Sometimes the initiatives paint with too broad a brush, sometimes they throw out the baby with the bathwater, sometimes they are poorly written, sometimes they cause more problems than they solve, but the final votes are the authentic voice of citizens who are rarely heard in the political process—and their decisions are wiser than those that any small group could ever make.

It is time to amend the United States Constitution to allow citizens to gather signatures and put national initiatives on the ballot every two years at the time of congressional elections. Concerns will quickly be raised by both liberal lobbies and conservative corporations about the cost of such campaigns and the specter of "dangerous" initiatives being placed on the ballot. In the end, however, all such concerns come down to a central question of whether the American people can be trusted to make educated decisions for themselves. Those who will oppose such an amendment fundamentally believe their countrymen and women are not smart enough to resist emotion-laden entreaties and slick election campaigns.

These national initiatives would be inconvenient first and foremost for a political class that would suddenly have to listen to the hopes and fears of average voters instead of just relying on getting their business done by making deals on the cushy couches of the plush back rooms. That's why this plan should not include measures placed on the ballot by Congress in order to shirk its responsibility to come to a decision. National initiatives are not about political punting, they are about the ability of the American people to put their concerns on the national ballot—and on the national agenda.

One new innovation that will make national initiatives feasible is the advent of the Internet in political life. This will help not only in gathering signatures and reducing the cost of campaigns, but—with the growth of Internet voting—help get Americans to cast their votes. The Internet is only beginning to revolutionize the way campaigns are waged. Yet, more households are now hooked up to the Internet than had radios when FDR delivered his Fireside Chats. Just as radio and then television changed politics in their own ways, the Internet will come to do so as well.

This is not to say that the older forms of communications media will disappear. Hearst's and Pulitzer's cheap daily newspapers a hundred years ago did not replace the more sedate journals; radio did not replace newspapers, TV did not replace radio. Yet each certainly had a large impact on its predecessors. The flashy, easy-to-read, colorful *USA Today* would never have been born if this was not an age of television. Each new communications tool diminished its predecessors' power. In 1900, when the United States had a population of 75 million people, there were 2,042 daily newspapers. In 1998, when the population had more than tripled but had also been exposed to radio and television, there were only 1,489 dailies. More important, each medium changed politics and favored candidates who could use the medium of the age. The rise of Theodore Roosevelt was chronicled and assisted by the sensationalist yellow journalists who adored TR's quote-worthiness and verve. In addition, Teddy Roosevelt came along as camera technology had advanced to the point where "action" shots were first possible—and no one was a better subject for such photos. Franklin Roosevelt understood and used the radio to rally the country around himself during the Great Depression and World War II. John F. Kennedy and Ronald Reagan might never have been elected to the presidency—and certainly would have been far less effective in office—were it not for the power of television and their ability to use it.

Soon the Internet will come to demand new kinds of politicians and new forms of political leadership. It is built on conversation, not monologues. It values mounds of detailed information that voters can scan to find the facts and proposals that they care most deeply about. And its central premise is the idea of individual empowerment. Dick Morris might have had some failings in his personal life, but, as a political observer, he is often on the mark. In his book, *Vote.Com*, he writes, "In the 1960s, it was common to hear people say that their leaders had access to more information, that it was wrong to judge them without knowing all the facts. Today, we would laugh at anyone who said that on television." He is right and his basic insight will come to transform political campaigns and elections themselves: "Voters want to run the show directly and are impatient with all forms of intermediaries between their opinions and public policy."

However, if this is true for Americans as voters, it holds even more for Americans as citizens. So far, those who have sought to bring the Internet into government and politics have offered up crimped ambitions, such as Internet voting. The Internet can be more than just a way voters communicate with elected officials, more than just a way in which they can conveniently access government services. The Internet can be part of a new spirit of democracy in America that lets citizens rule themselves—making their own decisions and making their own choices. Since America was born—and increasingly during the Industrial Age—we have defined democracy as electing representatives to make decisions for us. Some commentators have recently called for "New England town meetings" on a national scale. Yet, even such an innovation would merely set policies for the elite establishment to carry out. Democracy in the Information Age can be something far richer. It need not just be something that happens every two years at election time. It need not just be something that happens at the ballot box. Democracy—the people ruling themselves—can happen every day. If Americans were able to decide for themselves which school their children attended, which health plan they joined, which means of saving for their retirement they chose, which avenue to job training benefits they selected—and if the Internet gave them access to the information they needed to make these choices—then democratic power, the power to rule, would be vested in their own hands.

The elite of both parties shudder at this thought. Sometimes it is because they think so highly of themselves, but often it is because they just don't know any better. We have all been reared in the shadow of the Progressive Era and the New Deal, which believed that the only way to help citizens was to take power from the wealthy and give it the selected, expert, enlightened few; to substitute bureaucracy for plutocracy. But as the world has changed, our politics can change too. The Choice Revolution would substitute democracy for expertocracy—creating a government built on the energies of the many, not the expertise of the few.

Two centuries ago, in his Inaugural Address, Jefferson observed that "Sometimes it is said that man cannot be trusted with the government of himself. Can he, then, be trusted with the government of others?" American democracy must be strengthened with the conviction that those who make decisions at the ballot box for everyone should be trusted to make life decisions for themselves and their families every day. "Let history answer this question," Jefferson said. The question still rings in our ears.

In *Efficiency and Uplift*, his study of how Frederick W. Taylor's scientific management shaped Progressive thinking, the historian Samuel Haber writes, "'Let the people rule' is, in part, a rhetorical phrase. Exactly how one lets the people rule is decisive. The progressives who greeted efficiency with enthusiasm were often those who proposed to let the people rule through a program in which the bulk of the people, most of the time, ruled hardly at all." Such a program, in an Information Age defined by personal decision-making, can no longer be satisfying. By putting government's decision-making power into the hands of individual citizens, the people will rule as they never have before. The meaning and spirit of democracy would be enriched and Americans would believe more strongly in the responsibility it conveys.

With his glory years behind him and with sadness creeping into his eyes, William Jennings Bryan waged his last campaign for the presidency in 1908. His campaign slogan asked America a question: "Shall the People Rule?" The answer then was no. In the coming years, a centralizing, hierarchical Industrial Age led Americans to construct a top-down government that took personal choices out of their hands and made decisions for them in exchange for security and protection from a cruel world's troubles. Today, as the economy and society change again and bring new values to the fore; as the Choice Generation rises to accept and demand personal responsibility; we can finally give a different answer. We can return to the bottom-up spirit of Jefferson. We can reenergize Wilson's vision of returning power to the people. We can renew Boy Bryan's faith in American self-rule. In fact, we can do no less.

PART III

The New Responsibility

As a nation we are becoming civically illiterate. Unless we find better ways to educate ourselves as citizens, we run the risk of drifting unwittingly into a new kind of Dark Ages—a time when small cadres of specialists will control knowledge and thus control the decision making process.

—*Woodrow Wilson, 1912*

*T*he Choice Revolution in government will not work unless it is coupled with a New Responsibility. While government should give Americans the freedom to make decisions about their children's schools or their own retirement, it must also demand that they do so, demand that they do so responsibly, demand that they accept the consequences of their choices, and demand that they work with each other toward common goals.

The Choice Revolution both depends on and breeds this New Responsibility. The Choice Revolution is impossible unless Americans are willing to accept the proposition that they can put their faith in their fellow citizens. Without stronger bonds of community, people will not trust one another to act wisely and with justice. The skeptical eyes we now turn on our neighbor are part of what has forced us to rely on a bureaucratic government to ensure our safety and well-being. At the same time, if citizens would have a greater say, they would have a greater stake—an investment in the world around them that would lead them to spend more time and energy on its affairs.

In an ever more diverse America and in an Information Age that empowers individuals and personalizes their world, the New Responsibility means government must do for citizens what the most successful modern businesses do for their employees—remind them of the duties they owe to one another and require them to work together to achieve common goals.

The Choice Revolution's support for the individual is a brand of individualism that should not be confused with a base breed of selfish narcissism. It is, rather, a building block for what Alexis de Tocqueville called "individualism rightly understood": a type of individualism in which individuals take responsibility for both themselves and those around them.

WE MANY, WE HAPPY MANY

A great city is that which has the greatest men and women. If it be a few ragged huts, it is still the greatest city in the world."
—*Walt Whitman*

On a snowy Christmas Eve in 1945, shortly after 10:45 P.M., an apprentice guardian angel named Clarence Odbody showed George Bailey the importance of community bonds and mutual obligations. In an attempt to convince George not to throw his life away, Clarence allowed him a peek of the world as it would be if George had "never been born at all" and if his Bailey Building and Loan had not served as a reminder to the citizens of Bedford Falls of what can be accomplished when people "stick together" and "have faith in each other." If Julian West in *Looking Backward* had seen a utopian world of a paternalistic, centralized government providing for the needs of its people, George Bailey in Frank Capra's film *It's a Wonderful Life* saw a dystopian vision of what happens when the attachments of community atrophy and when the idols of the marketplace reign supreme.

Despondent over the fact that he faces "bankruptcy and scandal and prison" because of the loss of $8,000, depressed that his childhood dreams of "shaking the dust of this crummy little town off my feet" and seeing the world have been dashed, George contemplates suicide until Clarence appears and shows him the world as it would have existed without him. The Bedford Falls that George knew was idyllic, but not perfect. Although its citizens struggled and pinched pennies, they were rich in friendships and the connections of community. People had time for their neighbors and the inclination to act as neighbors. And, though nobody seemed to realize it, what made this wealth of associations possible was the Bailey Building and Loan—the only "place where people can come without crawling to Potter," the wealthy businessman who ran "everything in this town *but* the Bailey Building and Loan."

Clarence shows George that without his Building and Loan, Bedford Falls descends into Pottersville—a world ruled purely by the marketplace's transactions and the government's laws. As the script notes to *It's a Wonderful Life* comment, "The character of the place has completely changed. Where before it was a quiet, orderly small town, it has now become in nature like a frontier village." Where the Building and Loan once stood, a sign flashes, "Welcome Jitterbugs." Pottersville is a world of neon lights and dancing girls; panhandlers, pawnshops, and peepshows; a harsh, hard-drinking world of burlesque halls, burly bouncers, bullets, and broken families; of fights and prostitution; of frayed nerves and short tempers; of sirens, smoke, and cold suspicion. This was the free and unfettered world that Clarence demonstrated results from a state of "no obligations."

"Strange, isn't it? Each man's life touches so many other lives, and when he isn't around he leaves an awful hole, doesn't he?" Clarence tells George. Introducing the Choice Revolution without a New Responsibility would leave "an awful hole" in Americans' civic life; a gaping chasm stemming from the belief that each can retreat into themselves and that they are not inexorably bound up into the fabric of their community. Trying to hold America together with the bureaucratic bonds of the present-day Social Security or public school systems is a poor way to unite a nation. Loosening these strictures with no notion of what can replace them is not much better.

Today, the same forces of technology and social change that are transforming the economy and government are also rendering outdated many of the community customs and institutions that served to define twentieth-century life. These forces are also slowly beginning to replace the old customs and institutions with new habits and means for the new century. Under the New Responsibility, government's task in this area would be to help speed that change in community life and play the role only it can as the focal point for common exertion.

Academics often term community the "third sector" between the market and government. But for most Americans it comes first in what they think of as their everyday lives. Community is Habitat for Humanity, a Fourth of July parade, talking to a neighbor across the fence, the NAACP, the Rotary Club, Little League and youth soccer teams, the Sierra Club, one's own family, the local soup kitchen, the National Rifle Association, the church choir and the temple sisterhood, Alcoholics Anonymous, the neighborhood watch, trick or treating, book clubs, and bowling leagues. Most of all, it is the values and bonds that result from all these activities and institutions.

With the end of the era of big government and the beginnings of the Information Age, conservative and liberal thinkers alike have converged on the idea of community—"civil society," as many political scientists call it—as a means of furthering their goals in this new environment. As political scientist William Galston has argued, civic institutions—real-life versions of the Bailey Building and Loan—"lean" against both the market and against government. They prevent each from over-reaching and create an arena where people can live their lives without the interference of either. However, leaning against something can also hold it up and prevent it from falling down. Community does this as well. It nurtures the cords of trust between people that philosopher Francis Fukuyama and many others have pointed out are needed for the functioning of capitalism. It gives people ways to come together and forge the shared beliefs needed for the functioning of democracy.

From this point of view, "community" does not just mean "a community." It is more a set of values than a place; it means neighborliness, more than a neighborhood. Yes, a community "is a place in which people know and care for one another—the kind of place in which people do not merely ask 'How are you?' as a formality but care about the answer," writes philosopher Amitai Etzioni. But, he adds, "communities speak to us in moral voices. They lay claims on their members." Communities are the breeding ground of active, involved citizens.

The state of those communities has become a source of more and more worry for Americans even in an era of economic prosperity. In a 1999 survey, 57 percent of Americans said they believed that civic life had weakened in recent years. At the heart of this anxiety is the belief that America's basic bargain—the notion that with opportunities come obligations—has been breached. In that same 1999 survey, 71 percent believed that "people are focused too much on their rights instead of their responsibilities."

It was this balance that President Clinton promised to help recalibrate. Along with opportunity and responsibility, community was to be the philosophical touchstone of his administration. In his New Covenant address, he promised to help build a "community where people look out for each other, not just for themselves." On the night of his 1992 election, before a cheering crowd in Little Rock, Clinton said that "We need a new spirit of community, a sense that we're all in this together." That same night, Vice President Gore explained that "While we give supreme value to the rights of the individual, we expect that freedom to be exercised with respect toward others and with decent restraint." Yet, while they fought for policies to strengthen opportunity and responsibility, the push for stronger bonds of community often fell by the wayside. By the second term, the Clinton administration rarely used the word "community" except in reference to racial harmony or the inner cities. When, in January of 1999, the White House released the

"Clinton/Gore Administration's Agenda for Communities," it was a set of promises including more empowerment zones, more low-income housing, and an increase in the minimum wage. There was no mention made of the balance of rights and responsibilities or of the need for citizen action, which Clinton and Gore had once made the defining features of their vision of community. The Republicans have proven even worse. In 1998, George W. Bush campaigned for reelection as governor on a bus emblazoned with the words "Opportunity" and "Responsibility." Even though aping Clinton's formula, "Community" was nowhere to be found.

Perhaps this reticence among politicians is due to the implications of what "community" really means. For a community is not a set of promises, but demands—demands we make of one another as citizens that are the price we pay for being enveloped in the community's warming arms. At its heart, a community is a set of often subtle obligations we have toward one another. When they become too harsh and demanding—when there is pressure to dress the same way or to worship the same God—these obligations create authoritarianism or conformity. Yet, without these obligations, we witness the very atomization of life and civic culture that is found today in too many towns and cities around America—where strangers and neighbors are often one in the same.

Despite all of America's progress—economically and socially—over the past decade, the country begins the twenty-first century with too many Americans convinced that the "give and take" of democracy involves only "take"; confused about what our country can do for us and what we can do for our country; and concerned that our political debates often descend into wars between "every man for himself" and "something for nothing"—the crude brands of self-indulgence practiced by economic conservatives and social liberals, respectively. In truth, however, the issue of community divides both parties in rather ugly ways. This cleavage of community breaks down both liberals and conservatives into authoritarians and libertarians.

The authoritarians in both parties seek to impose their narrow vision of morality on the general public. They want to limit the Constitution's basic freedoms in order to foist their personal agenda onto the nation. On the Republican side are those social conservatives who use their personal religious beliefs not to wisely inform their viewpoint, but to undermine the barest of barriers between church teachings and state decisions. The liberals have their authoritarian wing as well. The PC speech code crowd attempts to police the personal thoughts and opinions of ordinary Americans in order to ensure that they conform to that which this group has deemed acceptable.

On the other hand, both parties also have libertarian wings that offer up a hollow vision of community—barren of bonds and devoid of duties. The liberals' version believes in an absolute freedom to say and do what you want wherever and whenever you want; in the total freedom to shout "fire"—and every other four-letter word beginning with "F"—in a crowded theater. Conservatives insist on a libertarianism in which individuals and corporations have no obligations to the community beyond their self-interest. This is a "lazy-fair" view of the world which says that true justice only comes when we sit back, let the market take its course, and trust that social justice and equal opportunity will be produced by the magic of the invisible hand.

Both of these opposing viewpoints—authoritarianism and libertarianism—leave much to be desired. As Amitai Etzioni has written, "We do constantly need to be on guard against self-centered communities, just as we need to watch out for self-centered individuals." The task for politics in the years ahead is to break down both forms of self-centeredness.

Perhaps ironically, the first step in building strong, but not stultifying, communities is strengthening the hand of the individual. The Choice Revolution will help, not hinder, the task of strengthening community because true community depends on people feeling comfortable in their individuality. British Prime Minister Tony Blair has said he believes in "the notion that for individuals to advance you require a strong and fair community behind you." Philosopher Robert Bellah has written of his belief that "Individuals are realized only in and through communities, and that strong, healthy, morally vigorous communities are the prerequisite for strong, healthy morally vigorous individuals."

While this is true, the reverse is true as well. Vibrant communities are only possible when each person feels able to stand on their own two feet. Independence is a prerequisite for interdependence.

For instance, between 1973 and 1993, the percentage of Americans who said that they've "attended a public meeting on town or school affairs" in the past year dropped by more than 40 percent. In a certain sense, who can blame these frustrated parents? Why would they want to seemingly waste their time attending a city council meeting or school board meeting and take part in a system that does not trust them enough to give them any power other than the biennial ability to check a box in the ballot booth? The Choice Revolution would give Americans a say and a stake in these meetings and a role bigger than just butting their heads against the barrier of bureaucratic regulation.

Without the power conveyed to people by the Choice Revolution, Americans will continue to believe that they can—and must—retreat from a public sphere that seems to have little place or need for them. With that power, they will come to believe that they can—and must—take part in the community around them. In *Self-Rule*, Robert Wiebe argued that "personal choice from a range of alternatives defines human freedom, conferring dignity on choice and chooser alike." This basic dignity would help build individual self-confidence—the only secure means of building the bonds of community.

In the instances where the principles of the Choice Revolution have already been introduced to government programs, citizen involvement has flourished. At the Vaughn Next Century Learning Center in Los Angeles, parents of children attending the charter school—almost 100 percent minority, most of them very recent immigrants with an average annual family income of less than $15,000—spend nine thousand hours a year volunteering on campus. It turns out that the sense of control they have at such institutions does not lead them to retreat into themselves, but builds the belief that community involvement is an expectation, not a frill.

The combination of the Choice Revolution and the New Responsibility—the trade-off between more individual power and more responsibility to the community—would not be altogether foreign to most Americans. It is the kind of trade-off that Cheryl McCormick and millions of other American workers now experience every day. McCormick is a beer-canner at a Miller plant that has empowered its workers with a greater degree of flexibility in how they approach their jobs in exchange for the promise that they will produce results and that they can work in teams. This is the deal most Americans in the Information Age are now being offered in their workplaces. McCormick and the eight others on her team decide for themselves how to do their jobs and how to handle any problems which might arise—and this empowerment has bred an expectation that each team member will do their fair share. "At my old plant," she says, "the supervisor was the only person I had to please. Here, I feel like I have eight bosses I have to please. If you walk in late, you've got eight people who want to know where you were." Still, she says she likes this new system better. Time and again, Americans in the workplace have shown a willingness to accept more responsibility when it comes with more trust to make decisions.

With the Choice Revolution, Americans will loosen the strictures of government, but will be better able to accept the demands placed on them by those in their community. The Choice Revolution and the New Responsibility are flip sides of the same coin; they are also indelibly linked—each necessitates the other. If Americans want to make their own choices, they will no longer be able to rely on the decisions meted out by government. That means parents will have to care enough about their children's educations to research the schools they choose from, those who opt to invest their Social Security funds will have to do so responsibly and accept the consequences of their decisions, Americans will have to use information to compare health care plans and choose the one best suited for them and their families. Taken together, a deal that includes both the Choice Revolution and the New Responsibility both gives more to Americans and asks more of them. It means government will have to grant citizens more individual decision-making power and personalized services while citizens will have to be more involved in the life of their country and community.

Today, viewing individual choice and community life as opposites misrepresents both. "To worship choice and community together is to misunderstand what community is all about," wrote journalist Alan Ehrenhalt in his overtly and candidly nostalgic book about industrial, urban Chicago, *The Lost City*. "Community means not subjecting every action in life to the burden of choice, but rather accepting the familiar and reaping the psychological benefits of having one fewer calculation to make in the course of the day." If community and choice were once in conflict, the rules of the Information Age mean both will have to adapt in order to thrive. True and lasting community does not mean bowing down to imposed strictures of authority, but having the power to reach out freely to one's neighbor—and then doing so. When power is vested in hands far away, responsibility is as well. When individuals have choices and a voice in their community, they care more about what occurs there.

The character of this connection can be seen in the behavior of the Choice Generation—a generation raised on the philosophy of "Just Do It!" that turns out to be doing what's right in greater numbers than its predecessors. The Choice Generation is bringing with it a regeneration of many of America's basic civic values. With more choices than ever in every aspect of life, this generation has realized that the price of choice is acting responsibly in their own lives and toward their community. The one place they are still left without choices and decision-making power—the government sphere—is the arena they continue to shirk. The Choice Generation's decision to retreat from involvement with a distant, inaccessible, outdated government while throwing itself into community service at the local level is echoed in a similar trend among the public at large. In 1984, 44 percent reported that they had volunteered for a church, charity, or other community group in the past year. By 1997, 58 percent made this claim. Another poll showed that the percentage of Americans involved in volunteer activities has basically doubled since the late 1970s. Charitable giving has more than tripled since the 1960s. The fact that much of the Choice Generation and many of its elders are involved in community life does not absolve government from taking actions to further this cause. It does mean that there is a receptivity to the idea that individualism and community can be strengthened by government at the same time. Arthur Schlesinger wrote that goal of *The Vital Center* was "to reunite individual and community in fruitful union." The Choice Revolution and the New Responsibility would combine to do the same—giving Americans a voice and a duty to use it.

INTER-ACTION

Men do not form a community in our present restricted sense of that word, merely in so far as the men cooperate. They form a community . . . when they not only cooperate, but accompany this cooperation with that ideal extension of the lives of individuals whereby each cooperating member says: "This activity which we perform together, this work of ours, its past, its future, its sequence, its order, its sense,—all these enter into my life and are the life of my own writ large."

—*Josiah Royce*, Problems of Christianity, *1913*

"These are interesting times," Calvin told Hobbes while they read the newspaper in a 1995 comic strip. "We don't trust government, we don't trust the legal system, we don't trust the media, and we don't trust each other! We've undermined all authority, and with it, the basis for replacing it! It's like a six-year-olds' dream come true." As a 6-year-old, Calvin can be excused for confusing community life's latest transformation with its destruction. His elders should know better. While America's community life is in a moment of transition, this transition should not be confused with the inevitable decline seen by hand-wringers on both sides of the traditional political chasm. The same forces that have transformed America's economy and government over the course of the nation's history have also continuously changed the ways in which Americans interact with one another. A century ago, the trends of centralization and hierarchy that altered the nature of government and the economy also changed Americans' notions of community life. Today, just as they already have with the economy and must with government, Americans need to reimagine what community life should look like to fit the twenty-first century.

More than the ways in which they work or are governed, the ways in which people interact with one another are central to their lives. That's why changes in community life are met with even more fear and distrust than changes in the economy and government. This has been a basic fact of American life from its very beginnings. In the Jeffersonian America of the early nineteenth century, a community was only as strong as its self-confident individual members. This was an understood assumption of American life. The word "individualism" was introduced to the country by an 1840 translation of Tocqueville's *Democracy in America*. It took a strange visitor from another continent to point out to us what we had accepted as a fact of life. Yet, Tocqueville took great pains to contrast individualism with selfishness. He pointed out that "Americans combat the effects of individualism by free institutions" that bound individuals to the community. "When the members of a community are forced to attend to public affairs," he wrote, "they are necessarily drawn from the circle of their own interests and snatched at times from self-observation. As soon as a man begins to treat of public affairs in public, he begins to perceive that he is not so independent of his fellow men as he had first imagined, and that in order to obtain their support he must often lend them his co-operation." With this emphasis on mutual obligation, the local community institutions which Tocqueville witnessed in action created bonds in what might otherwise have been an atomized nation of disconnected farmers.

The transformations in technology, communication, and transportation at the dawn of the Industrial Age ended not only the isolation of old communities, but their insulation as well. The lure of the train whistle and the open road served to break up families that had once been tied to each other, and the old spirit of community started to disappear when it had to contend with industrial forces. Between 1898 and 1906, a system of rural free delivery of mail was constructed to bring the post to

people's front doors. The twin forces of urbanization and industrialization changed the geography of American communities. In 1850, there
were 6 cities with a population of over 100,000 people. Ten years later,
there were 9. By 1900, there were 38. In 1910, just before Roosevelt and
Woodrow Wilson faced off, there were 50. Cities and the Industrial Age
went hand in hand.

A significant part of the original Jeffersonian vision of community
that Tocqueville had found upon his visit was the notion of space—of
room for Americans to stretch out in their independence and not sit on
top of one another as in the walled-in old centers of Europe. Jefferson
saw the growth of cities as a danger to the very spirit of what made American communities and made them work. "I view large cities as pestilence
to the morals, the health, and the liberties of man," he wrote at one
point. "The mobs of great cities add just so much to the support of pure
government as sores do to the strength of the human body," he wrote at
another. Jefferson simply could not see how the free and dignified community life that Americans had known could continue in urban cores.
His fears were, of course, justified. The values and institutions of community had to adapt to meet new circumstances.

That adaptation was a slow process. As late as 1885, Josiah Strong's
best-selling *Our Country* reviewed seven deadly "perils" to America's
well-being: immigration, "Romanism," Mormonism, intemperance,
socialism, wealth, and, finally, "the city." Even later, William Allen
White sang the praises of small-town Emporia, Kansas, as a place where,
when the residents read the announcement of a birth or a wedding, "we
have that neighborly feeling that breeds the real democracy." In contrast,
he wrote, "the city is a wilderness of careless strangers whose instincts of
humanity are daily becoming more blunted to suffering, because in the
nature of things suffering in the cities must be impersonal." In truth,
America has never completely overcome its suspicions about city life.
Even those who never knew any other life but that of sidewalks and skyscrapers, idealize and idyllize life far from the city. Plains, Georgia;
Dixon, Illinois; Hope, Arkansas; Russell, Kansas; Carthage, Tennessee;
and Midland, Texas—all still have a mythic place in American life. In

fact, to this point, only one president can truly be said to have grown up in a big city—and not surprisingly, it was Industrial Age reformer Theodore Roosevelt.

Just as they adapted Americans' conceptions of government, Roosevelt and his fellow Progressives adapted Americans' conceptions of community life to the age of industrialization and urbanization. The new technologies and the new ways of working they brought with them affected the way Americans viewed each other. The old notion that community life was based on independent farmers and villagers united in local clubs and associations was overwhelmed by the force of technologically driven change. Some saw these changes as an exciting prospect that would tear down the barriers of distance and turn a continental nation into a Jeffersonian village. William Allen White believed that the wondrous new developments of science would transform the country into Emporia writ large. "Steam has given us electricity and has made the nation a neighborhood," he wrote. Others were less sanguine. They saw that the old vision of community would not survive the Industrial Age. "The Great Society created by steam and electricity may be a society, but it is no community. The invasion of the community by the new and relatively impersonal and mechanical modes of combined human behavior is the outstanding fact of modern life," wrote John Dewey.

These "impersonal and mechanical modes" would come to destroy the old idea of community life—one built on the bedrock of individualism—and replace it with a new notion: that of centralized power in the hands of elites running national organizations. "Democracy's individual and collective components, after moving in tandem throughout the 19th century, uncoupled early in the 20th," explains Robert Wiebe. "Democracy in the 19th century held individuals within bounds—family, community, universal law—with a promise that groups and individuals benefited one another through mutual reinforcement. When the European visitor Adam Gurowski described the core of American democracy as a 'union of the utmost individual independence with a well-regulated social and political organization,' he was reflecting his hosts' sense of a harmony, not a tension." But as the stature of the individual shriveled in the Industrial Age, this "mutual reinforcement" and its obligations fell by the wayside and harmony gave way to tension.

The power of the individual was retreating in all aspects of American life. It would have been strange if community life had been any different. As was often the case, Woodrow Wilson saw the big picture. "Yesterday, and ever since history began, men were related to one another as individuals. To be sure there were the family, the church, and the State, institutions which associated men in certain wide circles of relationship. But in ordinary concerns of life, in the ordinary work, in the daily round, men dealt freely with one another. Today, the everyday relationships of men are largely with great impersonal concerns, with organizations, not with other individual men." In such a world—as Americans lived and worked in very different ways than their parents—the definition of community life changed for many from one of interaction with other individuals to one of joint membership in large-scale organizations of every conceivable variety of profession, interest, hobby, and cause.

With the old individualized community of the farms and small towns disappearing, Americans created forms of community practice for the world they lived in. Many Americans sought to establish links based on the new forms of work replacing agriculture. In 1880, there were 16 state and local bar associations. By 1916, there were 671. In 1900, more than 50 years after its founding, the American Medical Association had 8,400 members. Ten years later, its membership had grown to over 70,000. In its first 11 years, from 1886 to 1897, the American Federation of Labor gained 256,000 members. Over the next 7 years, the membership grew to 1,676,000. But it wasn't just professional and labor organizations that were gaining prominence and providing new links. Everywhere one turned new national organizations were springing up that, like the new economy of the day, were hierarchical, centralized, and built according to the rules of planning and regimentation. Like the Parent-Teacher Association—originally founded in 1897 as the National Congress of Mothers—many of these new associations were created to bring expert knowledge to communities throughout the country.

The Progressive Generation was responsible for constructing much

of the associational framework modern Americans associate with community life. Between 1880 and 1920, they created an enduring structure that allowed Americans to relate to one another in the Industrial
Age.* What these associations had in common was their national reach.
Just as businesses grew in strength and scope due to industrial technologies, just as government sought to follow suit, community life
became nationalized as well in the Industrial Age. As generations came
and went, Americans came to accept that community was defined by

---

*The familiar names of these organizations—and the breadth and depth of the
areas they cover—serve as a monument for the manner in which the Progressives changed what it meant to be involved in one's community. In the forty
years between 1880 and 1920, they founded organizations including the American Red Cross (1881), the American Civil Liberties Union (1920), the League
of Women Voters (1920), the National Association for the Advancement of
Colored People (1909), the American Automobile Association (1902), Planned
Parenthood (1916), the United Way (1918), the Urban League (1910), and the
Anti-Defamation League of B'nai B'rith (1913). The National Association of
Manufacturers (1895), the Chamber of Commerce (1912), and the Jaycees
(1920). The Farmer's Union (1902) and the Farm Bureau (1919). The Actors'
Equity Association (1913) and the Theatre Guild (1919). The National
Audubon Society (1905) and the Sierra Club (1892). The American Society of
Agricultural Engineers (1907), the American Institute of Chemical Engineers
(1908), the American Society of Heating, Refrigerating and Air-Conditioning
Engineers (1894), the American Society of Mechanical Engineers (1880), and
the Society of Motion Picture and Television Engineers (1916). The American
Historical Association (1884) and the Organization of American Historians
(1907). The American Astronomical Association (1899) and the American
Anthropological Association (1902). The American Legion (1919) and the Vet-
erans of Foreign Wars (1899). The Boys Club of America (1906), the Boy
Scouts of America (1910), the Girl Scouts of America (1912), and the Camp
Fire Boys and Girls (1910). The Author's League of America (1902), the Amer-
ican Society of Composers, Authors, and Publishers (1914), and the American
Booksellers Association (1900). The American Cancer Society (1913) and the
American Lung Association (1904). The Association of American Universities
(1900), the College Board (1900), and the American Council on Education
(1918). Catholic Charities (1910), the Catholic Daughters of America (1903),

large cities and big organizations—a concept that would have been totally antithetical to Thomas Jefferson's vision.

Industrialization built up the centralized forces of the economy while breaking apart bonds of what had once been thought of as community. Today, the Information Age is challenging large entities and, with them, what we have long thought of as marking community. Yet, like industrialization, the present changes in the economy and society present the duty to rethink community for our own time. This means that modern innovations in community life must center around creating arenas wherein people can make stronger individual ties to one another.

Urbanization and national organizations—the Industrial Age's contributions to American's notions of community—are no longer the cutting edge. Suburbs and "edge cities"—products of the Information Age—have displaced urban cores as the places most Americans call home. At the same time, the large-scale, hierarchical associations of the Progressive Era are also in decline. As sociologist Theda Skocpol points out, "With several notable exceptions, such as the Christian Coalition,

---

and the American Catholic Historical Society (1884). The American Jewish Congress (1918), the American Jewish Historical Society (1892), the Jewish War Veterans (1896), the National Council of Jewish Women (1893), and Hadassah (1912). The Sons of the American Revolution (1889), the Daughters of the American Revolution (1890), the Daughters of the Confederacy (1894), and the General Society of Mayflower Descendants (1897). The American Federation of Teachers (1916) and the International Brotherhood of Teamsters (1903). The National Assocation of the Deaf (1880) and the National Society to Prevent Blindness (1908). The National Genealogical Society (1903), the National Geographic Society (1888), and the Geological Society of America (1888). Kiwanis International (1915), Rotary International (1905), and Optimist International (1919). The Lions Clubs (1917) and the Loyal Order of Moose (1888). The American Newspaper Publishers Association (1887) and the Magazine Publishers of America (1919). The American Philatelic Association (1886) and the American Numismatic Association (1891). While exhausing, this list is nowhere near exhaustive of the organizations the Progressives formed in the years surrounding the end of the nineteenth and the beginning of the twentieth centuries.

few new local-state-national federations have been founded since the 1960s and 1970s. And many of the 30–40 nationwide voluntary federations that flourished in mid-20th-century America have gone into absolute as well as relative membership decline." But this does not necessarily mean that community life is atrophying. It means that Americans are choosing new forms of involvement better geared to a less hierarchical, less centralized age. For instance, the late Everett Carll Ladd showed that while the national PTA might be far less popular than it once was— only one-quarter of all schools had chapters by the mid-1990s—new, local independent parent-teacher organizations had sprouted up to pick up the slack. "The PTA has been getting beaten by local entrepreneurs who are more concerned with their hometowns than with the [PTA's] Chicago headquarters," wrote Ladd. "It would seem that the trend is away from centralized national organizations to those decentralized and local." The energy and excitement in community life today is not found, as it was a century ago, in the formation of national organizations. It is found in local community groups such as Friends for Life in Waco, Texas, and the Puente Learning Center in East Los Angeles.

This new local vibrancy has not prevented a spate of hand-wringing about America's loss of community. Much of this perceived crisis is built on nostalgia. For many, it is anything but easy to imagine new vessels for the values of community after a century of certitude that community could only be found on city streets and in national organizations. In a special issue of the *Brookings Review* devoted to "civil society," noted sociologist Alan Wolfe rightly wrote that "Americans retain their social and civic instincts, but they have little choice but to shape them to the new realities of two-career families, suburban lifestyles, and rapid career changes." Yet the magazine's cover was a painting of a bustling city street scene—a picture far removed from most Americans' "new realities."

Even more than the rise of suburbs, even more than the decline of national organizations, what leads many "civil society" nostalgists to worry about the Information Age is its personalizing technologies— especially the Internet. At a Washington, D.C. discussion on civil society in 1999, E. J. Dionne began his remarks by picking up on a comment made by a previous speaker. "At a meeting about civic renewal, we shouldn't be talking about Amazon.com, but about your local book-store." His tongue was firmly planted in his cheek, but the joke represents a central problem for those who seek to build community spirit in the twenty-first century. They cannot succeed until they see Amazon.com and the Information Age as allies in their efforts, not enemies. Like the Progressives a century ago, they must rethink community for their own times, not hold on ever tighter to increasingly outdated forms of civic life. Today, that means harnessing the power of technological change to create new forms of community life.

There are two basic visions of the impact of the Information Age on community. One sees an atomized society where people never leave the house—ordering their groceries on-line and never making friends in the cereal aisle. The other sees a networked society where people use the Internet to form friendships and make connections with those who have similar interests and outlooks. Although Americans are generally split on this question, this divide is partly generational. Among the populace at large, according to a 1999 poll, 43 percent believed that "new technologies have made Americans more isolated and drawn them farther apart," while 49 percent said that these technological advancements "have opened up new lines of communication and brought people closer together." However, when it came to young people—the Choice Generation that is comfortable with these technologies—64 percent believed that technology had brought Americans closer together, while a mere 29 percent felt it had pulled them farther apart.

While it will be a long time before the Internet replaces handshakes or hugs, millions of Americans now communicate instantaneously with e-mail and just around the corner lies a future where Americans will be able to have face-to-face conversations with friends and family halfway around the world with video communication. Moreover, the Internet can form communities based on shared interests and not just shared geography. By bringing a universe of information to every citizen, the Internet affords individuals the opportunity to shape their surroundings as never before and to make the connections that strong community life depends on.

Finally, the Internet can also be used as a way to empower individuals themselves so that they can build the local communities that a decentralizing nation needs. As Walter Lippmann identified the problem in 1914, "The Golden Rule in a village, and the Golden Rule for a nation of a hundred million people are two very different things. I might possibly treat my neighbor as myself, but in this vast modern world the greatest problem that confronts me is to find my neighbor and treat him at all."

Instead of the fear of traditionalists that modern technology will result in an America of loners sitting in front of their computer screens, technology can be harnessed to provide real connections between individuals. With "Link Point," an experimental demo from Microsoft, a neighborhood can form an on-line community that allows neighbors to contact one another by phone or e-mail, that lets people know about clubs and organizations in the area that might interest them, and that informs local residents of events where they can come together and ways in which they can help one another. It would make the often ad hoc activities of a community, such as carpools or canned-food drives, much easier—harnessing an on-line community to build more traditional forms of community.

The civil society skeptics who confuse transformation with inevitable decline rarely pause to consider whether the new community being produced in the Information Age might, in fact, be stronger than that which it replaces. Once, Americans accustomed to the rhythms of farms and small towns could not imagine that community connections could be built in an industrial urban nation. Today, too many American civic leaders believe that community can only be found in tightly knit cities and assembly line factories. However, it is possible that the community Americans are constructing in the Information Age might indeed prove deeper and stronger. "The industrial system was a cooperative scheme in the sense that it coordinated the efforts of many individuals; but unless the individuals took an interest in the whole and regarded its activity as an expression of their identity, it did not constitute a genuine community," writes philosopher Michael Sandel. What drives today's economy—and soon hopefully its government and community—is the notion of providing connections between individuals. Community built on this foundation is potentially much stronger than the mechanistic processes it replaces.

In his preface to *Leaves of Grass*, Walt Whitman warned that the nation's newfound largeness could become "monstrous" without a corresponding largeness of spirit. In the Progressive Era, farsighted leaders on every level created associations and organizations that instilled that largeness of spirit in the American people. Today, the nation's decentralization could become monstrous without a willingness to decentralize our spirit—a commitment from every citizen to look into the forgotten corners of American life and accept responsibility for the conditions of their fellow citizens. The New Responsibility means a strengthening of this commitment. More than anything else, however, it means matching the increased freedom of the Choice Revolution with the recognition that freedom has a price that no American can shirk paying.

WHAT YOU CAN DO FOR YOUR COUNTRY

> If freedom is worth having, if the right of self-government is a valuable right, then the one and the other must be retained exactly as our forefathers acquired them, by labor, and especially by labor in organization, that is in combination with our fellows who have the same interests and the same principles.
>
> —*Theodore Roosevelt, age 24,*
> *The Duties of American Citizenship*

When a sweater-clad Jimmy Carter addressed the nation and called for the "moral equivalent of war" in confronting the energy crisis, skeptical commentators pointed out that its acronym was MEOW. But when William James first summoned forth the doctrine in a 1906 speech to the Stanford student body, it was a roar. He recommended the "conscription of the whole youthful population in a civilian army" in order to "inflame the civic temper." His address was reprinted numerous times as an essay in the magazines of his day and sold more than thirty thousand copies on its own. "To coal and iron mines, to freight trains, to fishing fleets in

December, to dish-washing, clothes-washing, and window-washing, to road-building and tunnel-making, to foundries and stokeholes, and to the frames of skyscrapers would our gilded youths be drafted off, according to their choice, to get the childishness knocked out of them." The heart of the New Responsibility is an update of this Progressive Era dream for our own time: the call for a year of mandatory national citizen service for every young person in America.

This type of Citizen Corps—where young Americans at age 18 would fulfill their requirement through either military or civilian service—would transform the face of American life. But it is not a new idea. After William James first proposed it in 1906, it lay dormant for years. Then, contemplating America's postwar future, Franklin Roosevelt spoke in 1943 of mandating young people to make a "year's contribution of service to the government." His idea was to marry the wartime draft with the New Deal visions of his National Youth Administration and Civilian Conservation Corps. However, fearing encroachment on their turf, union leaders fought FDR's efforts in Congress and labeled them "forced labor."

Yet, with a short gap between World War II and the Korean War, the military draft continued until 1973—during times of both war and peace. For a generation, young Americans were called out of their personal lives in order to serve their country. The draft not only ensured America's security, it brought together Americans from all walks of life—creating social stability, a sense of equality, and bonds of community. As Mickey Kaus points out in *The End of Equality*, serving with snotty young John F. Kennedy aboard PT-109 in the South Pacific were high school dropouts, a fisherman, a refrigerator engineer, a son of Polish immigrants, factory workers, and a jazz pianist. Americans who might never otherwise meet were thrown together to achieve a common goal. The nation was better off for it—then and in years to come. All Americans were reminded that with the opportunities of American life come obligations to serve. The draft reached rich and poor, white and black and every other color conceivable. As Kaus reminds us, "They even drafted Elvis."

However, in the agony of Vietnam, the draft consensus got all shook up. As exemptions became increasingly possible, service became a system to game—and the more fortunate were clearly better players. The percentage of young people serving dwindled and those who did don a uniform were more likely to be poor and minority. Eventually, the military moved to an all-volunteer force and notions of patriotism and the duty of service came to be seen as embarrassingly outdated. Slowly, however, such notions seem to be coming back into style. In the past two decades Senators Bill Bradley, John McCain, Sam Nunn, Gary Hart, Bob Torricelli, and Bob Kerrey all have—at some point and sometimes obliquely—called for universal national service. Building on the success of Kennedy's Peace Corps, President Clinton introduced the AmeriCorps program, which has seen hundreds of thousands of young people devote a year or two of service in exchange for satisfaction and help in paying for college. After a bumpy start, it has built bipartisan support as an idea in line with the best of American values.

However, a program of universal national service for every young person is an entirely different matter. It would be clearly coercive (seemingly constricting choice instead of expanding it), it would be expensive (tens of billions of dollars a year—real money, even in an age of trillion-dollar surpluses), and it would be huge (approximately 4 million young Americans presently turn 18 every year). So why such a program and why now? Universal national service is a main part of the New Responsibility because it provides a necessary counterbalance to the individual autonomy of the Choice Revolution. It would provide a means for government action in a postbureaucratic age, forge bonds of community at a time when technology is pushing all aspects of society toward individual customization, instill a sense of public spirit and community obligation in the Americans whom the Choice Revolution will give more decision-making power, and build on the Choice Generation's own synthesis of both exercising personal power and taking responsibility for others.

First, and above all else, a Citizen Corps is necessary because of the gaping national need for such service. Many of America's most pressing concerns can only be solved by human interaction, not bureaucratic regulation. Unfortunately, the comfortable continue to peddle the idea that all is basically well in American life—that "peace and prosperity" have made every rough place plain and every crooked place straight. At a time when, despite progress in recent years, about one out of every five American children lives in abject poverty, such a claim is offensive. There is work enough for every 18-year-old in America to do—and then some. An army of Americans committed to tackling some of the nation's most intractable problems could make an unbelievable difference in the life of the country. Millions of children need extra reading and math tutoring; thousands of homeless are looking for help in moving off the streets and back into society; parents need, but often cannot afford, child care for their young children; after-school care is needed to keep older kids off the streets, away from the television, and in a classroom; an overburdened and expensive health care system needs an infusion of nurses aides; the Peace Corps needs to expand its efforts in nations around the globe without reducing its quality; soil erosion needs to be battled; streams need to be cleaned; classrooms need more teacher aides; and the police need help in organizing neighborhoods against crime.

Caring for America's aging population would be one of the biggest challenges the Citizen Corps could undertake. In nursing homes, elderly Americans blow through their entire life savings in a matter of weeks. Millions of the old could stay out of nursing homes for years if someone could come visit them once a day, making sure that they are all right and that small household chores are performed. This visit to make sure they have groceries and that their burnt-out light bulbs are changed could shine a ray of light into an otherwise lonely existence.

The Citizen Corps would also make clear that a military stint is the highest form of service. With dropping enlistment rates and grave difficulties with recruitment, universal national service would revitalize the armed forces and bring young Americans of all colors and backgrounds into soldierly life.

Second, national civilian service would tie together Americans who are being pulled apart by the Information Age's personalization. This personalization is clearly positive for the individual Americans who will be better able to shape their lives to their liking. However, it does present a challenge to the nation as a whole. Today, very few institutions still tie together Americans of all walks of life. In 1992, Kaus wrote that even popular culture was no longer the bond it once was. "Instead of everybody watching Milton Berle, young professionals watch the 'Arts and Entertainment' network while the less cultured watch 'Married . . .With Children.'" Today, even this is no longer true. New technologies allow Americans to watch their favorite television programs whenever they want to watch them. The days of people gathering around the office coffee machine on Friday morning and discussing the previous night's episode of "ER" are coming to an end. Technology now allows Americans to pause the program they are watching while they get up to use the bathroom or fix a snack, and then resume when they sit back down. The winning Super Bowl touchdown could appear on the screen in millions of households at different times. MyCNN.com advertises itself as a service that lets Americans "Decide what's news to you. Choose your stocks, weather, sports and stories." If people can design their own individual Nikes and their own Barbies, if they can now decide "what's news" to them, something needs to be there to hold us together. Universal national service is part of that something.

Moreover, young people would be coming together not just for social cohesion, but for constructive work. Shared goals and tasks would build bonds and demand that young Americans work with each another. "People do not live together merely to be together," wrote Spanish philosopher Ortega y Gasset. "They live together to do something together." It is this act of doing something—something positive, patriotic, and uplifting for one's nation—that allows for the shared experiences and common rite of passage that national service will produce. When a senator and a janitor can meet and each ask the other, "How'd you serve?" a disparate and diverse nation will be more united than ever. As was the case with John Kennedy and his buddies in the South Pacific, everyone would come to understand that they are ultimately in the same boat. This unity—in service and afterwards—would also breed a spirit of civic equality where the worth of each American is seen as equal and deserving of equal respect. This is the spirit of an old Hungarian immigrant saying: in America, "The President is Mister and I am Mister, too."

Third, the Citizen Corps would inculcate in Americans the belief that they must live up to their mutual and civic obligations. While both parties have taken up the language of personal responsibility over the past decade, both have shied away from talking about Americans' reciprocal responsibilities: the standard of duties and honor we all owe to one another—rich to poor, poor to rich; white to black, black to white. The national service rite of passage would also, hopefully, speed the passage of the rights mentality that has impelled many Americans to push the boundaries of the acceptable past the breaking point simply because they are entitled to do so.

With this year of service, Americans would begin their adult lives by thinking about the well-being of others instead of focusing solely on their own. It would also move this thinking process into the realm of action—imprinting on Americans the importance of service to others throughout one's lifetime. Whether it is as civilian soldiers or citizen servers, the work they do over their year of service will be of immense importance to the country; the work that they will likely continue to do for the rest of their years will be of perhaps even more importance. From this perspective, a year of universal national service is not about mobilizing moralizing Do-Gooders, but about creating lifelong Good-Doers—inculcating the values of community responsibility and active citizen service for a lifetime.

Universal citizen service would also serve as a tangible reminder to *all* Americans of their civic obligations—democratic duties and republican responsibilities that are the price of living in this country. AmeriCorps and other voluntary service programs accomplish great things, but they have fallen short in convincing every American that there are requirements in being a citizen. They appeal to some of the more public-spirited young people, but fail to reach those raring to start running a rat race from which they will probably never turn back. Service should not be a special chance, but a way of life.

Proposals like the one supported by former Senator Sam Nunn and former Representative David McCurdy, which would require service in exchange for government financial aid in attending college, fall short for a similar reason. While noble in premise, such a system imposes requirements on poor and middle-class Americans while leaving the rich off the hook. It fails because it posits that citizen obligations are required only of those who receive direct government benefits, not of every American.

Citizens are built, not born and not bought. Sometimes we seem to forget this. At a time when many political leaders seem to preach that the responsibilities of citizenship entail nothing more than voting and thus putting your civic duty in hock to politicians for another two years, national service would serve as a very tangible reminder to Americans that they owe more than this to their nation. Not everyone agrees. Donald Regan, while secretary of the treasury, said the issue of universal national service had to be answered based on whether America needs young people "picking up trash rather than earning their first million." Similarly, Jack Kemp has said that, "At the age of 18, you should be focusing on your dreams and ambitions, not picking up cans in Yellowstone." Part of the appeal of universal national service is that it would force—yes, force—18-year-olds to spend a year focusing on the dreams of the nation and realize that their personal ambitions are part and parcel of the country's.

Fourth, and finally, universal national service molds and melds with the spirit of service that the Choice Generation has already exhibited. Their high rates of voluntarism and interest in service to the community can be adapted and harnessed to service to the nation. Ultimately, the Choice Generation's voluntarism, which is often wonderful and good, is no substitute for service's core commitment to community and country. National service is not charitable altruism, but a duty owed by citizens to their country. This duty—what Will Marshall called "a strong ethic of civic obligation," of "equal sacrifice for the common good"—is a notion the Choice Generation has never really been exposed to.

For those young people who have lost their way, national service is one way to link them back to their moorings. After the Columbine High School tragedy, Michael Brown, co-founder of the highly successful City

Year service program, commented, "Everyone is saying: 'What do we do for our children?' It's time we ask something of our children." A year of citizen service would work wonders in counteracting both young people's natural self-involvement and the destructive influences they oftentimes fall under.

"When the Athenians finally wanted not to give to society, but for society to give to them, when the freedom they wished for most was freedom from responsibility, then Athens ceased to be free," wrote Edward Gibbon. Universal national citizen service must be seen as an expansion of, not a limit on, Americans' freedoms. Using coercive means to make every young person give a year of service to their country is not something to be taken lightly. But neither is the atrophying of the bonds of community, the weakening of the spirit of mutual obligations, the loss of basic civic equality, and—most of all—the major challenges facing America in the coming years that cannot be fully met by either government or business action alone. A standing army of Americans—committed to fighting against the nation's ills and enemies wherever they be found—would be awesome force for national good.

VALUING COMMUNITY

The Lord above made man to help his neighbour,
No matter where: on land or sea or foam.
The Lord above made man to help his neighbour but
With a little bit o' luck,
With a little bit o' luck,
When he comes around you won't be home.

—*Alan Jay Lerner*, My Fair Lady

Instituting universal national service would be an important way for government to build new bonds of community, but the New Responsibility must call on individual Americans to do more on their own as well. All over America, citizens are taking the lead in creating new local community institutions based on a set of values that is different from that which Americans have grown accustomed to. It is these values that can inspire the New Responsibility the nation needs—an attitude that accepts responsibility not only for one's own personal actions, but for one's own community. The nation's connective tissue can be repaired if individual Americans resolve to strengthen the use of public pressure to remind Americans of their mutual obligations.

According to one story, French statesman George Clemenceau was wearing a bowler hat to a garden party, when he encountered British statesman Lord Balfour, who was wearing a top hat. Balfour said, "They told me top hats would be worn." Clemenceau replied, "They told me, too." Few of us have such fortitude to buck conformity. That's why few forces have a greater impact on human behavior than the desire to fit into a group. Driving on the highway as the sun sets, drivers usually turn their headlights on not because they start sensing the impending darkness, but because they see that other drivers have turned theirs on. The pressure to follow suit becomes ever greater as more and more drivers shine their lights on the road. Only an awfully obstinate person will leave their lights off when everyone else has turned theirs on. This pressure is only magnified when people know those who are around them. Each weekend, millions of Americans heave themselves off the couch on a quiet Saturday afternoon and mow the lawn, not because of an unshakable desire for neatly trimmed grass, but because of a fear of standing out and having their neglect noticed by the neighbors. Without creating a nation of intrusive busy-bodies, this fear should be channeled to public ends—strengthening the pressure that already exists to participate in community activities and to exercise one's rights responsibly. To butcher the Bard: thus cowardice doth give conscience to us all.

Public pressure can be applied, not to breed conformity, but to build community and strengthen the notion of the public citizen. Public citizenship is defined by what one contributes to the life of the nation and how one fulfills the obligations inherent in being an American. These obligations are something deeper and more committed than conventional volunteerism which—while both noble and needed—can often be done more out of pity than a shared bond of citizenship.

The tale of old-time rural barnraisings is instructive. A whole community would come together to help a family do what they could not do alone—raise up the huge barn needed for farming success. We often consider those barnraisings—when neighbor came to lend neighbor a helping hand—as a powerful metaphor for pulling together as one community. But this point of view leaves out half the story. A barnraising was not something one did out of kindness or a desire to be helpful, it was something one was simply expected to do. Neighbors came from all over and worked all day not just because they knew their neighbors would do the same for them when the time came, but because a barnraising was about a mutual obligation everyone shared to each other and the community. The accepted rules of community life simply did not permit you to be absent.

Today, modern barnraisings happen all around us—even if we don't notice them. Of America's 1.5 million firefighters, 85 percent are volunteers. Seattle has a low rate of death from heart attacks because a public education campaign has resulted in half of the population knowing CPR—and a widespread expectation that the citizens of Seattle have a duty to each other to know this lifesaving technique. Chances are that if your heart stops while you are walking down the street there, someone will be there to help you and perhaps save your life. As Morley Safer said in a 60 Minutes report on this phenomenon, "If you're going to have a heart attack, have it in Seattle." Such cooperation is not only beneficial, it provides people with broader vistas and tighter ties of community—it not only raises barns, it raises awareness.

Americans should insist on more of such thinking—laying plans which require fellow citizens to, in Franklin Roosevelt's words, "shoulder our common load." The lives of those who engage in such community enterprises are not only fuller, they are richer as well. For it is in the act of raising these barns—like the Bailey Building and Loan—that many hands come together in a common purpose and build the bonds which, in turn, give Americans the ability to require more of their neighbor and of themselves.

A Newer World

I know of no safe depository of the ultimate powers of the society but the people themselves.

—Thomas Jefferson

O n July 4, 1902, as hundreds of thousands of Americans lined the streets of Pittsburgh, the parade carrying the visiting president of the United States moved slowly through town. As the procession passed under the window of 2208 Fifth Avenue, Bernard Lager's wife gave birth to a baby boy. They named him—naturally—Theodore Roosevelt Lager.

Starting in the Progressive Era and continuing through most of the next century, visionary American leaders built a government and a community life fit for the Pittsburgh and the world that Theodore Lager had been born into—powerful, centralized, hierarchical, expert-driven, top-down ruled. They had to fight to do so, but they were convinced it was an effort worth undertaking. America is a better nation because of their work.

A child born exactly one hundred years after Teddy Lager will be born into a very different world and a very different economy—one marked by hugely expanded choices, dispersed decision-making power, personalized services, bottom-up thinking. However, as things stand now, he or she will grow up in an America that has only begun to adapt its community life to this new situation and whose government has, by and large, remained stagnant in its outlook. This child deserves better. Like Teddy Lager, he or she deserves an America that has kept pace with the times in all its facets. He or she deserves leaders who have the courage, convictions, and capabilities that marked the farsighted politicians of the Progressive period.

Fortunately, Americans need not wait meekly for such leadership to arise. In the opening pages of *The Vital Center,* Arthur M. Schlesinger took the occasion of its halfway mark to look back at what he called "this ghastly century." He contrasted its auspicious beginnings to the world-weary disillusionment of its midpoint. "Nineteen hundred looked forward to the irresistible expansion of freedom, democracy, and abundance," he wrote, "1950 will look back to totalitarianism, to concentration camps, to mass starvation, and to atomic war." He didn't know it, but 1950 looked forward to a mixed record. A nearly half-century of global balance of terror, of the killing fields of Cambodia and the ethnic cleansing of Sarajevo, of the fall of the Prague Spring and the crushing blow at Tiananmen Square. But there was more to this century, progress as well as perturbation. The nations of the world were freed from the shackles of colonialism, the globe was linked to instantaneous communication, cures were found for the most dreaded diseases, and man fulfilled his oldest dream—to walk among the stars. In the end, the twentieth century was a human century—showing both the best and worst that people, individually and in community, are capable of.

If there is a final image of the century's last years, it must certainly be that of men and women dancing on the tattered carcass of the Berlin Wall. If there is a lasting lesson that the twentieth century teaches the twenty-first, it should be the one they taught us. For after forty years of worldwide confrontation—year after year of lives lost and fortune spent—the Berlin Wall was torn down by neither an M-1 tank nor an MX missile. It was the bare hands and garden tools of ordinary citizens rising up to dismantle their old shackles and substitute the promise of freedom that finally brought the story of this century full circle to the beginning that Schlesinger described. Perhaps their example is not a bad vantage point from which to look forward to the century ahead. "An invasion of armies can be resisted, but not an idea whose time has come," wrote Victor Hugo. The story of the close of the twentieth century and the opening of the twenty-first is that faith in the wisdom and power of people is an idea whose time has come.

Americans are building a New Economy on the foundation of individual choice and personalized decision-making power. Now, they are coming to demand—ever more firmly—that government follow suit; that the industrial, Hamiltonian top-down model be displaced and Jefferson's bottom-up vision be returned to its preeminence. Once, there was a leader who promised to do just that. Running for president in 1968, Robert Kennedy proposed a government that put its trust in the people and put its power back into their hands. In his campaign book, *To Seek a Newer World*, he decried "the frightening vision of people as interchangeable units, the middle class as powerless as the poor to affect government." Although he recognized that "we are far removed from Jefferson's time," he still believed in Jefferson's "vision of participating democracy." That vision was propelling him to the point of making a decisive break with the government created by Theodore Roosevelt and Franklin Roosevelt. "Bigness, loss of community, organizations and society grown far past the human scale—these are the besetting sins of the 20th century, which threaten to paralyze our capacity to act," RFK told an audience in rural Minnesota, "Therefore the time has come . . . when we must actively fight bigness and over-concentration, and seek instead to bring the engines of government, of technology, or of the economy fully under the control of our citizens." He never reached that point. His campaign to put humans behind the wheel of government ended on the cold floor of a Los Angeles hotel kitchen.

Perhaps he would have failed in any case. Perhaps what he called "the giant organizations and massive bureaucracies of the age" would have caused him to lose this battle. If Woodrow Wilson was too late, Robert Kennedy was too early. The long day of the Industrial Age was waning, but it still had a few good years left in it. Nevertheless, his vision reached Americans who had begun to sense that the world was changing. As the train carrying Robert Kennedy's body rumbled toward his final destination, the tracks were lined with Americans paying their last respects—men and women with different color skins and different color collars; inspired hippies and incipient yuppies; hard-hats and housewives. They came to express sadness for a family that had already suffered so much. They came to ask what might have been. They came because in the midst of the most divisive decade since the Civil War, he had been able to unite Americans across lines of age and color and background.

But perhaps they came for another reason as well. Perhaps they came because they shared Kennedy's dream of an America run by the many, not the few; one ruled by the people, not an elite; one governed from the bottom up, not the top down. It is a vision that has lain dormant in the years since his death—rejected by both political parties. But his dream need not have died with him. Its time has finally come. "Hamiltons we have today. Is there a Jefferson on the horizon?"

Acknowledgments

Staring at a blank screen at 2:00 A.M., the process of writing a book seems to be as lonely and solitary as it can be. In fact, this book—like all books—is the product of many hands.

Every politician for whom I have written speeches has fretted about the acknowledgments they are supposed to deliver at the beginning of the speech. There is always the fear that they will inadvertently omit someone who should be included. I now know how they feel. Nevertheless, my debt to so many is so great that I undertake this list and do so with the hope that those accidentally absent from these pages will know they are very much in my heart.

Thank you to those whose help, advice, counsel, support, assistance, and faith over the years helped me reach the point where I was able to write a book and to write this book in particular. They include Chuck Alston, Don Baer, Stan Beiner, Howard Berman, Rick Berke, Sarah Bianchi, Marland Buckner, Charles Burson, Louis Caldera, Heather and Chuck Campion, Laura Capps, Catherine Denn, Jim Gelb, Richard Gephardt, Matthew Granade, John Gurrola, Mark Halperin, Bob Hertzberg, Elaine Kamarck, Cathy McLaughlin, Nick Mitropoulos, Richard Neustadt, Jeffrey Nussbaum, Bruce Reed, Thomas Rosshirt, Rabbi Moshe Rothblum, James Sasser, Jonathan Shapiro, Philip Sharp, Mark Sheridan, Brad Sherman, Jeffrey Shesol, June Shih, Tom Soto, Ginny Terzano, Thomas Umberg, Marcella Urrutia, Henry Waxman, Lowell Weiss, Michael Whouley, Ted Widmer, David Wilhelm, Doug Wilson, Alan Wolfe, and Michael Woo.

Thank you to my teachers over the years, especially Elaine Roukema,

Aiko Utsumi, Will Carney, the late Bernard Kaplan, Paul Mertens, Patrick Kelly, the late Douglas Price, Maxine Issacs, and Theda Skocpol.

Thank you to the staffs of the White House Library, the Northeast branch of the Washington, D.C. Public Library, the Library of Congress, the Amelia Earhart Branch/North Hollywood Public Library, the Library System of the University of California, and the Historical Society of Western Pennsylvania for their assistance in the research for this book.

Thank you to my agents, Bill Leigh and Wes Neff, for believing in this book long after they should have given up; to Tim Bartlett for his thoughtfulness and insight; to Vanessa Mobley for so ably shepherding this project to completion; to Christine Marra for her diligence and dedication; and to John Donatich for bringing this project to the light of day.

Thank you to Al From, Bill Galston, Will Marshall, and Simon Rosenberg for their willingness to offer feedback on an early draft of the book. When I was in high school and college, these men were giants to me. Since I have had the good fortune to get to know them, my esteem for them has only grown.

"Think where man's glory most begins and ends, and say my glory was I had such friends," wrote Yeats. Writing this book has reminded me how glorious it is to have such wonderful friends. I will not attempt to name them all here, but merely will thank them for their everlasting kindness, patience, support, and wonderful ability to bring a smile to my face.

Few impositions on a friendship are more substantial than the request to read a book manuscript. Emily Berning, Lauren Hammer, and John Turner responded to this request by going far above and beyond the call of duty. This book would be far worse without their careful edits, considered erudition, and aversion to alliteration. It would probably be far better if I had taken more of their advice.

Thank you also to Anne Aaron, Kenny Baer, John Gomperts, Chris Kelly, Daniel Pink, Robin Swanson, and Jeffrey Yarbro for looking over and offering thoughts on all or part of the book at various stages of the process.

Thank you to the staffs of the Democratic Leadership Council and Progressive Policy Institute for their friendship and tireless efforts.

Thank you to President Bill Clinton, Vice President Al Gore, and their staffs for the opportunities they gave me and, much more important, for the opportunity they gave the country by laying the foundation for a new mission for government.

Finally, thank you to my parents—for everything.

VALLEY VILLAGE, CALIFORNIA
June 2000

Recommended Reading

ON THE AGRICULTURAL AGE

The Jefferson Image in the American Mind, Merrill D. Peterson (New York: Oxford University Press, 1960)

Jefferson and Hamilton, Claude Bowers (New York: Houghton Mifflin Company, 1925)

The Age of Jackson, Arthur M. Schlesinger Jr. (Boston: Little, Brown and Company, 1945)

The Life and Selected Writings of Thomas Jefferson, Thomas Jefferson (New York: Random House, 1944)

ON THE SHIFT TO THE INDUSTRIAL AGE

The Promise of American Life, Herbert Croly (1908)

The New Nationalism, Theodore Roosevelt (New York: The Outlook Company, 1910)

The New Freedom, Woodrow Wilson (New York: Doubleday, Page & Company, 1913)

The New Democracy, Walter Weyl (New York: The Macmillan company, 1912)

The Old Order Changeth, William Allen White (New York : Macmillan, 1910)

Drift and Mastery, Walter Lippmann (New York: M. Kennerley, 1914)

Looking Backward: 2000 – 1887, Edward Bellamy (1888)

Rendezvous with Destiny, Eric F. Goldman (New York: Alfred A. Knopf, 1952)

The Search for Order, Robert H. Wiebe (New York: Hill and Wang, 1967)

The Era of Theodore Roosevelt, George Mowry (New York: Harper, 1958)

A Very Different Age, Steven J. Diner (New York: Hill & Wang, 1997)

The Progressive Movement, Richard Hofstadter (Englewood Cliffs, NJ: Prentice-Hall, 1963)

The American Political Tradition, Richard Hofstadter (New York: Alfred A. Knopf, 1948)

The Age of Reform, Richard Hofstadter (New York: Vintage Books, 1955)

The Reckless Decade, H. W. Brands (New York: St. Martin's Press, 1995)

The Americans: the Democratic Experience, Daniel J. Boorstin (New York: Random House, 1973)

The Warrior and the Priest: Woodrow Wilson and Theodore Roosevelt, John Milton Cooper (Cambridge, MA: Belknap Press of Harvard University Press, 1983)

Progressivism, Arthur S. Link, Richard L. McCormick (Arlington Heights, IL: Harlan Davidson, Inc., 1983)

The Progressive Years, Otis A. Pease (New York: G. Braziller, 1962)

The Burdens of Progress, Richard M. Abrams (Glenview, IL: Scott, Foresman, 1978)

The Administrative State, Dwight Waldo (New York: Ronald Press Co., 1948)

The Tyranny of Change, John Whiteclay Chambers (New York: St. Martin's Press, 1992)

The Crossroads of Liberalism, Charles Forcey (New York: Oxford University Press, 1961)

Efficiency and Uplift, Samuel Haber (Chicago: University of Chicago Press, 1964)

America as a Civilization, Max Lerner (New York: Simon and Schuster, 1957)

The Vital Center, Arthur M. Schlesinger Jr. (New York: The Riverside Press, 1949)

Self-Rule, Robert H. Wiebe (Chicago: University of Chicago Press, 1995)

ON THE SHIFT TO THE INFORMATION AGE

Government's End, Jonathan Rauch (New York: PublicAffairs, 1999)

The Wealth of Choices, Alan S. Murray (New York: Random House, 2000)

Building the Bridge, Will Marshall ed. (Lanham, MD: Rowman and Littlefield Publishers, 1997)

Reinventing Democrats, Kenneth S. Baer (Lawrence, KS: University Press of Kansas, 2000)

Reinventing Government, David Osbrone, Ted Gaebler (Reading, MA: Addison-Wesley, 1992)

Taking Control, Morley Winograd, Dudley Buffa (New York: Henry Holt and company, 1996)

Middle Class Dreams, Stanley B. Greenberg (New York: Random House, 1995)

They Only Look Dead, E. J. Dionne Jr. (New York: Touchstone, 1996)

The Work of Nations, Robert B. Reich (New York: Random House, 1991)

Intellectual Capital, Thomas Stewart (New York: Currency, 1997)

Prosperity, Bob Davis, David Wessel (New York: Random House, 1998)

13th Gen, Neil Howe, Bill Strauss (New York: Vintage Books, 1993)

Millennials Rising, Neil Howe, William Strauss (New York: Vintage Books, 2000)

The Long Boom, Peter Schwartz, Peter Leyden, Joel Hyatt (Reading, MA: Perseus Books, 1999)

ON COMMUNITY LIFE

The End of Equality, Mickey Kaus (New York: Basic Books, 1992)

The Spirit of Community, Amitai Etzioni (New York: Touchstone, 1993)

Citizenship and National Service, Will Marshall (Washington: Democratic Leadership Council, 1988)

Democracy's Discontent, Michael J. Sandel (Cambridge, MA: Belknap Press of Harvard University Press, 1996)

About the Author

A Senior Speechwriter to Vice President Al Gore at age 21, Andrei Cherny was the youngest White House Speechwriter in American history. He has also written speeches for President Bill Clinton, Richard Gephardt, cabinet members, senators, governors, and members of the House of Representatives.

He is the author of the 2000 Democratic Party Platform. He was the founding Editor of *Blueprint: Ideas for a New Century*, a policy journal geared toward finding the next set of new ideas for American politics. He presently is the Contributing Editor of *The New Democrat* and the Senior Policy Advisor to the Speaker of the California State Assembly.

A graduate of Harvard College, he was born, raised, and currently resides in Los Angeles's San Fernando Valley. For more information, visit www.andreicherny.com.

Index

Printed in the United States
117004LV00004B/128/A